Introduction
to the Intertestamental
Period

INTRODUCTION
to the
INTERTESTAMENTAL
PERIOD

Raymond F. Surburg

CPH.
SAINT LOUIS

Library of Congress Cataloging in Publication Data
Surburg, Raymond F   1909-
    Introduction to the intertestamental period.
    Includes bibliographies.
    1. Judaism—History—Post-exilic period. 586 B. C.–210
A. D. 2. Bible. O. T. Apocrypha—Introductions.
3. Apocryphal books (Old Testament)—Introductions.
I. Title.
BM176.S94   296'.09'014   75-1115
ISBN 0-570-03237-7

6 7 8 9 10 11 12 1 3 14 15   06 05 04 03 02 01 00 99 98 97

To
MY WIFE, LILLIAN
*For all that this book owes
to her and for all that
I owe besides*

Contents

PART ONE

The Historical Background

CHAPTER I

Introduction

When readers of the Bible turn its pages from Chapter 4 of Malachi to Chapter 1 of the Gospel According to St. Matthew, they pass not only from the Old to the New Testament, a fact of which they are well aware, but they also pass over a number of centuries, a truth to which most readers give little thought. Between Malachi and the appearance of John the Baptist there is an interlude of about four centuries. Certain scholars in the past have characterized these centuries as the "silent centuries," and have relegated them to oblivion, not considering them of much significance for Jewish history or for an understanding of the history and theology of the New Testament.

In a larger sense than is often realized, these centuries are the key for the understanding and adequate comprehension of the life and literature of the New Testament. While the setting for both the Old and New Testaments is the Mediterranean world, yet the intellectual, social, and religious backgrounds of both testaments is different. The fact is that the atmosphere in which the New Testament is written is in large part the product of the period between the testaments, and no amount of study of the Old Testament can solely explain it. On the other hand, no survey of the life of the Roman era is able to give the Biblical reader explanations of many New Testament phrases and ideas.

During the intertestamental period important developments took place: great dynastic changes occurred; the face of Europe was changed two or three times; the geography of European and Asiatic countries was greatly altered; and new civilizations appeared.

The political and religious history of the intertestamental period is one with which the serious Bible student ought to be acquainted. The literature of this period is no less noteworthy. The Hebrew, Aramaic, and Greek intertestamental writings of this period represent what Eissfeldt has called "die Wirkungsgeschichte des Alten Testaments," the story of the influence of the Old Testament in the history of the world and of the Christian church.

PART ONE: HISTORICAL BACKGROUND

The history of the interim between the testaments is invaluable for understanding the New Testament. It bridges the gap between the political and social conditions at the time of Malachi and the world that confronts the reader of the gospels. In many respects institutions found in the last books of the Old Testament are not continued in the New Testament. During the intervening centuries world control has passed from the Persians to the Romans; the West is now in control instead of the East. The whole face of Jewish society has changed by New Testament times. The student of the New Testament finds that new facts and situations challenge him; a score of questions suggest themselves to him. Studying the developments of the intertestamental period will enable him to understand many of the changes that have occurred.

In the days of Malachi the population was scanty; the cities were heaps of rubbish; the land everywhere bore the marks of long desolation; the poverty of the many was aggravated by the rapacity of the few. In early New Testament days Palestine appears as one of the most densely populated parts of the Roman Empire. Its cities are crowded; its terraced hills are cultivated to the last inch. The merchants of Palestine share in and largely control the trade of the Mediterranean world.

Greek is universally used throughout the Roman Empire as the language of the New Testament. Aramaic replaces Hebrew as a spoken language, although the discoveries of Qumran negate the conception that after the return Hebrew became a totally dead language. At the end of the Old Testament period Aramaic had become the lingua franca of the Persian Empire; this helps to explain the origin of the practice of using a methurgeman (interpreter) in the synagog services. At first the Aramaic paraphrases for both the Law and the Prophets were given orally, but eventually in the post-Christian centuries they were written down and known as Targums, of which there were a number. From where did the Greek language come? Why did the Jews in the Dispersion not read their Scriptures in Hebrew instead of in Greek, in a translation known as the Septuagint, written in a language that has been identified with the language of the Koine Greek of the Egyptian papyri? The answer is to be found in the years between the last books of the Old Testament and the coming of John the Baptist in the New.

A characteristic of Judaism of the New Testament is the passionate devotion of Israel to one God and the avoidance of all polytheism and idolatry. There are also the beliefs in the immortality of the soul and the resurrection of the body that receive emphasis in the New Testament. These eschatological views are delineated with greater clarity in the first century after Christ than in the last century of the Old Testament.

On the pages of the Gospels we meet the Sanhedrin, read of the traditions of the elders, and are confronted with the activities of the scribes. The Gospel writers report that on numerous occasions Jesus resorted to the synagog, not for sacrifices but to read the Law and for religious discourse and prayer. When Jesus graced this earth with His presence. Palestine was divided into three parts: Judea, Samaria, and Galilee. Whence did this division of Biblical geography arise? The answers to all these questions are found in a study of the geography, history, and religious development of the Jews and the peoples with whom they came into contact during the time between the Testaments.

Sources covering the intertestamental period are the writings of the Egyptian historian Manetho, the geographer Strabo, the histories of Polybius, the writings of Flavius Josephus and Philo, the Jewish apocryphal and pseudepigraphical writings, the Zadokite documents from Damascus, and the manuscripts from the Dead Sea caves.

The purpose of this volume is to treat briefly the Jewish literature which originated in Palestine and in the Dispersion, concentrating especially on the Septuagint, the Apocrypha, the Pseudepigrapha, the writings of the Qumran Sectaries, and the writings of Josephus and Philo.

A portrayal of the historical development of the Near Eastern world from the time of the Babylonian captivity till the end of the religious development of the Jews as experienced by them in Egypt, Palestine, and the Jewish Dispersion, should help in a better understanding of the Septuagint, the Apocrypha, the Pseudepigrapha, the noncanonical literature of Qumran, and the writings of Philo and Josephus.

CHAPTER **II**

The Jews Under Persian Rule

The period from 596 B. C. to A. D. 70 was a decisive one for the children of Israel. It was during this time that "Judaism" came into existence. Beginning with the deportations in 605 B. C. and 596 B. C., the Jews concentrated in Judea for centuries now became a religious community which eventually scattered throughout the Near East, Middle East, Asia Minor, and Europe. The historical works that shed light on this period of history are: the Books of Nehemiah, Ezra, Esther; and the Books of the Maccabees, the *Jewish Antiquities,* and the *Jewish War* of Josephus. Additional data is also found in Haggai, Zechariah, Malachi, and the Apocrypha and Pseudepigrapha, together with the newly found scrolls from the area of the Dead Sea.

Judaism has its birth and development in the years between 605 B. C., the date of the first Babylonian deportation by Nebuchadnezzar, and 538 B. C., when the decree of liberation was issued by Cyrus. Not all

Jews were deported by Nebuchadnezzar in 605 B.C., 597 B.C., and 587 B.C., but those who were taken by Babylon represented the flower of the social and religious people of Judah (2 Kings 24:14-16; 25:11-12). The deportees grew to enjoy living in their new Babylonian homes and were successful in their agricultural and commercial endeavors.

In contrast to their brethren of the Northern Kingdom, the Jews from the Southern Kingdom did not intermarry in exile but preserved their identity by existing as separated communities in a heathen environment. In Babylonia the Jews maintained themselves as a religious community probably under the direction of elders (Neh: 8:1; 13:1). Under the leadership of the prophet Ezekiel and other religious leaders, the Jews were strengthened in their national unity by spiritual instruction from their leaders. "They sought to fix their minds upon and to shape their conduct according to the Mosaic ideal and the teaching of the Prophets, especially that of Isaiah (40—66), which was intended for this period. The God of Israel was not overthrown in the defeat of His people, for He is the God of the nations. As God of all, He will give life to the people whom He has chosen. (Ezek. 37:1-14)." [1] During the Exile it became apparent that the Jews could exist as a religious community without a king and the cultus of the temple. Fidelity to the law of Jehovah became the force that solidified the people and helped them remain a religious unity. During the Babylonian Exile, scribes skilled in the Law explained the meaning of the sacred writings to gatherings of the Jews and thus anticipated the synagog, which played such a vital role in the subsequent history of Judaism. The scribes emphasized personal prayer, the observance of the Sabbath, and the practice of justice in brotherly relationships.

The result of this religious activity was the formation of a small nucleus of Jews who were determined to guard the deposit of God's revelation. Babylonia, therefore, became an important center for the maintenance and promulgation of the ideals of Judaism, and for many centuries there kept alive the flame of Judaism.

In 538 B.C., in fulfillment of the prophecy of Jeremiah (626—587 B.C.), the Jews were given permission by Cyrus to return to their native land, and in accord with his policy of toleration, religious liberty was granted to all peoples heretofore made vassals by the Babylonians. When these expatriates of Babylonia returned to Judea, they endeavored to reform the lax morality that had been adopted by the Jews who had remained in Judea.

Ezra and Nehemiah record three returns to Palestine by Jews from exile countries. The first return took place under Cyrus in 538 B.C. (Ezra 1:5; 2:67); the second was led by Ezra in 457 B.C., and the third by Nehemiah in 444 B.C. The various groups that eventually returned to Palestine from Babylonia numbered over 50,000 people, among whom were 4,229 priests (Ezra 2:2-67). Most of these exiles settled near Jerusalem, where together with those who had remained, they constituted a Jewish district, a nation of Judeans: the Yehudim. The lot of the repatriated Jews was a difficult one: wrecked houses had to be laboriously rebuilt or bought from their owners, and fields ruined by the ravages of war had to be recultivated. The territory assigned to the returned Jews was very small, Keilah, Beth-zur, and Tekoa to the south.

In the seventh month after their return, the Jews began rebuilding the temple completely destroyed in 587 B. C. Their determination, however, to preserve the purity of their race and religion created difficulties for them with their neighbors, the Samaritans, Arabians, Ammonites, and others. This resulted in opposition to the building of the temple, which was halted by official decree of the Persian king, and thus the building of the temple ceased in 537 B. C. The next 15 years were spent in agricultural efforts and in the rebuilding of their homes. The great religious enthusiasm that the repatriates had upon their first return to Judea began to wane. God then caused two prophets, Haggai and Zechariah, called "the prophets of the temple," to prophesy and galvanize the people into action, arousing them from their sinful lethargy and indifference. In 515 B. C. the rebuilding of the temple was completed under the stimulation furnished by Haggai and Zechariah, both of whom began to prophesy in 520 B. C.

Under Zerubbabel, the governor, and Joshua, the high priest, the temple was restored. The Book of Ezra, which has furnished us with most of the historical material thus far, omits a period of over 57 years that followed the completion of the temple. In 457 B. C. Ezra, a man of priestly lineage and a scribe of the Law, sought permission from the Persian Emperor Artaxerxes to lead another group of Jews to Palestine to investigate the religious conditions there. The Persian emperor allowed Ezra to requisition supplies and funds needed for the rehabilitation of the Jews of Judea and Jerusalem from the Persian governor closest to the Jews of Palestine.

In 457 B. C. Ezra returned with 1,700 men and the temple vessels that had not been brought back from Babylonia. Upon his arrival in Jerusalem, Ezra was shocked to find that the Jews had violated the law of Moses through intermarriage with foreign and Canaanite women. He gave himself to prayer and confession of the sins of the people. Ezra succeeded in persuading the priests to put away their heathen wives, but later Nehemiah had to take the same action.

The efforts of Ezra were especially concerned with instructing the Jews in the law of God as it was revealed in the Pentateuch. This resulted in a strict observance of the Sabbath, the conducting of the liturgy as prescribed, the suppression of mixed marriages, and the dismissal of foreign wives.

Nehemiah was a layman who played a prominent role in the 5th century B. C. in Palestine. He occupied an important position at the court of Artaxerxes I at Susa (Shushan). When Nehemiah was apprised of the plight of the Jews in Palestine, he prevailed on the Persian king for a leave of absence so that he might help his countrymen. Nehemiah was appointed governor of Judea, was given letters of recommendation to the provincial governors en route, and was provided with a military escort from Susa to Jerusalem.

In 444 B. C. he came to Jerusalem and immediately upon arrival made a night tour of inspection of Jerusalem, after which he called the people together and urged them to rebuild the walls of Jerusalem. Within less than two months this was accomplished despite the opposition of Sanballat (a representative official of Artaxerxes, Neh. 2:10; 4:2), the Samaritans, and other hostile neighbors.

Ezra and Nehemiah cooperated to improve the religious and social conditions of the people. In this effort they were also assisted by Malachi, the prophet. Chapter 8 of Nehemiah records how the Law was read to the people as they were assembled at the Feast of Tabernacles:

> Ezra the scribe stood upon a pulpit of wood, which they had made for the purpose. . . . And Ezra opened the book in the sight of all the people (for he was above all the people); and when he opened it, all the people stood up; and Ezra blessed the Lord, the great God. And all the people answered, Amen, Amen, with lifting up their hands; and they bowed their heads and worshiped the Lord. . . . So they read in the book, in the law of God, distinctly and gave the sense and caused them to understand the reading. (Neh. 8:4-6, 8)

The people promised that the covenant with God would be kept and that they would maintain separation from their heathen neighbors. Nehemiah instituted drastic marriage reforms (13:25) and extirpated Sabbath desecration (13:21). Some years later Nehemiah obtained another leave of absence from Artaxerxes and returned to Jerusalem. He enforced strict observance of the Sabbath and removed from the court of the temple the chamber which Tobias, the Ammonite, had been permitted to erect through the indifference of the high priest Eliashib, who had married a daughter of Sanballat. Tobias fled to his father-in-law in Samaria. At this time the oldest transcription of part of the Hebrew Bible was undertaken by these outcasts, and it became known as the Samaritan Pentateuch. These exiles also built a temple on Mount Gerizim.

At the close of the Old Testament period (circa 400 B. C.), Judea had been a province of Persia for 138 years, and Jews were scattered throughout the 128 provinces of the Persian empire. Persia had been a world power for over 140 years. The Persian kings of the 5th century before Christ, under whose sovereignty the Jews had enjoyed for the most part a mild and enjoyable rule, were Artaxerxes I (465 – 425 B. C.), during whose reign the walls of Jerusalem had been rebuilt; Xerxes II, who ruled only a year; and Darius II (Nothius) 423 – 405 B. C.

Not much is known of what happened in Judea between 432 B. C. and 411 B. C. During the next decade Bagoas was the governor of Judea. Johanan, the high priest, grandson of Eliashib, was an important political leader at this time. He murdered his own brother in the temple in 408 B. C., thereby fell into disfavor with Bagoas, and was shortly replaced by his son Jedaiah.

THE JEWS UNDER PERSIAN RULE

The Elephantine Papyri, discovered in 1903 on the Island of Elephantine at the First Cataract of the Nile River in Egypt, opposite Syene, present students of the Old Testament with an interesting glimpse of one of the outlying regions of the Persian empire during the 5th century. They also inform us about the closing years of the Old Testament period. The Aramaic papyri from Syene have shed light on a Jewish military colony which had settled in Upper Egypt and received lands for themselves and their descendants. They engaged in business or pursued a profession, spoke and wrote Aramaic, kept their own customs, and enjoyed self-government. During the reign of Darius II, Jedonia, the son of Gemariah, ruled with the elders over the military colony. Contrary to the Law, this Jewish colony built a temple of its own to JHWH.

In 419 B. C. a certain high official named Hananiah wrote to Elephantine and cited the text of an edict of Darius II, fixing the details of the Passover. We also learn from the Elephantine Papyri that the Jewish temple had just been sacked in an anti-Jewish pogrom around 411 B. C., instigated by priests serving the ram-headed Khnum [Chumis]. The Jews wrote to Jerusalem asking permission to rebuild their temple. After receiving no reply from Jerusalem, they wrote a second letter in 408 B. C., but at the same time forwarded a request to the Samaritans, petitioning them for permission to rebuild their destroyed temple. This time the Jerusalem authroties responded quickly in the affirmative. How long the colony lasted is not known; the last dated document from the area comes from 400 B. C.

In addition to worshiping JHWH, the Jews at Elephantine honored other divinities which they probably had brought along from Canaan, e. g., Anathbethel, Ashim-bethel, and Cherem (or Charam). However, Yahweh remained their primary deity.

The Touna-el-Gebel letters indicate the existence of other Jewish colonies in Upper Egypt during the 5th century B. C. It seems that the Jews of these colonies maintained contact with their coreligionists in Jerusalem. The postbiblical period of Jewish history is marked, according to Bickerman, by a unique polarity: "on the one hand, the Jerusalem center and, on the other, the plurality of centers in the Diaspora. The Dispersion saved Judaism from physical extirpation and spiritual inbreeding. Palestine united the dispersed members of the nation and gave them a sense of oneness." [2]

The first signs of the decline of Persian power came in the reign of Artaxerxes II (404—358 B. C.), when revolts in different parts of the empire threatened to terminate the rule of the Persians. Already in the reign of his predecessor, Darius II, who was dominated by his wife Parysatis, a considerable number of revolts had occurred. The Libyan Amyrtaus expelled the Persian garrisons from Egypt and proclaimed himself king. In 401 B. C. Artaxerxes had to abandon the campaign against Egypt, when his brother, Cyrus the younger, challenged his right to the crown. Cyrus fell at Cunaxa, north of Babylon, but his Greek mercenaries, "the ten thousand," whose famous march has been described by Xenophon in *The Anabasis*, were able to reach the Black Sea, showing that the might of the Persian empire was weak. For nearly 40 years (378 – 340 B. C.) Egypt enjoyed freedom from the control of Persia.

Artaxerxes III Ochus (358 – 338 B. C.) was forced to suppress an uprising in the western parts of the empire. In 350 he tried to reconquer Egypt but failed. Then Syria under the leadership of Sidon revolted. In 338 Artaxerxes III was poisoned by his general, Bagoas. Darius III, the last of the Persian kings, strengthened his hold over the Greek cities and reconquered Egypt in 334. It appeared as if the stability of the Achaemenian rule had been restored, but it was not for long, for in the same year Alexander the Great set out to liberate the Greek cities of Asia Minor from Persian domination.

Already during the Babylonian period the Jews had adopted what Semitic scholars call *Reichsaramaeisch* (Imperial Aramaic) in place of the old classical Hebrew language. Aramaic had been a Semitic and Syriac dialect spoken in the Babylonian Valley and was closely related to Hebrew. However, the difference between Hebrew and Aramaic was sufficiently great to necessitate the paraphrasing of the read Hebrew synagog pericopal selections (from the Torah and the Prophets) in the Aramaic by a *methurgeman* or interpreter. The Hebrew of certain books of the Old Testament showed Aramaic influence insofar as the figures of speech came from the Babylonian and Persian environments. A noticeable difference can be seen in the style of Ezra, Nehemiah, Haggai, Zechariah, Esther, and Malachi, all products of the post-exilic period. In these books it is noted that the Jews reckoned time according to the kings of Persia. (Cf. Hag. 1:1; Zech. 1:1; Ezra 1:1; Neh. 2:1.)

Some scholars contend that a number of important influences in Judaism and its literature are to be traced to the Persian period and to the contacts the Jews had with non-Jews in Elam and Persia. It is claimed that the Persian Jews obtained from Zoroastrianism their monotheistic concept of God. With this view the facts as revealed in the Old Testament are not in agreement. The Jews were essentially monotheistic throughout their entire history. This does not militate against the fact that the Jews on numerous occasions were guilty of idolatry.

The two eschatological doctrines of immortality of the soul and the resurrection of the body are alleged to have been acquired by the Jews as a result of their contacts with Zoroastrianism. Long before the Babylonian Captivity, the Jews expressed their hope in an afterlife and their belief in the resurrection of the body. Passages in Job and Isaiah clearly set forth these doctrines.

Another doctrine supposedly acquired during the stay of the Jews in Babylonia and Persia is the belief in angels. However, the historic episodes of the patriarchs give sufficient evidence of their belief in angels, so that the doctrine of Old Testament angelology does not have its origin in the post-exilic period.

CHAPTER **III**

The Jews and Alexander the Great

Before the time of Philip of Macedon, the city states of Greece had never formed a united government. Heretofore the Persian kings had been able to manipulate one Greek state against another. Ever since the days of Xerxes, the power of Greek states had been increasing, but their lack of unity prevented them from becoming an offensive power in world politics. It was Philip of Macedon who achieved this unity, although not all Greeks were a part of the Hellenic League, which became the instrument for the conquest of the Persian Empire.

Philip of Macedon, the father of Alexander the Great, highly esteemed Greek culture. He entrusted his son Alexander to a teacher named Symmachus, who acquainted him with the Iliad of Homer. When Alexander was 13, the great philosopher Aristotle was appointed as his teacher. From him Alexander learned to know and appreciate Greek literature and art, and he developed an intense admiration for Greek religion, culture, and civilization and eventually became "the Apostle of Hellenism."

Alexander ascended the throne of his father when he was a mere youth, bringing to fruition the plans that had been conceived by his father. He spent a year warring in Greece and winning its allegiance, especially after the destruction of Thebes in 335 B. C., whose population was assassinated as a warning that the alliance between Alexander and the Greeks must be respected. After a winter of preparation, Alexander in 334 left Europe for Asia, and Macedonia never again saw him.

With the aim of conquering and making himself ruler of the Persian Empire, he crossed into Asia Minor with about 30,000 infantry and 5,000 cavalry, less than half of whom were Macedonians.

After visiting Troy, made famous for him by the Homeric legends, he engaged in a battle with the Persian satraps of Asia Minor at the little river Granicus, near ancient Troy. The Persian nobles were put to flight, and Sardis submitted without resistance. The Lydians were allowed to resume their self-government, which they had lost about 200 years before.

Alexander then advanced against the Ionian cities of Asia Minor, which were taken and "liberated," often against their will. By autumn of 334 Ephesus, Miletus, and Halicarnassus had fallen. During the winter of 334 – 333 the southern part of Asia Minor capitulated. In October 333 at Issus, Alexander met a great Persian army of 600,000 footmen under the command of Darius III. The Persian army was several times as large as Alexander's and included 30,000 Greek mercenaries. But the Persians were put to flight, and their defeat marked the beginning of the downfall of the great Persian Empire. Damascus at this time was taken by surprise. Alexander, however, did not pursue Darius but decided to secure his own rear position.

After his victories over the Persians, Alexander turned to the conquest of the cities along the eastern coast of the Mediterranean. Sidon, Byblos, and Aradus sent envoys to Alexander and offered their submission. Tyre, however, refused to yield. To capture the city, Alexander had to build a causeway from the mainland to the island. In its construction he took the ruins of old Tyre, the city of the mainland, and laid it "in the midst of the water." Her dust was scraped from her, and Tyre was made "like the top of a rock," "a place for the spreading of nets in the midst of the sea" (Ezek. 26:4, 5, 12-14). After seven months of siege, Tyre was captured in August 332, with 8,000 Tyreans slain and 30,000 sold into captivity. With the fall of Tyre the maritime supremacy and commercial predominance of the Phoenicians ended.

Gaza, which also refused to surrender, was likewise besieged and taken after two months. The punishment visited on Gaza was greater than that on Tyre. The prophecy of Zechariah was fulfilled: "Gaza also shall see it and be very sorrowful . . . and the king shall perish from Gaza." (Zech. 9:5)

Alexander next went up to Jerusalem, which like Tyre and Gaza would not surrender. According to Josephus and the Talmud, Jaddua, the high priest, attired in his priestly garments and followed by a multitude dressed in white garments, came out to meet Alexander. When he saw the multitude, headed by the high priest adorned in his priestly garments and miter and with the golden plate whereon was the name of God, Alexander drew near and adored the name of God and saluted the high priest. He told the high priest he had seen him in a dream. When the high priest showed Alexander the passage in the Book of Daniel predicting that he would be the first king of Greece and would destroy the Persian Empire, Alexander believed it was a prophecy about him. From that time on Alexander became a friend of the Jews. Although this account is considered unhistorical by most scholars, yet it indicates that Alexander was kindly disposed toward the Jews.

In 332 Alexander invaded Egypt, and its satrap surrendered. Alexander was welcomed as deliverer by the Egyptians, who hated the Persians. Entering the temple of Amon, Alexander gladly accepted from the Egyptian priest the robe of son of Amon, thereby being proclaimed as the legitimate son of Pharoah; he was also assigned a chapel in the temple of Karnak. Alexander at once began the introduction of Greek civilization in Egypt. In 331 he founded the city of Alexandria, laid out by the architect Dinocrates and constructed under his supervision. Alexander supplied the city with excellent harbors, intending that it should supersede Tyre as the commercial metropolis of the eastern Mediterranean and promote Greek commercial interests. Special consideration was accorded to the Jews, who were allowed to live in a separate part of the city and permitted to observe their own customs and retain their worship. The presence of many Jews in Alexandria was to have an important bearing on the subsequent history of the Jews and Christians in lower Egypt.

From Egypt Alexander pushed east again, and on October 1, 331, he met Darius in Assyria, who was arrayed against him with a million soldiers. The Persians were defeated with great loss of life. Alexander then marched south to Babylon, whose governor opened its gates to him. Mazaeus, satrap of Babylon, was retained as its ruler. Alexander restored the Babylonian temples and then proceeded eastward.

In Susa, capital of Elam, Alexander obtained great treasures. At Babylon and Susa he took gold and silver to the equivalent of 60 million dollars. At Persepolis he also acquired a vast treasure estimated at 100 million dollars. In 330 B. C. he spent the winter at Persepolis. While in a drunken stupor and at the instigation of the Athenian courtesan Thais, Alexander burned the royal palace of Xerxes. In the spring of 330 he took Ecbatana, the capital of Media. Darius was murdered by one of his own kinsmen, and his body was sent to Alexander for burial in Persepolis.

Before Alexander had completed his conquest of the Persian Empire, he changed his original plan of imposing Greek culture on conquered areas and peoples. He now adopted the idea of uniting Europeans and Asiatics into one world empire in which all people would have equal opportunity. After the battle of Arbela [or Gaugamela], where he had defeated Darius, Alexander appeared in Oriental garb and had the courtiers bow before him in Oriental custom. In Asiatic countries the rule of the government was turned over to Asiatics. This estranged the Greek and Macedonian soldiers.

Between 330 and 325 Alexander continued his victorious career as conqueror by adding to his empire northeastern Persia and what is now known as western and southern Afghanistan. He crossed the Hindu-Kush Mountains and marched into Sogdiana, conquering that part of Russian Turkestan lying between the Oxus River and the Jaxartes River. Three hundred miles from Kashgar in Chinese Turkestan he built another Alexandria. It was called Alexandria the Ultimate.

After spending two summers and a winter in the wild regions north of the Oxus, Alexander crossed over the Hindu-Kush Mountains into Afghanistan, entering into India by the Khyber Pass. He conquered the Punjab in India and would have pushed on as far as the Yellow Sea, but his Macedonian troops refused to go further. They felt it was folly to continue because they had more booty than they could carry. In 323 Alexander reached Babylon with an army that marched from India through Gedrosia, now called Baluchistan, traversing a land no European had ever penetrated.

In Babylonia Alexander proceeded with his plans of uniting the peoples of the East and West. This he hoped to achieve by planting European colonies in Asia and Asiatic colonies in Europe and by promoting intermarriage between the peoples of different races. The first of these objectives he had partially accomplished by founding along the line of march no fewer than 70 Alexandrias, cities in which he left his own troops who inter-married with the native population.

He then ordered his Macedonian soldiery to marry women of the Asiatic races. He himself married Roxanna, the Bactrian princess at Susa, and Statira, the daughter of Darius III, thus introducing polygamy, a practice disapproved of by the Macedonians. Alexander also married Parysatis, another Persian princess. He entered upon these marital alliances as an example to his subjects. Besides trying to blend the races and civilizations of East and West, Alexander even wanted to intermingle the floras of the European and Asiatic continents.

On his arrival in Susa in 324 Alexander found misrule on the part of the official responsible for the government of the city. Simultaneously he became aware of a growing resentment toward him. In Greece many turned against him when they heard that he had killed his own nephew, the historian Callisthenes. The Greeks were scandalized by the report that Alexander wished to be considered a god. A mutiny also took place because of his orientalizing practices.

In 323 Alexander planned a sea voyage around Arabia. However, in the same year, in the midst of further plans for the conquest of south Arabia, Africa, and western Europe, Alexander died of a fever in the thirty-third year of his life. He thus had ruled for 13 years and in that brief time had conquered and ruled over a larger territory than any other ruler in history.

Alexander was vainglorious and conceited. He had dreamed of having Mount Athos carved into a statue of himself holding the world in his hands. He wanted himself recognized as a god, but early death negated all his further ambitions. Some authorities take a different view of the designs of Alexander.[1]

The results of Alexander's conquests were both beneficial and evil. The chief beneficial effects were the following:

1. Hellenic civilization spread over Egypt and western Asia.

2. The distinction between Greek and barbarian was broken down to some degree and constituted an aid in preparing the minds of men for the Christian Gospel.[2]

3. The Greek language became the universal language, spoken and written by the cultured.

4. A sea route from Europe to India was discovered.

Among evil effects was demoralization of the Greeks after coming into possession of the great riches of the Persian Empire. Another was effeminization of the Greeks through contact with oriental vices and luxuries. One writer described the importance of the results as follows:

> If we think of the civilization of the Greeks we have no difficulty in fixing on its chief characteristics. High perfection of intellect and imagination, displaying itself in all the various forms of art, poetry, literature and philosophy — restless activity of mind and body, finding its exercise in athletic games or in subtle disputations — love of the beautiful — quick

perception—indefatigable inquiry—all these enter into the very idea of the Greek race. We have only to do with this national character so far as, under Divine Providence, it was made subservient to the spread of the Gospel.[3]

One of the important consequences of the conquest of Alexander was the widespread dispersion of the Jews, who helped prepare the way for Christianity. Alexander was favorably disposed toward the Jews, permitting them to settle in many cities he founded. Already in the time of Darius, three million Jews are reputed to have been scattered throughout the 127 provinces of the Persian Empire. Jewish settlements could be found throughout Asia, even as far as China.

No other person in history has been claimed in legends by so many different nations. The Egyptians have made him a god in their fable literature; the Islamic nations have depicted him as Iskander, the hero-saint; the Israelites have joined him to the house of David as a forerunner of the Messiah; the Ethiopian Christians have preserved Alexander in their hagiological literature as a saint; and in the saint tales so popular during the Middle Ages Alexander is portrayed as Alexandre le Grand looking for paradise.[4]

CHAPTER IV

The Ptolemies and the Jews

When Alexander died in 323 B. C., he left no heir old enough to rule in his place. A son was posthumously born to Alexander's Bactrian wife, Roxanna. However there were a number of relatives of Alexander, either by blood or marriage, who hoped to be the successor to rule his empire. Even before the burial of the great conqueror, the battle for his kingdom began. For a while Perdiccas, one of Alexander's generals, endeavored to keep the empire together for Alexander's unborn son. Philip Arridaeus, the demented half brother of Alexander, was proclaimed titular king until Alexander's son would be of age to rule.

The *diadochoi* or "successors" of Alexander contested the possession of his empire. One of them, Cassander, murdered Roxanna and her son. By 315 B. C., Ptolemy, Cassander, and Lysimachus formed an alliance aimed at thwarting the ambitious designs of Antigonus to become a second

Alexander. To Ptolemy, the son of Lagus, Egypt was assigned; to Lysimachus, Syria was allotted, and to Seleucus Nicator, the province of Babylon was allocated. Many students of the Bible believe that this happened in fulfillment of the prophecy of Dan. 11:4: "And when he shall stand up, his kingdom shall be broken, and shall be divided toward the four winds of heaven; and not to his posterity, nor according to his dominion which he ruled, for his kingdom shall be plucked up, even for others beside those."

The disruption of Alexander's empire led to a renewal of the agelong struggle for the possession of Palestine by the Egyptians and Mesopotamians. Ptolemy invaded Egypt in 320 B. C.; Jerusalem was surprised on a Sabbath day and taken without resistance. In 315 B. C. Palestine was lost to Ptolemy's rival, Antigonus; but after the Battle of Gaza (312 B. C.) Ptolemy reclaimed it. Seleucus, who cooperated with Ptolemy, made himself master of Babylon.

The year 312 B. C. marks the beginning of the Seleucid empire which inaugurated a calendar long in use among the Jews; in fact, it is still employed by some Jews in parts of the East. At the Battle of Ipsus, 301 B. C. Antigonus was killed; this presented Ptolemy I (Soter [Lagi] 305 — 285 B. C.) the opportunity to seize Palestine, but Seleucus (305 — 280 B. C.) won the victory and ruled over Syria from his capitol in Antioch.

Josephus in Book XII of *Jewish Antiquities* gives an account of Ptolemy's capture of Jerusalem as follows:

> And this king seized Jerusalem by resorting to cunning and deceit. For he entered the city on the Sabbath as if to sacrifice, and, as the Jews did not oppose him—for they did not suspect any hostile act—and, because of their lack of suspicion and the nature of the day, were enjoying idleness and ease, he became master of the city without difficulty and ruled it harshly. This account is attested to by Agatharcides of Cnidus, the historian of the Diadochi, who reproaches us for our superstition, on account of which we lost our liberty, in these words. "There is a nation called Jews, who have a strong and a great city called Jerusalem, which they allowed to fall into the hands of Ptolemy by refusing to take up arms and, instead through their untimely superstition submitted to having a hard master." [1]

The Letter of Aristeas says of Ptolemy:

> He had overrun the whole of Coele-Syria and Phoenecia, exploiting his good fortune and prowess, and had transplanted some and made others captive, reducing all to subjection by terror; it was on this occasion that he transported a hundred thousand persons from the country of the Jews to Egypt. Of these he armed some thirty thousand chosen men and settled them in garrisons in the country. [2]

The Jews were to be found in large numbers in Ptolemaic Egypt as is indicated by the Egyptian inscriptions and papyri. While many Jews had been in Egypt before the time of the rule of the Ptolemies, it is still true that many were brought to Egypt by Ptolemy Lagi.

The Jews enjoyed the same rights of autonomy which they had under the Persians and were allowed to live in peace and practice their religious and cultural traditions. The central government concerned itself only with the collection of taxes and did not interfere in internal affairs. The high priests were permitted to administer local affairs as they had done under Persian rule.

The early Ptolemies were capable and enlightened rulers with absolute and unlimited power over Egypt and its subjects, although their own personal lives were immoral and dissolute. During the rule of the Ptolemies, Egypt became one of the most important intellectual centers of the Helle- nistic world. No attempt was made to hellenize the natives. The govern- ment of the Ptolemies was concerned with securing the largest possible revenue from the Egyptians, whom they therefore refrained from oppress- ing. The Ptolemies preferred the Greeks over against the natives and showed them many favors.

Alexandrian Egypt became famous as the home of scholars and a great center of learning. It is claimed that at one time no less than 14,000 students pursued studies in conjunction with the museum and library at Alexandria. Scientific research characterized the endeavors of many scholars through the maintenance of botanical and zoological gardens by the museum and by dissection and astronomical laboratories.

From 319 – 198 B. C. Palestine was under the control of the Ptolemies. While they were in power, it was a propitious time for the Jews of both Egypt and Palestine. However, in the wars that ensued between the Ptolemies and the Seleucids, the Jews suffered as Palestine was trampled under foot by soldiers of the opposing army. Greek influence was strong in Palestine, although Hellenism was weak in Jerusalem and its vicinity.

The Ptolemies, the Greek kings of Egypt, were the following:

Ptolemy I	(son of Lagus)	323 – 283 B. C.
Ptolemy II	(Philadelphus)	283 – 247 B. C.
Ptolemy III	(Euergetes)	247 – 221 B. C.
Ptolemy IV	(Philopater)	221 – 203 B. C.
Ptolemy V	(Epiphanes)	203 – 181 B. C.
Ptolemy VI	(Philometor)	180 – 146 B. C.
Ptolemy VII	(Euergetes II)	145 – 117 B. C.

Ptolemy I (323 – 283 B. C.), Son of Lagus

The founder of the Ptolemaic dynasty was one of the great rulers of ancient times. It was he who was responsible for building the museum and the library at Alexandria. His fame as a patron of learning spread through- out the ancient world. The distinguished mathematician Euclid taught geometry at the court of Ptolemy.

Ptolemy I realized the need of a strong army which he secured by hiring Greek and Macedonian mercenaries. In addition he maintained a fleet by which he controlled the Mediterranean Sea. Alexandria became one of the important emporia of the ancient world. On his first invasion of Palestine, Ptolemy I had carried away to Egypt many Jewish captives, and the number grew into the thousands in subsequent expeditions. Those Jews who could bear arms were placed in various fortresses for military garrison duty. Later on Ptolemy II freed these Jewish slaves and was kindly disposed toward the Jews.

Ptolemy II, Philadelphus (283 – 247 B. C.)

The famous 370 – 400 foot high lighthouse located on the Island of Pharos, in the harbor of Alexandria is reputed to have been erected by Ptolemy II. It was destroyed in A. D. 1326 after having stood for nearly 1600 years.

Ptolemy II was the son of Ptolemy I and his wife Bernice. The private and family life of Ptolemy II in many respects followed the pattern of that of Oriental monarchs. He was married to Arsinoe I, the daughter of Lysimachus. Then he married his own full sister, Arsinoe II, widow of Lysimachus. At the beginning of his reign he murdered his own brother. According to some reports, Ptolemy Philadelphus was one of the richest kings in the world of his day. Ptolemy II is customarily regarded as the king who began the Ptolemaic ruler cult. The world was greatly impressed by the splendor of his inauguration. During his reign Egypt began trading with Italy.

Ptolemy II loved learning even more than did his father. He established a zoo at Alexandria and also promoted the learning of the natural sciences. He had animals in Ethiopia and South Africa captured and brought back to Alexandria. He was responsible for adding many new books to the museum and library founded by his father.

Ptolemy II Philadelphus was the ruler of Egypt during whose reign and at whose instigation the Pentateuch was translated into Greek. This precipitated the translating activity that eventually produced the Septuagint. The *Letter of Aristeas,* discussed in another part of this volume, records the part which Ptolemy II is alleged to have played in initiating this Greek translation.

As a patron of learning and Greek culture, it was the conviction of Ptolemy II that life's greatest satisfaction was derived from taking advantage of pleasures as they presented themselves. He was 62 years old when he died – prematurely old from having lived a wild and luxurious life.

Ptolemy III, Euergetes (Benefactor) (247 – 221 B. C.)

Like his father, Ptolemy III, Euergetes carried on war with the Seleucids. He fought a war with Antiochus Theos of Syria to save the life of his sister Bernice.

Ptolemy III followed in the footsteps of his predecessors regarding learning, particularly in the promotion of pure science. The mathematical astronomer Erastosthenes was custodian of the library at Alexandria and was encouraged in his scientific researches. He calculated the circumference of the earth, which he estimated to be 25,000 miles, by his "science of shadows." Another scientist who received encouragement from Ptolemy

III was Archimedes of Syracuse, the discoverer of specific gravity and the principle of the lever.

Ptolemy IV, Philopater (221 – 203 B. C.)

Antiochus III the Great, Seleucid monarch, declared war against Egypt and invaded Coele-Syria and Palestine. Ptolemy IV was compelled to defend this part of his empire; he defeated Antiochus III at the Battle of Raphia 217 B. C.; Antiochus was forced to return Palestine and Coele-Syria to Egypt.

Ptolemy IV celebrated his victory by a tour of the eastern Mediterranean provinces, including Palestine. As his father had previously done, Ptolemy IV visited Jerusalem and offered sacrifices of thanksgiving and bestowed rich gifts to the Temple. The Egyptian king was curious to know what was in the Holy of Holies and attempted to enter it but was prevented from doing so. According to Jewish legend he was struck down by paralysis. When he returned to Jerusalem he determined to punish the Egyptian Jews for his chagrin and humiliation by depriving them of all privileges they had heretofore enjoyed.

The non-Jewish population that resented the Jews, because of favors the Ptolemies had showered on them, followed the example of the king and persecuted the Egyptian Jews.

Under Ptolemy IV, Philopater, Egypt began to decline. He was voluptuous and indolent and found himself faced by rebellion at home. He succeeded in crushing the revolt, after which he continued to live in vice and luxury. His son, only an infant, succeeded him in 205 B. C.

Ptolemy V (203 – 181 B. C.)

The accession of Ptolemy V caused the kings of Macedonia and Syria to form a military alliance with the intent of attacking Egypt and stripping her of outlying provinces. When Antiochus III had invaded Palestine, the Jews were largely on his side. The exact reason for this change of allegiance on the part of the Palestinian Jews is not known, although Philopater's cruelty may have been a contributing cause.

Shortly thereafter the Egyptians under General Scopus drove the Syrians out of Jerusalem and occupied the Holy City for a time. However, in 198 B. C. Antiochus III, who at first had been defeated, turned defeat into victory by overcoming the Egyptians at Paneas in the Valley of the Jordan. When Antiochus III planned to attack Egypt, he was restrained by warnings of the Romans that Egypt had been declared a protectorate. Antiochus III hesitated to attack Egypt and instead made a peace treaty which was confirmed by a diplomatic marriage. Antiochus III's daughter was to be married to the young Egyptian king, but Phoenicia and Palestine were given to Syria, bringing the Palestinian Jewish population under control of the king of Syria. This took place in 198 B. C., after the Ptolemies had ruled Palestine for 122 years.

In characterizing the rule of the Ptolemies, Dorothy Miller wrote: "The entire history of the Ptolemies, and indeed the history of all the Hellenic dynasties, is an outstanding illustration of the fact that brilliancy of intellect, material splendor, and the highest civilization, without true religion, the presence of God in the life and the State, do not add one iota to morality or beneficence. It would seem that there are no crimes and no vices that were not common in the lives and families of the most enlightened princes of the era. The life of a mother, a brother, a sister, a child, or a friend was worth nothing if it stood in the way of personal desire or political ambition." [3]

CHAPTER V

The Jews Under the Seleucids

Syria under the Seleucids:

Seleucus I	Nicator	312 – 280 B. C.
Antiochus I	(Soter)	280 – 261 B. C.
Antiochus II	(Theos)	261 – 246 B. C.
Seleucus II	(Callinicus)	246 – 226 B. C.
Seleucus III	(Keroneos)	226 – 223 B. C.
Antiochus III		222 – 187 B. C.
Seleucus IV	(Philopater)	187 – 175 B. C.
Antiochus IV	(Epiphanes)	175 – 163 B. C.
Antiochus V	(Eupator)	163 – 162 B. C.
Demetrius I		162 – 150 B. C.
Demetrius II	and Alexander	
Balas' struggle for throne		
Alexander Balas		150 – 145 B. C.
Demetrius II		145 – 139 B. C.
Antiochus VII		139 – 134 B. C.

Seleucus I Nicator (312 – 280 B. C.)

The founder of the Seleucidae was one of the generals of Alexander the Great, Seleucus Nicator. He was able by military conquest to come into control of a large part of Alexander's empire, which reached from the Hellespont and the Mediterranean to the Indus River in the east. In 321

B. C. the satrapy of Babylonia was assigned to him, but in 316 B. C. Antigonus, ruler of Phrygia, drove him out. After the Battle of Ipsus in 301 B. C., Seleucus I received Syria and Asia Minor. The Seleucid era began at this time, and 1 Maccabees and other histories date historical events according to this era.

Seleucus I Nicator founded the famous city of Antioch on the Orontes, 16 miles from the Mediterranean, and made it the capital of his kingdom. When the Romans took over control of Syria, Antioch was designated as capital of the Roman province. The city, with a population of about half a million, became one of the great centers of Hellenistic culture in the Roman Empire. Here East and West met and their cultures fused.

The House of Seleucid imitated the example of Alexander in that they founded as many as 40 cities by means of which they hoped to Hellenize the territory subject to them. Other important Hellenic centers were Antioch of Pisidia and Seleucia on the Tigris. Apamea, Laodicea, Edessa, and Beroea were also founded as centers of Greek culture. Life in these great cities was characterized by Oriental luxury and vices, paired with intrigue and assassination — murder and bloodshed everywhere. The history of Syria, particularly in the latter part of this period, presents a series of sordid accounts of evil and cruel men and women living in an evil and degenerate age.

Daniel 11 sets forth events of this period affecting the Jews of Palestine in the 2nd century B. C.[1] In this chapter we will not present all the rulers of the Seleucids, but will refer to those kings under whom the Jews were either favored or persecuted.

Antiochus III (222 – 187 B. C.)

An outstanding Seleucid was Antiochus III, the Great. After a number of battles, Palestine eventually was transferred, at the Battle of Paneas [Panium] in 198 B. C., from the control of the Egyptian Ptolemies to that of the Syrian Seleucids. The Jews liked Antiochus III much better than they had some of the rulers of the Ptolemies. During the first part of Antiochus' rule, the Jews fared well, enjoying many privileges and favors which included the free exercise of their faith with its customs and freedom from taxes. Thus Jewish law was given government sanction as had been the case under the Persians. Traders were not allowed to carry into Jerusalem foods forbidden to the Jews. Antiochus III prevailed upon thousands of Jews to settle in the cities built by him. Unfortunately, however, these favors bestowed on the Jews were not continued for long.

At this time the Jewish Diaspora grew. Thus in the 2nd and 1st centuries B. C. Jews were found in Babylon, around Jerusalem, in Joppa, in Galilee and various parts of the country beyond the Jordan, in Phrygia and Lydia, in Hyrcania, in Egypt, and in Cyrenaica. Because of the transfer of Palestine to Syrian control, the Jewish communities in Egypt and Palestine became politically separated, a situation that was to have serious consequences for Judaism.

PART ONE: HISTORICAL BACKGROUND

With the encouragement of Hannibal, the Carthaginian general, Antiochus III undertook to fight the Romans; he was defeated with disastrous consequences. The decisive battle was fought at Smyrna in 190 B. C. All the territory west of the Taurus Mountains in Asia Minor had to be relinquished to the Romans, which eventually meant the surrender of a large part of Asia Minor. The Syrians were required to pay a heavy indemnity, 15,000 talents, which according to present monetary values was the equivalent of about $30,000,000. To guarantee the payment of this indemnity, twelve high ruling members of the Syrian nobility had to be given as insurance. The wealthy house of the Seleucids suddenly found itself ruined. In order to meet the exorbitant Roman demands, Antiochus III robbed the temples of the kingdom and also the temple of the Jews in Jerusalem. Temples were known to contain deposits of gold. When Antiochus III embarked upon stealing the gold from the temples of his realms, he met with opposition and was killed while confiscating the gold of a temple in the northeastern part of his kingdom.

Seleucus IV (187—175 B. C.)

Seleucus IV (187—175 B. C.) was required to continue the heavy financial payments to Rome. He also tried to rob the temple in Jerusalem and aroused the fanatical opposition of the Jews. The temple bank had deposits belonging to widows and orphans and also some money of Hyrcanus, son of Tobias, totalling 400 talents of silver and 200 talents of gold. (2 Macc. 3:11; Josephus *Ant.* xii, 196-235). This, together with a demonstration in Jerusalem, prompted the Syrian chancellor Heliodorus to forgo the confiscation of the temple gold. According to 2 Macc. 3:1-40 this was considered a miracle by the Jews. Seleucus IV was murdered by Heliodorus, who intended to take over the government for himself.

Antiochus IV (175—163 B. C.)

Antiochus IV (175—163 B. C.), surnamed Epiphanes, brother of Seleucus IV, followed on the Syrian throne, and he continued the oppressive policies of his predecessor. He operated as a typical Oriental king and showed adeptness at deception and dissimulation. He became famous for his wicked deeds. Besides being very ambitious and desirous of fame, he suffered from alarming aberrations and eccentricities. Polybius the historian dubbed him "Epimanes," "the madman," rather than Epiphanes, "the manifest god," because of the rashness of his acts. Hoping to realize the dream of imperial magnificence, his great passion was to make all the people of his realm devotees of Greek culture as he was. The Jews especially were obnoxious to him. Tacitus in his *Histories* (V,5) wrote as follows: "King Antiochus strove to overthrow the superstition of the Jews and to introduce among them Greek customs, but was prevented by the war with the Parthians from improving the condition of this most debatable race." Reicke wrote about Antiochus IV:

28

Strongly reinforcing a tradition of the Seleucids, he required men to worship him as Olympian Zeus (II Macc. 6:2; also on coins), thereby giving a special Western emphasis to his imperialism. Unlike his father, he was always careful to keep on good terms with Rome and its allies in Asia Minor.[2]

The Hellenization program while generally successful met with opposition in Judea. There were two parties among the Jews: the Conservative and the Hellenistic. The Jews in Palestine had been subjected to Hellenism for nearly a century and a half. Many Jews in Jerusalem wore Greek clothes, imitated Greek customs, and had acquired a speaking knowledge of Greek. Most of the Jewish people nevertheless loved their Jewish faith and customs.

It was the hope of Antiochus IV that the Hellenization of the Jews of Judea would be as easily effected as it had been in other districts of his dominion. The Syrian king expected to get help from the Graeco-philes who had forsaken the Jewish way of life. Antiochus IV built gymnasia, theaters, temples, racecourses, and public baths in the larger cities of Palestine. In Jerusalem (to the dismay of the orthodox) a Greek gymnasium was erected directly under the citadel. According to Josephus (XII:V.1) Greek fashions were introduced, and young men were seen attired in Greek caps; the priests of the temple neglected their priestly offices and instead engaged in worldly pleasures of the palaestra. The pious Jews were strongly opposed to the extravagance displayed everywhere as well as to the idolatry being committed, for many of the practices of Hellenism were completely incompatible with the teachings of the Hebrew Scriptures.

When Antiochus IV became king, Onias III occupied the position of high priest. His brother was Yoshua, a leader of the Jewish Hellenistic party. Onias III changed his name to Jason to show his compliance with the plans and decrees of the Syrian king and abandoned the customs and religion handed down to the Jews from the fathers. An offer of 440 talents was made to Antiochus IV for the high priestly position. Another 150 talents were proffered for permission to build a gymnasium in Jerusalem where Jewish youth might be trained in the athletic activities and games of the Greeks. Jason received the appointment and set about energetically to Hellenize Judea and Jerusalem.

In 172 B. C. Jason himself was replaced by another brother, Menelaus, because the latter had outbid Jason by 300 talents (2 Macc. 4:24). From the viewpoint of the orthodox Jew, conditions had deteriorated to a pathetic state when the highest ecclesiastical office in Judaism could be secured by bribery. The appointment of Menelaus was a flagrant violation of Jewish law and aroused bitter dissatisfaction in Judah. To pay for his bribes, Menelaus was forced to steal large sums of money from the temple treasury, which outraged the Jews to such an extent that they sent a delegation to the Syrian king protesting the actions of Menelaus. The aggressive Hellenistic party met with opposition, and a serious disturbance among the Jews broke out. However, Menelaus triumphed by resorting to further bribery, and the delegation that protested was put to death. According to 2 Macc. 4:34 — 35, Menelaus had Onias murdered.

Antiochus IV embarked on four campaigns against Egypt. The first was undertaken in 173 B. C., after the death of Ptolemy VI. Coele-Syria, Palestine, and Phoenicia were claimed by the Seleucid king. In the battle Ptolemy Philometor was taken prisoner, and Antiochus IV had himself proclaimed king of Egypt in Memphis in 169 B. C. Alexandria, however, revolted and elected as their king Ptolemy's brother.

The situation in Judah was to become even more critical. While Antiochus IV was conducting a second successful campaign against Egypt, Jason decided to regain his position by force. He believed the opportune moment was while Antiochus IV was engaged in fighting the Egyptians. A rumor was also spread that Antiochus IV had been killed. When the latter was apprised of what had occurred in Jerusalem, he became angry and marched against Jerusalem. Bloody revenge was taken upon the Holy City. According to Josephus, the Syrian soldiers were allowed to massacre 40,000 men, women, and children, besides selling many Jews into slavery. Philip, a very cruel man, was made governor of Jerusalem. Thereupon Antiochus IV dared to enter and ransack "the most holy temple of all the earth." The golden altar and all the consecrated vessels and ornaments together with many other priceless treasures were pilfered.

Besides these indignities, heavy tax burdens were placed on the Jewish population. Because of the luxurious standard of living maintained by Antiochus IV and also on account of the wars he constantly waged, he was in need of funds. He decided to obtain financial help from the Jews. Various types of taxes, such as the poll tax, crown tax, and temple tax, were imposed. A very heavy tax, amounting to a third of the grain harvest and up to half of the fruit harvest, was also levied on salt obtained from the Dead Sea. During times of war the Syrian soldiers were instructed to take cattle and other food stores as they were required for the army of Antiochus IV. The harshness and unreasonableness of this program of taxation becomes evident when it is realized that in general the Jews of Palestine were poor. Most of them were small farmers who tilled and harvested in primitive fashion. Force was employed in the collection of these different taxes, and failure to pay resulted in individuals and villages being sold into slavery.

In 167 B. C. Antiochus IV became involved in another war with Egypt which proved to be his last. When it appeared as if he would be successful, Egypt appealed to Rome for help, a request welcomed by Rome. As Antiochus was approaching Alexandria, he was met by G. Popillius Laenas, an ambassador from Rome, who demanded that the Syrians immediately leave Egypt. Antiochus left Egypt in disgrace, returning with apprehension to Syria because the Jews as an anti-Syrian party were settled on the southern border. Upon his return he decided to vent his fury on the Jews and forced them to become Greek in their religion and thinking, since opponents of the Hellenist party began to show a pronounced political orientation toward Egypt.

He sent Appollonius with an army of 22,000 men against Jerusalem, who secured entrance to Jerusalem by deception. As soon as he was within the city he proceeded in a fit of treacherous villainy to kill the citizens by the thousands. Women and children were sold as slaves; the city was burned; its walls were thrown down, and its materials were employed to fortify the old city of David, which remained for 26 years as a Syrian garrison.

A decree was then issued by Antiochus IV that all Jews were to conform to Syrian laws, customs, and religion. The worship of Greek gods and goddesses was to replace adoration of Jehovah. Distinctively Jewish customs, such as Sabbath observance, the rite of circumcision, and the avoidance of unclean food, were prohibited on penalty of death. Those mothers who had their babies circumcised were crucified with their babies hung around their necks. The required daily sacrifices were prohibited. A herd of swine was driven into the temple, and on the altar dedicated to the Olympian Zeus, swine flesh was sacrificed. This altar was used for two and one-half years; this is believed to be the source of the 42 months or the "time and one-half" of the Book of Revelation, where it is the stylized description of the period of evil. The holy utensils were desecrated by sprinkling broth made from swine flesh over them.

Indecent orgies polluted the sacred courts of the temple and became resorts for revelers. Profane foreign cults, included among them the rites of the barbaric Bacchic ritual, were substituted for the time-honored temple ritual. This outraged the religious sensibilities of the Jews. The Books of the Maccabees contained descriptions of the sad situation into which the Jews were forced.

> For the king had sent letters by messengers unto Jerusalem and the cities of Juda, that they should follow the strange laws of the land. And forbid burnt offerings, and sacrifice, and drink offerings, in the temple; and that they should profane the sabbaths and festival days: And pollute the sanctuary and holy people: Set up altars, and groves, and chapels of idols, and sacrifice swine's flesh, and unclean beasts: That they should also leave their children uncircumcised, and make their souls abominable with all manner of uncleanness and profanation: To the end they might forget the law, and change all the ordinances. And whosoever would not do according to the commandment of the king, he said, he should die. 1 Macc. 1:44-50.

A spirit of heroism seized many Jews. They preferred to be killed, yes, even martyred, rather than betray their faith and violate their conscience. As history has so clearly demonstrated again and again, oppression and persecution, far from extinguishing the strength and vitality of a people, nourish and fortify all its reserves of obstinacy, resistance, and national pride, confirming rather than dispersing its individuality. Of this truism the Jews have been and still are the most remarkable and constant witness. With holy determination and unfaltering courage the Jews set their faces grimly against this persecution; for nothing was more precious to them than their religion and the worship of the God of their fathers.

Although idol altars were conspicuous everywhere, the Books of the

Law publicly burned, and death the punishment for defiance, many Jews chose to remain faithful to the covenant of Jehovah. Thus 1 Maccabees asserts: "Howbeit many in Israel were fully resolved and confirmed in themselves not to eat anything unclean. Wherefore they chose rather to die, that they might not be defiled with meats, and that they might not profane the holy covenant." (1 Macc. 1:62–63)

The atrocities and inhumanities perpetrated on the Jews by the Syrians beggar description. All Jews, young and old, male and female, were maltreated and tortured for failing to comply with the decree enforcing Hellenization. An example of Jewish heroism is the case of the aged scribe Eleazar, who was flogged to death for his refusal to eat pork, is reported in 2 Maccabees.:

> It happened also that seven brothers and their mother were arrested and were being compelled by the king, under torture with whips and cords, to partake of unlawful swine's flesh. One of them, acting as their spokesman, said, "What do you intend to ask and learn from us? For we are ready to die rather than transgress the laws of our fathers." The king fell into a rage, and gave orders that pans and caldrons be heated. These were heated immediately, and he commanded that the tongue of their spokesman be cut out and that they scalp him and cut off his hands and feet, while the rest of the brothers and the mother looked on. When he was utterly helpless, the king ordered them to take him to the fire, still breathing, and to fry him in a pan. The smoke from the pan spread widely, but the brothers and their mother encouraged one another to die nobly. . . . (7:1-5)

This example of martyrdom was followed by his six brothers, and finally their mother was subjected to the same inhumanities and tortures.

Of these and other martyrs of the time of Antiochus IV, the author of the Epistle to the Hebrews asserted:

> And others were tortured, not accepting deliverance; that they might obtain a better resurrection. And others had trial of cruel mockings and scourgings, yea, moreover of bonds and imprisonments: they were stoned, they were sawn asunder, were tempted, were slain with the sword: they wandered about in sheepskins and goatskins; being destitute, afflicted, tormented; (of whom the world was not worthy); they wandered in deserts, and in mountains, and in dens and the caves of the earth. (Heb. 11:35-38)

The Jews experienced difficult times. However, force and brutality did not triumph over their faith, which ultimately resisted the onslaught of paganistic Hellenism. A party of opposition was formed, headed by scribes, whose origin is traced back to Ezra. These scribes were orthodox, legalistic, and strict. Among their objectives was that of fostering the study both of the Torah and of the traditions of the elders which had been transmitted orally from one generation to another. The scribes were opposed to everything that was Gentile. For example, they refused to use glass because it was made of material found in the soil owned by Gentiles.

At first this group was small and scattered throughout the land in villages and towns, purposely avoiding settling in Jerusalem. Then gradually they became the strong opponent of the movement to Hellenize the Jews and were rabid anti-Syrian in their activity. Known as the Chasidim, the pious or separated ones, it was from this group that eventually the sect of Pharisees sprang. They were willing to suffer persecution and martyrdom for their religion and persisted in adhering to the tenets of the ancient faith. Their fanatical legalism was a definite characteristic of the Pharisees of Christ's day. For more than a generation they had opposed the activity of the priestly aristocracy that had aided and abetted the Hellenizing ways of the Seleucid kings. They were not strictly a political party, although when the Jews decided to revolt, they joined them to fight for freedom of religion from oppression and tyranny. When, however, religious freedom had been won, the Chasidim refused to continue to fight for political freedom.

CHAPTER VI

The Jews Under the Maccabees

The opposition of the Jews to the efforts at Hellenization finally broke into open revolt, led by the family of the Maccabees. The revolt grew into a determined struggle for complete political independence. The climax of the struggle between Jews and Syrians came when Appelles, an officer of Antiochus Epiphanes, entered the village of Modin, in the hills between Jerusalem and Joppa.

Mattathias of the Asmonean line was commanded to bring a sacrifice to the heathen god on an altar set up for this purpose. A special appeal was made to the aged priest to comply, for he was told that his example would do much to influence the people. He was assured that he would be given position, honor, and wealth, and would be numbered among the friends of the king. To this command Mattathias responded: "God forbid that we should forsake the Law and the ordinances of our God. We will not hearken to the king's words to go aside from our worship, either to the right hand or to the left." He refused to comply. When another local headman came forward to make the sacrifice, Mattathias struck him down and killed him. He also killed Appelles and destroyed the altar.

Mattathias then called upon those who were loyal to the Jewish faith to follow him as he fled to the hills. His sons and those zealous for the Law followed him. At first the band was small but it kept increasing; Mattathias became their leader in conducting a type of guerilla warfare. Maccabees I described their activity as follows: Emerging suddenly from their hiding places in the mountains, they would fall upon neighboring towns and villages, destroying idols and heathen altars, forcing circumcision upon the apostate Jews, and reestablishing the synagog. Their ranks were swelled by zealots for the Law called the Chasidim; marching up and down Judah these patriots waged their war of purification, carefully avoiding the larger cities, hiding by day and attacking by night.

Judas Maccabaeus (165–161 B. C.)

Mattathias has five sons: John, Simon, Judas, Eleazar, and Jonathan. For a time the father of these five sons led the activities, but the strain was too much for him, and he died in 166 B. C. Before dying he appointed his third son, Judas, as successor (Josephus claims that he was the eldest). Judas (165–161 B. C.) was surnamed Maccabaeus, or "the Hammerer." He united all guerilla groups under him and became a capable and outstanding guerilla chief. With him a glorious period of Jewish history began. The Syrians tried to subdue Judas and his followers, but the invading hosts were routed by Judas Maccabaeus. Appolonius, the governor of Samaria, was ordered to subdue Judas but was unsuccessful. Another opponent, Seron, the governor of Coele-Syria, was defeated by Judas in the pass of Beth-horon.

During this period Antiochus IV Epiphanes had been fighting in the east against the Persians and Armenians, having left Lysias in charge of affairs at home. Lysias decided to send an army under the command of Nicanor and Georgias against the Judean Hills. Nicanor encamped on the plains of Ajalon. An army of 46,000 infantry and 7,000 horsemen was sent to wipe out the followers of Judas. Georgias with one-eighth of the force tried to surprise Judas at night but could not find him. Meanwhile Judas with an army of only 3,000 surprised Nicanor and routed him. The slave traders that accompanied the Syrian army were taken captive, and they themselves were sold into slavery. This battle occurred in the summer of 164 B. C.

Another successful engagement for the Jews is spoken of in 1 Maccabees as taking place in 165 B. C., and this time Judas is represented as defeating Lysias. Snaith believes that the author of 1 Maccabees is in error on this matter. Lysias is supposed to have come with 60,000 footmen and 5,000 horsemen, while Judas with his 10,000 men is portrayed as winning a decisive battle in which 5,000 Syrians were killed.

In 164 B. C. Judas entered the city of Jerusalem and restored the temple, cleansing it from all pollution, and reinstituting the former services required by the law of God. The Feast of Hanukkah or Rededication took place on Kislev 25, 164 B. C. Religious liberty had been won, and a new priesthood was inducted. In John 10:22 we read: "And it was at Jerusalem the feast of the dedication, and it was winter. And Jesus walked in the temple in Solomon's Porch." This festival was also known as the feast of lights and marked the end of the first phase of the wars of Judas Maccabeus.

The success of Judas was limited to achieving freedom for Jerusalem and the Jews in Judea. He had also been successful in his skirmishes with the Bedouin Arabs in the Negeb and had extended the boundaries of Jewish dominion into parts of Philistia. However, there were others Jews who were in trouble with the Gentile people of Gilead and Galilee. These troubled Jews asked Judas Maccabeus for help; this was sent them in the persons of Simon and Jonathan, together with a military force. They rescued the loyal Jews and settled them in Judea. As a result of these expeditions, Judas became confident of himself as a military leader, making excursions into Edom and Philistia.

Lysias' Attack on Judas

While Judas was winning these battles, Antiochus IV Epiphanes died on a campaign in the east. Before his departure to the battle in which he was killed, he entrusted his seven-year-old son (later Antiochus V, Eupator) to his general Philip, appointing the latter as regent and guardian of the boy. In view of this development, Lysias was willing not to coerce the Jews into becoming Hellenists. However, when Judas endeavored to drive out the Syrian guard from Akra, the citadel overlooking the temple, Lysias was forced to act. He attacked Judas from the south, up the valley through Beth-zur. Lysias came with 100,000 foot soldiers, 20,000 horsemen, and 32 elephants. A vivid description of this battle is found in 1 Maccabees 6:30 ff. The author of 1 Maccabees states that the elephants were made furious by being shown blood, produced from the juice of grapes and mulberries.

In the opening engagement between Lysias and Judas, the latter's oldest brother, Eleazar, was killed by an elephant he was trying to kill. The odds were too great for Judas, and he and his cohorts had to retreat to Jerusalem where he secluded himself in the temple fortress with a small number of supporters. But by this time Lysias' rival had arrived, making it necessary for Lysias to come to quick terms with Judas so that Lysias might be free to challenge the rulership of the Seleucid kingdom.

Lysias signed a treaty granting the Jews the right to live according to their own laws and to worship Jehovah in keeping with the precepts laid down in the Torah. Judas received a full pardon, although politically he and his compatriots remained under Syrian rule. The temple fortress was destroyed; Menelaus, the high priest, was deposed and put to death. His successor was a man named Jakim. He was better known by his Greek name Alcimus. Although of true Aaronic stock, Alcimus was pro-Syrian in his sympathies.

Chasidim Desert Judas

At this time Judas lost the help and support of the Chasidim who had only assisted the Maccabees while religious persecutions were raging against the Jews. However, when religious freedom was gained, the Chasidim refused to support any political ambition of Judas. The withdrawal of their forces represented a great loss to Judas' army. He drove the pro-Seleucid Jakim (Alcimus) out of Jerusalem; Alcimus appealed for help to Demetrius I, king of Syria, son of Seleucus IV, nephew of Antiochus IV. Demetrius sent one of his generals, Bacchides, with a good-size army. Judas was compelled to leave Jerusalem, and Alcimus was reinstated. Although he was accepted and trusted by the Chasidim, he massacred a number of them.

Nicanor, commander in Judaea under Bacchides, attempted similar tactics against Judas, but Judas saw through Nicanor's policy of feigning friendship and fled to the Judean Hills. (Historians believe that the two had actually become friends but that Alcimus ruptured their friendship.) Finally Nicanor and Judas met on the field of battle at Adasa, near Beth-Horon, on the 13th of Adar in 161 B. C. Even though Nicanor was slain, it was the last victory for Judas. Two months afterward Judas was besieged by a large army of Syrians at Elasa, a place north of Jerusalem, and killed.

According to 1 Maccabees 8, Judas sent a delegation to Rome to ask for help against the Syrians. The author of Maccabees describes the Romans: "They were very strong and well-disposed toward all who made an alliance with them, that they pledged friendship to those who came to them . . . . Men told him [Judas] of their wars and of the brave deeds . . . among the Gauls . . . they had defeated them and forced them to pay tribute" (8:1-3 RSV). Judas also had been told that the Romans had defeated Antiochus the Great, with his 120 elephants, cavalry, chariots, and a very large army. The Romans forced Antiochus to pay a heavy tribute, but they kept peace with their friends. "They have subdued kings far and near, and as many as have heard of their fame have feared them." They were, according to Judas, a great and exalted nation, yet no one wore a crown or was clothed in purple. A Senate composed of 320 ruled the Roman people, and from this group one was chosen each year to rule over the Senate.

Eupolemos and Jason were sent as ambassadors by Judas to make a treaty with the Romans. It was to be a defensive and offensive alliance. If either power was attacked, the other was to come to its aid. No food or war materials were to be given to the foe of the other party of the agreement. This gave the Romans an opportunity to interfere in the affairs of Syria and the Near East.

Before the Jewish emissaries returned, Judas had been killed in a battle against overwhelming odds: an army of 20,000 footmen and 2,000 horsemen. Judas Maccabeus must be considered one of the great military men that the Israelite nation had produced. After his death, a state of chaos developed in Israel. At this particular time the Jewish nation was divided into three groups: the Maccabees, the Chasidim, and the Hellenists. Upon the death of Judas, the Hellenists, previously forced underground, appeared and reasserted themselves. Alcimus, a Greek lover, was the high priest. He placed unbelieving Hellenists in important positions and tore down the partition of the temple separating the court of the Jews from that of the Gentiles. The condition of the Maccabees was disastrous; famine and persecution added to their woes; their party approached extinction. Three of the surviving Maccabee brothers were driven out of the land and fled to the marshes beyond the Dead Sea; one of them was killed. Jonathan, the younger brother of Judas, was elected to take his place. Jonathan and Simon, the two survivors, withdrew to the wilderness southeast of Jerusalem.

Jonathan (160 – 142 B. C.)

Jonathan (160 – 142 B. C.) embarked upon guerilla warfare; he retook from the Syrians one important stronghold after another until only Jerusalem remained. Thus Jerusalem remained in the control of the Syrians and of the pro-Hellenistic party of the Jews for 7 years; during this time Jonathan only waged small skirmishes.

However, a revolution in Syria in 153 B. C. helped Jonathan achieve his goal of getting control of Jerusalem: there were two claimants for the Syrian throne. Demetrius I, the occupant, was challenged by Alexander Balas, claiming to be the rightful heir, the son of Antiochus IV Epiphanes. Balas had the support of the kings of Cappadocia and Pergamum and especially that of Rome and Egypt. The Egyptians, Romans, and other neighboring rulers seized this opportunity to involve themselves in the internal affairs of Syria.

Both Demetrius and Balas offered Jonathan many privileges for his military support. While the offer of Demetrius was very generous, Jonathan did not trust him and decided to accept the offer of Alexander Balas. In the ensuing conflict between the two claimants, Demetrius was defeated and killed. As a reward for his support, Jonathan was appointed high priest; Balas made him one of the "king's friends," and sent him a purple robe and golden crown. This made Jonathan king-priest.

In 153 B. C., at the Feast of Tabernacles, Jonathan officiated as high priest at the altar. Since the House of Mattathias was of priestly descent, the offerings made by Jonathan were not illegal; in fact, the Chasidim joined the party of Jonathan permanently at this time. Jonathan now combined in one office two positions – that of priest and king. The Chasidim were a religious party, mainly concerned about religion and the Law.

Alexander Balas did not remain king long. He became an immoral individual, given to drunkenness and debauchery and hated by the people. Demetrius II attacked Balas, claiming the right to the Syrian throne. Balas, who had married Cleopatra, daughter of Ptolemy VI of Egypt, endeavored to take away the Egyptian throne from his father-in-law. Balas was defeated and killed as he was fleeing. Demetrius II Nicator then assumed the rule over the Syrian Empire.

In Syria's troublous times, Jonathan consolidated his own position. He attacked and subdued a number of cities southwest of Jerusalem. He acquired cities, including Joppa, which was used as a seaport for Jerusalem. The Hellenistic party of Jerusalem informed Demetrius II of Jonathan's action. The Syrian ruler sent an embassy to Jonathan demanding that he discontinue the attack. Upon receipt of this demand, Jonathan left his troops and proceeded to meet Demetrius to pacify him and if possible to arrange favorable terms for the Jews. Jonathan's overlord was so impressed by him that he confirmed all the privileges that had been granted to Judas by Alexander Balas and most of the privileges promised by Demetrius I.

Jonathan, the fugitive of a few years ago, now was one of the arbiters of the Syrian throne, courted alike by the man in possession and the man who wanted to be. Thus by diplomacy Jonathan strengthened his position and acquired considerable territory, especially west of Jerusalem: several Philistine cities, and the land northward up to Mount Carmel. Jonathan became master of Judah to a degree that Judas Maccabeus had never attained. While Judas had conquered by his great courage, force, strategy, and determination, his brother Jonathan resorted to diplomacy as his chief weapon. Jonathan, the youngest of the five sons of Mattathias, was called "The Cunning."

Trouble in Syria resulted in death for Jonathan. A pretender known as Antiochus VI had been placed on the Syrian throne by Trypho, an officer in the Syrian army. The latter had personal aspirations for the throne. Trypho realized that Jonathan, faithful to his master, constituted a roadblock on his path to the throne. Under the guise of friendship he invited Jonathan to a meeting for negotiations. When Jonathan entered the city for negotiations, Trypho seized and killed Jonathan's bodyguard and later had Jonathan treacherously assassinated.

Simon Succeeds Jonathan (142 – 134 B. C.)

Simon, the third son of the Maccabean leader Mattathias, and the last living son, became the leader of the party. According to 1 Maccabees 13, he addressed the people of Jerusalem as follows:

> Ye know yourself what great things I and my brethren and my father's house have done for the laws and the sanctuary. It is battles and it is troubles which we have seen. All my brethren have been slain for Israel's sake, and I am left alone. Now, therefore, be it far from me that I should spare my life in a time of trouble for I am no better than my brethren. Doubtless I will avenge my nation and the sanctuary and our wives and children, for all the heathen are gathered to destroy us of very malice. (Vv. 3-6)

When the people heard these words, they shouted: "Thou shalt be our leader, and we will follow you."

One of Simon's great accomplishments was the unification of the three opposing parties of Judaism: the Hellenists, the Chasidim, and the Maccabees. As soon as Simon became leader, he effected a treaty with Demetrius II, the rightful king of Syria. Trypho was defeated and killed in his battle against Demetrius Nicator. The latter released the Jews from all payment of taxes and granted them political independence, giving them the status of an independent ally. That for which Mattathias and his four sons gave their lives was now realized by his last son, Simon. This took place in 142 B. C.; from this time the Jews date their independence. A great festival of thanksgiving was celebrated, and for many years the day was observed annually, according to the author of 1 Macc. 13:43-52.

The Jewish people conferred upon Simon the position of absolute sovereign, and made the office of ruler of the nation hereditary in his family. Simon also dispatched an embassy to Rome with instructions to make a treaty with the Romans, who gave recognition to the political independence of the Jewish kingdom.

After Simon had secured complete control over the Judean territory, he set about diligently to restore his desolated and war-torn territory. To safeguard the temple Simon drove the enemies out of the fortifications in the Shephelah Hills and thus made safe the road connecting Joppa and Jerusalem. In May 141 B. C. the garrison in the citadel of Akra surrendered, and Simon entered Jerusalem amid great jubilation. Whenever possible he also freed Jewish prisoners of war, restoring these individuals to their former lands. The author of 1 Macc. 14:4-15 says the following about Simon:

> As for the land of Judea, that was quiet all the days of Simon: for he sought the good of his nation in such wise, as that evermore his authority and honor pleased them well. And as he was honorable in all his acts, so in this, that he took Joppa for an haven and made an entrance to the isles of the sea and enlarged the bounds of his nation, and recovered the country. And gathered together a great number of captives and had the dominion of Gazara, and Bethsura, and the tower, out of which he took all the uncleanness, neither was there any that resisted him. Then did they till their ground in peace, and the earth gave her increase, and the trees of the field their fruit. The ancient men sat all in the streets, communing together of good things, and the young men put on glorious and warlike apparel. He provided victuals for the cities, and set in them all manner of munition, so that his honorable name was renowned unto the end of the world. He made peace in the land, and Israel rejoiced with great joy; for every man sat under his vine and his fig tree, and there was none to fray them: Neither was there any left in the land to fight against them: yea, the kings themselves were overthrown in those days, moreover, he strengthened all those of his people that were brought low: the law he searched out; and every contemner of the law and wicked person he took away. He beautified the sanctuary, and multiplied the vessels of the temple.

He made a treaty with Rome which gave security and prestige to the Jews against all their enemies; the Roman Senate sent official letters to kings of Cappadocia, Pergamum, Syria, and Egypt telling them of the alliance and warning them against making war against the Jews; Simon issued a coinage of his own money. It was always considered a sign of sovereignty when a ruler was able to issue his own coinage. Coins have survived from the time of 141 – 136 B. C. On one side, the coin read: "Jerusalem, the Holy," and on the other the value of the coin was designated, either the shekel or half-shekel.

Simon ruled well and wisely. The only dark spot on his record was the treatment given apostate Jews, whom Simon either deported or executed. Sorcerers were hanged and pagans exiled. The successful activities of

Simon fostered the fires of nationalism and made its flame burn brightly. During this period of prosperity and renovation, the hope of the Messiah's coming was keenly aroused in the minds of the faithful Israelites. Simon's rule was designated as the beginning of a new era—"and the people of Israel began to write in their instruments and contracts: in the first year of Simon, the great high priest and captain and leader of the Jews."

Simon's Death

Unfortunately for Simon, he did not live too long to enjoy the fruits of his valiant efforts and planning. Like his brothers, he suffered a violent death. In 135 B. C. while Simon was inspecting the fortress of Dok in the Jericho Plain and attending a banquet in his honor he and his two sons were slain by his own son-in-law Ptolemy, who planned to become his successor; Simon's wife was held as a hostage for a time and then brutally murdered.

Thus died the last son of the noble Mattathias, all of whose sons met with violent deaths while fighting and working in the interest of the Jews. Two sons, Judas and Eleazar, met death on the battlefield; three others were killed by treachery. All were buried in a beautiful and impressive monument at Modein, built by Judas.

With the death of Simon a period of 30 years during which five of the Maccabees rendered valiant service came to an end. Great things were achieved during these three decades. The result was that the small city-state of Jerusalem, harrassed by its enemies and threatened with complete annihilation, had grown into a united nation. Israel had an army that was respected and feared by her enemies. The temple had been cleared of all pagan abominations. The Jews once again had a high priest and a hereditary prince and were enjoying religious liberty and almost complete political independence.

CHAPTER **VII**

The Jews Under the Hasmoneans

Although Ptolemy had planned to exterminate all of Simon's descendants, son John Hyrcanus escaped. Being warned of Ptolemy's murderous design, John Hyrcanus proceeded to Jerusalem and assumed the dignity of the high priest in the place of his father. He did not inherit the title of king, for even Simon had not been permitted to use the designation of king. One of the Hasmoneans had applied this title to himself, but it is doubtful that the people ever acknowledged him as such.

The death of Simon spelled trouble for the Jews, for when the Syrians heard of the murder of Simon, they proceeded to attack Jerusalem. After a long siege, Hyrcanus was forced to accept the terms of the Syrian king, Antiochus VII Sidetes, who meant to effect the subjugation of Israel to the Syrians and bring about the loss of Israel's political liberty. However, this state of affairs did not last long, because contests over the Syrian throne made it possible for Hyrcanus to regain independence and gave him enough time to control his kingdom. Without interference from the north, Hyrcanus was able to extend his dominion by successful military expeditions. The kingdom was enlarged to the extent that it practically covered the same territory over which Solomon had ruled in the 10th century B. C. The chief military expeditions of Hyrcanus were directed against the Samaritans and the Idumeans. The temple of the Samaritans on Mount Gerizim was destroyed and the Samaritans subdued. Hyrcanus forced the Idumeans to accept the Jewish religion and to become circumcised. Herod the Great was an Idumean and even though he was not of Jewish ancestry, he was a Jew according to religion.

Hyrcanus did not treat the Chasidim well, failing to appreciate the important role they had played as supporters of the Maccabeans from the time of Mattathias to the death of Simon. The Pharisees were more concerned with the proper observance of the Law than they were with the political progress of the Jewish nation. The antagonistic attitude of Hyrcanus over against the Chasidim resulted in internal tension. From this time forward the existence of three sects is dated: the Pharisees, who came out of the Chasidim, the Sadducees, and the Essenes. Hyrcanus was the first Jewish prince to stamp *his name* upon the coinage he issued. Josephus (*Jewish Antiq.* XIII, X, 7) says that Hyrcanus "administered the government in the best manner for 31 years." His reign was a prosperous one, yes, even brilliant. He died in 106 B. C.

Aristobulus I (104 – 103 B. C.)

Aristobulus I succeeded his father Hyrcanus, although the latter had appointed his wife Salome as successor to the throne and Aristobulus as high priest. He seized the throne, imprisoned his mother, and allowed her to die of starvation. He also murdered his brother Antigonus and had another brother Alexander Jannaeus incarcerated. Only one brother, Antigonus, he spared, and him he allowed to share the rule of the government. Aristobulus I called himself "king." He was ruthless, cruel, and extremely ambitious. His favorite brother Antigonus was murdered by people who were jealous of him, and Aristobulus I had unwittingly contributed to carrying out the dastardly plot. In an agony of remorse for the death of his brother, Aristobulus I died. In his sympathies he was pro-Hellenic and did much to promote Greek culture. His role departed extremely from the ideals for which the Maccabees had fought. He increased the boundaries of his realm by extending its boundaries northward, beyond Samaria and Scythopolis, and by conquering those Itureans who lived in "Galilee of the Gentiles." Turner asserted about Hyrcanus: "Hyrcanus' move toward the more politically minded and aristocratic party [the Sadducees] had the greater significance and importance in that it set the direction for the future development in the Hasmonean dynasty." [1] John Hyrcanus gave the Jewish state a different direction "by developing Hellenistic sympathies" and so departed from ideals held by the earlier members of his family.

Alexander Jannaeus (103–76 B. C.)

Alexandra (his wife) had been appointed by Aristobulus as his successor. After his death she freed her brother-in-law Alexander Jannaeus from prison and appointed him high priest. She then married him and made him the king. Like Aristobulus I, Alexander Jannaeus was ambitious, ruthless and without scruples. Being a Hellenist in his sympathies he favored the Sadducees at the expense of the Pharisees. He ruled as an oriental despot, departing greatly from the standards set by the Maccabee brothers. Alexander Jannaeus extended the boundaries of Judah into Galilee, Philistia, and central Jordan. In Alexander Jannaeus the Hasmonean dynasty reached its height territorially. However, Turner points out that "the subjugation of so many cultured Greek cities had a demoralizing effect on the civilization of Coele-Syria; prosperity declined in field and city, and everywhere the scars from the wars from which his reign was scarcely ever free were visible." [2]

He had numerous clashes with the Pharisees, who owed their origin to the Chasidim, "the pious ones," during the reign of Antiochus Epiphanes. The Chasidim had helped the Maccabees in their struggle to be free from Syrian power. At other times however, the Chasidim had remained neutral, especially after Judas Maccabeus began to exhibit political ambitions. When the Pharisees now revolted against Alexander Jannaeus, he put down the revolt by harsh methods, killing 6,000 of his enemies. On another occasion when his enemies within Israel rebelled, he crushed the revolt by crucifying 800 of the ringleaders in the sight of a banquet given by Jannaeus for his followers and concubines. Before the eyes of those dying of crucifixion, the cruel king had their wives and children massacred. Many in his realm came to hate him. Alexander Jannaeus died at the age of 49 and left his widow, Alexandra, to rule in his place.

Alexandra (76–67 B. C.)

Before Alexander Jannaeus died, he had advised his spouse to cast her lot with the Pharisees. Alexandra was the first woman to rule over the Jews in her own right. She heeded the advice of her husband and favored the Pharisees and thereby gained their support. She was an able woman, and in contrast to her husband's reign hers was one that promoted peace and prosperity. Alexandra was able to restore the happy and palmy days of the reign of Simon. She was greatly helped by an advisor, Simon ben Shatach, who was assisted by the Jewish scholar Tabbai of Egyptian origin.

Simon ben Shatach introduced a number of important reforms in Israel: 1. Those Pharisees who had been driven into exile were welcomed back, those in prison were freed, and important positions were assigned to the Pharisees in the kingdom; 2. Jewish ceremonies which had been neglected were restored; 3. Every Israelite was to pay a poll tax of half a shekel for the support of the temple, a payment required of proselytes and freed men. This was aimed at freeing the temple and its upkeep from its former support by wealthy Sadducees; and, 4. Compulsory education for all Jewish children.

During the reign of Alexandra, the Sanhedrin increased in power and prestige. The Pharisees gained an advantage at this time that henceforth they never relinquished. Alexandra ruled for 9 years with great success and earned the love and affection of her subjects.

Aristobulus II (67 – 63 B. C.)

The position of high priest had been conferred upon Hyrcanus II during the reign of Alexandra, who designated him as her successor. However, he did not rule very long. Character-wise he was an indolent weakling with no inclination to offer any opponent resistance. Alexandra's son Aristobulus II had the opposite qualities and decided to usurp the throne. With the aid of the Sadducees he inaugurated a successful revolution. In a battle near Jericho, Hyrcanus II was defeated and forced to abdicate his position as king and high priest.

This arrangement might have continued had it not been for the governor of Idumaea, whose name was Antipater, the father of Herod the Great. Antipater was afraid that Aristobulus II would deprive him of his position and so prevailed upon Hyrcanus II to nullify his agreement and attempt to regain the throne. With the help of the Nabatean king, Aretas II, Antipater and Hyrcanus II defeated Aristobulus II and imprisoned him in Jerusalem. A civil war then broke out between the two sons of Alexandra; this continued until 63 B. C.

To terminate the struggle, both brothers appealed to Rome, which at this juncture inaugurated Roman politics in Palestine, and from this time forth Rome was to exercise a lasting influence upon Judea and the period of the New Testament.

Pompey had been successful in defeating the pirates in the Mediterranean and had defeated Mithradates VI, the strongest ruler of a small kingdom in northern Asia Minor. With the defeat of Mithradates, Rome was now definitely interested in Syria and Palestine. The request for help by Aristobulus II and Hyrcanus II gave the Romans the opportunity they were seeking: interference in the affairs of Palestine. The Romans were glad to come to Palestine to arbitrate and remain there permanently. However, in comparison with the beginning of the century when Simon had made a treaty with the Romans, the policy of Rome had changed. Rome was now definitely aiming for conquest and power.

When Pompey heard of the rulers in Palestine, he sent his General Scaurus south to capitalize on the situation. Both sides offered the general bribes, but since Aristobulus II offered the greater sum, Scaurus favored him. Scaurus ordered Aretas of Arabia to withdraw from Judea; this left Aristobulus II in power from 67 – 63 B. C.

In 63 B. C. Pompey summoned both parties to appear before him so that he might conclusively settle the dispute. Pompey decided in favor of Hyrcanus II. However, Aristobulus II would not capitulate and fled to a fortress called Alexandrium, from where he tried further negotiations with Pompey. When Pompey was adamant, Aristobulus II was driven from this stronghold. He fled to Jerusalem which was then besieged by Pompey.

Again Aristobulus II tried to negotiate, offering a large sum of money and surrender of the city. When Babinus, the general of Pompey arrived, he found the city closed to him and there ensued a siege which lasted three months, during which time war was raging inside and outside of Jerusalem. The followers of Hyrcanus II were willing to surrender, but those of Aristobulus II insisted on fighting to the end. When the city finally capitulated, 12,000 Jews had died, Jerusalem was burned, and Pompey marched into the holy of holies in the temple. However he did not despoil the temple, and he desisted from taking the huge quantities of stored gold he found.

Hyrcanus II again found himself high priest and ethnarch. Those who had served as leaders in the revolt under Aristobulus II were put to death. From this time forward the Jewish race was confined to the province of Judea. All the outlying territory, which Simon and some of his successors had conquered and incorporated into the Maccabean and Hasmonean kingdoms, was severed from Jewish control and given independence. Samaria, destroyed by John Hyrcanus, was restored, rebuilt, and given the name of Sebaste. Antipater was made governor of Judea and ruled till his assassination in 43 B. C.

Aristobulus II and many of his followers were taken to Rome to march in Pompey's triumphal procession. Thus the Jews, who on frequent occasions before had parleyed for the friendship and protection of Rome, now felt the invincible grip of her conquering hand from which they were destined never to escape as an independent nation.

CHAPTER VIII

The Jews Under the Romans (63 B. C. — A. D. 135)

The Roman period of Jewish history begins with 63 B. C. and extends to the suppression of the rebellion of Bar-Cochba by Hadrian with the concomitant disintegration of the life of the Jews. For the New Testament student this period ends with the destruction of Jerusalem and its temple in 70 A. D. When the Jews were obedient and submissive to the laws of the Roman rule, they were treated with consideration. Judaism was recognized as one of the licensed religions in the Roman world. The Jews were required to pay a tribute which, even though it was small and not burdensome, they nevertheless resented. They had their own Sanhedrin, a judicial and legislative body, and were permitted to settle civil and minor cases. Not since Persian domination were the Jews given such fair treatment as under Roman rule, yet the extremists, known as the Zealots, kept Israel in constant unrest and provoked the Jews to break out in rebellion a number of times.

The years between 63 B. C. and 43 B. C. were troubled ones for the Near Eastern world, especially between 53 B. C. and 43 B. C. Caesar and Pompey had become estranged in 49 B. C.; there was civil war between them till at Pharsalus in Thessaly Pompey was defeated (48 B. C.). He was later killed in Egypt. In the struggle between them for the control of Rome, Aristobulus II and his sons were on the side of Caesar. Aristobulus II was poisoned while on his way to Judea with the troops furnished him by Caesar. In the year 44 B. C. Caesar was murdered; after this war ensued between Brutus and Cassius on one side and Mark Anthony and Octavian on the other.

The history of Judaism under Rome may be divided into five parts: (1) the Idumean dynasty; (2) the first procurators; (3) the reign of Agrippa I; (4) the later procurators, and (5) the Jewish revolt.[1]

The Idumean Dynasty (63 B. C. — A. D. 6)

Antipater, who had been a loyal partisan of Pompey, cleverly succeeded in winning the favor of Caesar by assisting Mithradates of Pergamus, an ally of Caesar, to traverse the Desert of Sinai. While Caesar allowed Hyrcanus II to retain his figurehead titles of ethnarch and high priest, Caesar conferred upon Antipater the status of Roman citizenship and made him procurator of Judea. At this time the Jews were granted many privileges in Palestine, Alexandria, and Rome — not the least among them was religious liberty. After Antipater had implanted himself in his position, he conferred high honors upon his two sons, Phasael and Herod, making Phasael the military governor of Judea and Herod the tetrarch of Galilee.

Antipater was loyal to Rome and at the same time devoted to the civil and political good of Judea. However, because Antipater was an Idumean, he was hated. For centuries there had been an ineradicable repugnance existing between the Jews and the Edomites. When Herod, the governor of Galilee, broke up a robber gang which had infested Galilee, and executed their leader, Hezekias, Herod was summoned to appear before the Sanhedrin in Jerusalem because he had arrogated unto himself the power to execute capital punishment. Instead of appearing before the Sanhedrin, Herod appealed to the Syrian proconsul, Sextus Caesar, who at once appointed Herod governor of Coele-Syria.

Following the assassination of Caesar, Cassius went to Syria to claim the proconsulship of Syria and to gather troops and procure money. Antipater and his two sons succeeded in winning the favor of Cassius by collecting tributes for him. In return, Cassius appointed Herod procurator of all Syria and even promised him the kingship of Judea. Antipater had ambitious plans for self-government but in 43 B. C. a fanatical Jew named Malichus poisoned him and thus ended Antipater's career. Herod at once exercised his prerogative and had Malichus killed. After the death of Antipater, Judea was left in the hands of Phasael and Galilee under the control of Herod. Difficult days were ahead for the two sons of Antipater because of developments in the Roman Republic.

Matters were now in a confused state in Palestine. The Battle of Philippi in 42 B. C. resulted in the defeat of Cassius and Brutus by Octavian (Augustus) and Anthony. As soon as Anthony came into control of Asia, Herod approached him and by bribery won his favor; as a result Anthony appointed Herod and Phasael as joint tetrarchs of Judea and allowed Hyrcanus II to continue only as high priest.

Antigonus, the son of Aristobulus II, called for help from the Parthians, who promptly responded and captured Jerusalem. Phasael was seized and committed suicide. Herod evaded his enemies and fled to Rome, where he requested Anthony to appoint Aristobulus III to the throne of Judea. Anthony did not trust the Hasmoneans and offered to confer the kingship on Herod as an appointment conferred by the Roman Senate. This took place in 40 B. C. Three years later he was able to recapture Jerusalem and take possession of the territory assigned to him by the Romans.

Herod the Great

Historical records show that Herod gave the Jews a strong and efficient government.[2] His creed, inherited from his father (Antipater), was loyalty to Rome no matter who was in power there. So long as Anthony's power in the eastern Mediterranean was supreme, Herod was loyal to him. After the Battle of Actium in 31 B. C., Herod shifted his loyalty to Augustus (Octavian) who, appreciating Herod's worth, confirmed his appointment as a *rex socius* and extended his kingdom to include practically all of Palestine.

Herod had embarked on a thorough program to eliminate his opponents. Antigonus and most of the Sanhedrin were liquidated. Young Aristobulus had been "accidentally" drowned by Herod's henchman. The aged Hyrcanus was murdered. Mariamne, his beautiful wife and most beloved, was killed because she was accused of unfaithfulness by Herod's sister, Salome.

Herod was a great admirer of Graeco-Roman culture. After his first campaign of bloodshed he undertook the improvement of his kingdom. The avoidance of unnecessary wars allowed his kingdom an opportunity to develop. He gave the Jews a strong and efficient administration. Many new buildings were constructed; others were rebuilt. Herod evinced real administrative ability in his architectural program. In the years 20 — 19 B. C. he began to reconstruct the temple because the temple of Zerubbabel was shabby in comparison with the surrounding new buildings. The cities of Samaria and Caesarea were completely reconstructed and adorned with magnificent buildings.

For 11 years Herod enjoyed peace, but the last 10 years of his reign (14 — 4 B. C.) again saw family feuds. Toward the end of his reign he became an embittered and murderous old man. At no time during his reign did he hesitate to exterminate people considered dangerous to his throne or interests. He had many wives and children. Jealousy and rivalry manifested themselves often in his family. Mariamne, sister of Aristobulus III, and granddaughter of Hyrcanus II was a Maccabean princess and had been his favorite wife. Herod had loved her greatly and favored her sons. Herod's mother-in-law, Kypros, and his sister Salome, representing the Idumeans, resented and plotted against Alexandra and Mariamne, representatives of the Hasmoneans. Through such intrigue Herod was induced to put Mariamne to death. Later, realizing his mistake, he embarked upon another wave of bloodshed that prompted the emperor at Rome to say: "It is better to be Herod's swine than his children." Three of his sons were executed. When Herod became afflicted with an incurable disease, he frequently resorted to cruelty and murder. One such act of cruelty associated with the last years of Herod's reign was the killing of the innocent babes at Bethlehem, probably in 6 or 5 B. C. The people loathed Herod with an undying hatred. To insure mourning upon his demise, he gave orders that the principal men of the nation were to be incarcerated in the hippodrome and at the moment of his death were to be executed by his troops. Fortunately, this order was countermanded. After reigning for 34 years, Herod died in 4 B. C.

According to the will of Herod, his kingdom was to be divided among his three sons: Archelaus was to be king of Judea (including Samaria and Idumea), Herod Antipas, tetrarch of Galilee and Perea, and Herod Philip, tetrarch of Trachonitis and adjacent regions. These arrangements of Herod required the approval of Rome, particularly in the matter of the kingship, for Rome did not allow any king to make the throne hereditary. All three brothers went to Rome to seek approval; Archelaus and Antipas sought the kingdom, the former having the support of Philip. An embassy of the Jews went to Rome purporting to rid themselves altogether of the sons of Herod and requesting that Judea instead be placed under direct Roman rule. "A certain nobleman went into a far country to receive for himself a kingdom, and to return . . . but his citizens hated him . . . saying: 'We will not have this man to reign over us.' " (Luke 19:12-14)

Archelaus

Archelaus was confirmed as ethnarch of Judea, Samaria, and Idumea. From the outset he was unpopular as a ruler, and the longer he ruled, the more he was disliked. Even before Archelaus went to Rome to represent his cause, he had suppressed a riot in Jerusalem, and his troops murdered 3,000 Jews at the Passover festival. Chaos and bloodshed characterized his entire reign. Archelaus did not possess the capabilities to deal with the difficulties left by the death of Herod. His marriage to a divorced woman alienated him from the loyalty of the Jews and increased their hatred of the Herodean family. On two different occasions he removed the high priest from office and conducted himself in a barbarous and high-handed manner. The one redeeming feature of his administration was his building program. The outcome of all the friction between Archelaus and the Jews after 10 years of administering his ethnarchy incompetently was his banishment to Gaul by the Romans. Judea then received a procurator in the person of Coponius. (A. D. 6 – 9)

Herod Antipas

The rule of Herod Antipas as tetrarch of Galilee and Perea was much more successful and enduring than that of his brother Archelaus. Herod Antipas engaged in extensive building and fortified his frontiers. He is mentioned a number of times in the New Testament especially in connection with the ministry of John the Baptist. From the strictly Jewish point of view, his illegal marriage with Herodias was a violation of the Law as was the beheading of John the Baptist, whom he had imprisoned because John denounced Herod's sin of adultery. This was the same Herod to whom Pontius Pilate sent Jesus on Good Friday morning (Luke 23:7-12). Herod Antipas was persuaded by Herodius to go with her to Rome and beseech Caligula to bestow upon him the title of king. However, Herod Antipas failed to gain his request and instead was deposed and banished.

Philip

Philip, the third son of Herod, was tetrarch of the district east and northeast of Lake Galilee. Of all the Herods he was by far the best. Philip does not have much connection with the New Testament. The evangelists report that when the Pharisees' hatred imperiled the life of Jesus, the

Master withdrew into the territory governed by Philip. In Schürer's opinion, the reign of Philip was "mild, just, and peaceful."

The Roman Procurators

The first three Roman procurators seem to have governed the country in a wise manner. At the request of the Jews, Judea was placed under the rule of the governor of Syria and received the first of the procurators who ruled from A. D. 6–40.[3]

The province of Judea contained all the land east of the Jordan area, south of Esdraelon, which in turn was divided into 11 toparchies of which Jerusalem was the head. A toparchy consisted of a major town and its adjacent country with its villages. The residence of the procurator was in Caesarea, although at the great feasts of the Jewish calendar he would reside in Jerusalem.

The procurator was chiefly a fiscal agent for Rome. His prerogatives: "to collect the taxes levied by the Roman government; to command the military forces of the provinces; to act as judge in the more important judicial cases." Since Judea was considered an imperial and not a senatorial province, the taxes collected were sent directly to Caesar (cf. Matthew 22:17 ff.).

Many Jews found employment in the tax collection program. The procedure: an individual would purchase the right to collect taxes in a certain district for a stipulated sum each year and any amount he collected over and above what was legitimate became his profit. There were many opportunities for extortion. The tax collectors (Latin: *publicani*) were hated by the Jews both as workers for a foreign power and as extortioners. They collected various taxes: export and import duties on goods transported from city to city, taxes on shipments from province to province, and taxes on salt—also tolls taken at bridges and harbors.

The judicial function was also in the hand of the procurator, and all capital offenses were decided by him, while minor cases were left to the lower Jewish courts to handle. The Sanhedrin did not have the power to carry out the death penalty but had to present the case to the procurator as was done in the case of Jesus. Ordinary civil and criminal cases were relegated to local sanhedrins.

The procurator was also a military commander. It was not unusual to see troops stationed at various places in Palestine. A contingent of soldiers was sent to Palestine to keep order, for Judea, being an eastern outpost of the Roman Empire, was inclined to revolt. As soon as Judea had been made a Roman province, the Syrian governor commanded that a tax be levied; this fomented a revolt by the Jews. While the Jews were accorded freedom in matters of religion, the procurators nevertheless found it difficult to satisfy them. Pontius Pilate was in charge of Judea in the days of Jesus, holding the office of procurator for 10 years, but finally in A. D. 36 he was banished to Gaul by Caesar Tiberius because of extreme cruelty to the Jews.

Herod Agrippa I (A. D. 41–44)

After Herod Antipas had been deposed and transported to Gaul in A. D. 39 he was eventually succeeded by Herod Agrippa I, who as a youth had been raised in Rome in great luxury and extravagance. As he was approaching middle life Herod Agrippa I was exiled by Claudius and sought refuge in an obscure place in southern Palestine. Faced by poverty and bankruptcy, he contemplated suicide, but his faithful wife prevented him from carrying out his intention. After a number of frustrating experiences in Palestine he set out for Rome, successfully eluding his creditors.

In Rome he contrived to become companion to the adopted son of Emperor Tiberius, Caius Caligula. All was going well for Herod Agrippa I until one day, while riding in a chariot with Gaius, he commented that it would be good if the emperor were dead. Tiberius had Herod Agrippa I put in jail for this remark. In A. D. 37 Tiberius died, and Caligula became his successor. Herod Agrippa I was freed by Caligula, won his royal favor, and was appointed king in A. D. 39. Agrippa received from Claudius the tetrarchy of Philip, and a little later Judea, Idumea, and Samaria were added to his dominions. He waited as "king," however, for a few years before he returned to Palestine to take possession of his kingdom. After his return from Rome, Herod Agrippa I ruled with marked success for four years. He tried to win the favor of the Jews, particularly the approval of the Pharisees, as was evident in his killing John and planning to kill Peter (Acts 12). Herod Agrippa I exercised tact and shrewdness. In Jerusalem he sought to avoid giving offense to the Jews. He helped maintain peace in Jerusalem when he prevailed upon Caligula not to set up his statue in the temple at Jerusalem. While Herod Agrippa I professed interest in Jerusalem, he really was a lover of Hellenism and indulged in Graeco-Roman amusements. He became ill with a serious disease and died a loathsome and horrible death in A. D. 44.

Herod Agrippa II

Herod Agrippa I was not succeeded by his 17-year-old son Herod Agrippa II, but the latter was given the region of Cholchis, in the Lebanon district. Later, however, he did receive the former tetrarchy of Philip, the territory adjacent to Galilee and the upper Jordan. Herod Agrippa II's kingdom was increased by Emperor Nero who added parts of Galilee and the city of Julias in Perea to his domain.

The capital of the kingdom was Caesarea Philippi, although Herod Agrippa II maintained a residence in Jerusalem. The Jews did not like him, realizing that his profession of Judaism was nominal. For Jewish history his reign was inconsequential. He is mentioned by Luke as a participant in the trial of Paul, recorded in Acts 24:13–26:32. During his rule there occurred the disastrous Jewish war (A. D. 66–70). He died about the year A. D. 100.

Second Series of Procurators

Between A. D. 44—66 Palestine had seven procurators: Fadus, Alexander, Cumanus, Felix, Festus, Albinus, and Florus. When Herod Agrippa I died, Claudius placed Palestine under procurators. The years of these seven procurators were years of great turmoil and stress. Fadus (A. D. 44—48) found Palestine in a state of unrest when he came into power. Judea was split into three opposing parties. The Pharisees were fanatical regarding their legalistic practices, and the Zealots were determined to drive the Romans out of Palestine. Fadus freed Judea from an infestation of robbers. The vestments of the high priest were seized by Fadus and kept in the tower of Antonio. The Jews, however, sent a delegation to Rome appealing for custodianship of the vestments. Claudius granted their petition. The administrations of the first two procurators, Fadus and Alexander, were comparatively mild and peaceable, although there were occasional uprisings against them. Serious disturbances characterized the administration of Cumanus (A. D. 48—52). At Passover time there was a gruesome massacre of the Jews who had rioted because a Roman soldier had defiled the temple. Another episode involved war between the Jews and the Samaritans. This brought about the banishment of Cumanus because he favored the Samaritans instead of punishing them. In three instances Cumanus was responsible for killing many Jews and acting cruelly against others.

Felix (A. D. 52—60) was even harsher in his treatment of the Jews than his predecessors in office. The land was terrorized by a band of men known as the Sicarii, "dagger carriers," feared because of their assassinations. These Sicarii were constantly urging the people to revolt against the Roman government. Messianic outbreaks also occurred often; one is referred to in Acts 21:38. According to Acts 24 the apostle Paul was brought before Felix. Conditions were considerably improved during the time of Festus, but he was unable to cope with the Jews, so he was recalled. Between the years A. D. 44—66 the Jews were in a perpetual state of rage and frenzy and were preparing themselves for a great and bloody conflict with Rome.

The Jewish Revolt (A. D. 66—70)

As a result of the revolutionary activity of the Zealots the Jews had allowed themselves to be filled with an irrepressible hatred against Rome and everything Roman. Many Jews who were not in favor of revolt against Rome were killed by the Zealots.

The revolution against Rome broke out during the procuratorship of Florus (A. D. 66). The plunder of some of the temple treasure by Florus was considered an insult by the Jews and resulted in an attempt by them to throw off the Roman yoke. King Agrippa's attempt to assuage the anger of the Jewish people was futile. The governor of Syria, Cestius Gallus, unsuccessfully attempted to quell the Jewish rebellion but was defeated and escaped to Antioch with only a remnant of his original army.

This victory greatly encouraged the Jewish revolutionists to proceed with their attempt to throw off the Roman yoke; the advocates of peace had to yield, though they realized the futility of the action of their fellow countrymen. Josephus was placed in charge of Galilee, though convinced that the Jewish revolt would fail. In various districts of Palestine military leaders were placed to prepare the land for war.

The Romans then sent Vespasian, one of their outstanding generals, to crush the rebellion in Judea. Within a year most of the strongholds of Palestine had fallen, and Vespasian was knocking on the gates of Jerusalem. Just then Nero died, necessitating Vespasian's return to Rome, where he was declared emperor. Instead of taking advantage of this development to strengthen themselves, the Jews conducted a civil war among themselves. Titus, the son of Vespasian, took his father's place and renewed the siege of Jerusalem with a force of four legions. After five months Jerusalem fell, the temple and city were destroyed, and hundreds of thousands of Jews were either killed or made prisoners.

The destruction of Jerusalem meant the loss of the identity of Judaism. The temple sacrifices ceased to be offered, thus eliminating the priesthood as an influential class of Judaism. Another influential body, the Sanhedrin, passed into history never to be revived. After the fall of Jerusalem the center of Judaism became located at Jamnia, where a number of leading rabbis had fled prior to the destruction of Jerusalem.

Two subsequent attempts by the Jews to assert their independence failed. In A. D. 115—117 the Jews in Cyrene, Egypt, Cyprus, and Mesopotamia revolted against Rome, but Trajan put it down with great slaughter. The other was the attempt of Bar Kochba or Bar Koziba, A. D. 132 —135 to throw off the Roman dominion with its severe restrictions for the Jews. Hadrian utterly defeated this insurrection, practically destroyed the scattered remnants of the Jews in Palestine, and placed heavy restrictions on Jews throughout the Roman Empire. From that time Palestine became the property of the pagans, and Palestinian Judaism was ended until in 1948 the sovereign state of Israel was proclaimed.

PART TWO

The Religious Background

CHAPTER IX

The Religious Sects of Judaism

After the return of the Jews from the Babylonian Captivity in 538 B. C., two tendencies began to manifest themselves. One was concerned with continuing the temple worship and ceremonies. In the postexilic period the high priest became important in the life of the Jewish nation; even the political interests of the Jews became centered in him. This was especially true after the revolt of the Maccabees, when the priestly and kingly offices were exercised by the same person.

The other tendency in postexilic Judaism was the new interest of the scribes in the Law—its inculcation and interpretation. At first both these interests coincided; the cleavage between them developed later. Thus the temple and the Law, originally assumed to have common responsibility in a common task, became separated; the one concerned itself with political problems, the other with religious affairs. This does not mean that the priests were not conversant with nor greatly interested in the Law, but as a class the priests directed their efforts mainly toward political questions, while the scribes were more devoted to the maintenance and development of the Law.

The Pharisees

Of all the parties found among the Jews in the centuries before and after the birth of Christ, the Pharisees constituted the largest and most influential sect. There are more references to them in the New Testament (mostly in the Gospels and Acts) than to any other sect of Judaism. It was the strictest group. (Acts 26:5)

Scholars are generally agreed that the origins of the Pharisees and other Jewish sects are shrouded in obscurity. Snaith asserts: "All these sects were largely the product of the period between the completion of the Old Testament and the beginning of the Christian Era, though some of their differences go back in their origins to the early postexilic period." [1]

Josephus in *Antiquities* mentions three sects of the Jews: the Pharisees, the Sadducees, and the Essenes in the time of Jonathan, high priest from 166/159 – 141 B. C. (References found in Josephus to the Jewish sects: *Antiq.*, XIII, 5:9; 10:6; XVII, 2,4; XVIII, 1, 3-4; XX, 9,1; *Wars*, II, 8-14.)

The name Pharisee, according to some, is derived from the Hebrew *perush*, meaning "separated" or "divided from." The first occurrence of the name Pharisee goes back to 135 B. C., when John Hyrcanus reigned. After A. D. 70 the name disappears from the annals of Judaism, although the spirit of the Pharisees continued.

There were a number of factors that contributed to the development of Phariseeism: One was legalism, the religion of the Torah, which began at the time of the Babylonian captivity. After the return from Babylonia, emphasis was on the study of the Law in the synagogs at the expense of worship in the temple. Under the influence of Ezra and Nehemiah the traditional interpretation of the Law was studied and applied to life. This period probably found its best expression in the Pharisees.

A second factor was the spirit of nationalism. Persecutions and isolation fostered the development of this spirit, which was advanced among the Jews during the Babylonian captivity, where they were a minority, and after their return, when conditions forced them to again stress their identity and national origin. To maintain themselves as a distinct people became a necessity when the Jews had to fight the Syrians undertaking to Hellenize the Near East in a series of campaigns.

A third factor contributing to the progress of Phariseeism was the rise of the Chasidim. This group was alarmed by the secularization of religion among the Jewish people and was shocked by the pagan spirit dominating their lives. Greek culture and ideals were a great danger to the Jewish communities of Palestine. In the chief cities Greeks settled in considerable numbers. The Decapolis, the region east and north of the Jordan, was populated by Greek-speaking people. Greek art and learning were in evidence all over Palestine. The brilliance of Greek culture attracted many Jews; some were influenced by it and capitulated. Adoption of Greek ways, manners, and speech was the road to social and political advancement. Thus the faith of Judaism was challenged by pagan philosophy, literature, and religion.

In the Jewish nation some favored a compromise position, and for this attitude they were called Philhellenes or Hellenists. The Chasidim became a special class in the nation, opposing with all possible means the efforts of the Hellenizers. The former came into prominence in the days of the Maccabean revolt, defending the Law and the worship of Yahweh, the religion of their forefathers, for which they were willing to make supreme sacrifices. The Chasidim continuously supported the Maccabeans when they revolted against the Seleucids and until the time of the open break between them and Hyrcanus. Because of their persecutions, the Chasidim developed a pride in their activities and eventually also felt superior to other members of the Jewish nation. The Chasidim were the forerunners of the Pharisees without bearing that name; their doctrine became that of orthodox Judaism. Under Alexandra (76 – 67 B. C.) the Pharisees regained their power, and she granted them a high place in the affairs of the Jewish people. Jewish historian Josephus relates of Alexandra's reign that "she was nominally ruler, but that the Pharisees held the authority" (*Antiq.* XIII, 16, 21). They retained authority until the destruction of Jerusalem in A. D. 70.

Around 135 B. C. the separation of the Pharisees from the rest of the nation was effected. John Hyrcanus (134 – 104 B. C.) had been a disciple of theirs but left them and joined the Sadducees (Jos. *Antiq.* XIII, 10, 5 and 6). Up to this time the Pharisees had been called *chaberim,* that is, companions and brothers. Now they became a closely knit group. They were persuaded that when the Law would be perfectly obeyed, the Messiah would appear and would free the Jews from the domination of their enemies. The Pharisees practiced tithing on all their possessions. They also avoided contact with anyone who had touched the carcass of a dead animal or in any way had become defiled. They refused to mingle with the Gentiles and the common people; intermarriage with Gentiles was strictly prohibited.

The Pharisees distinguished themselves by their garb. Matt. 23:5 states that they made broad their phylacteries and enlarged the borders of their garments. The phylacteries, made from calfskin, were wrapped around the forehead and left arm as in Deut. 6:6-8, 11, 18, and Ex. 13:1-16. In the leather pockets of the phylacteries were placed the Shema (Deut. 6:4-5) and the promise of the blessing of God, which served as an easy identification of the Pharisees. According to Josephus there were about 6,000 Pharisees.

The party obtained members from all classes of the Jewish world. There were few priests among the Pharisees; the majority were laymen. The pious Pharisaic confraternity had poor and rich among its members. To join, Tricot asserts, "it was necessary to have an exact knowledge of the commandments and traditions, to adhere to the teaching of the Doctors of the party, and to distinguish one's self by the exact performance of all the precepts relating to the Sabbath rest, to ritual purifications, and to Levitical tithes." [2] The chief men among the Pharisees were the scribes, who in the New Testament always appear in close association. A majority of the scribes belonged to the Pharisees, and it was through the scribes that the party exercised strong influence among the people and in the Sanhedrin.

Pharisees were not only in Jerusalem but in all parts of Palestine. They were loved by the lower classes because of their devotion to the Law and their religious zeal but were feared by the upper classes on account of their power over the people. The Sadducees were their great opponents. John Hyrcanus, who had favored the Sadducees at the expense of the Pharisees, at his death advised his wife to restore the Pharisees to their former position of power. Pontius Pilate feared the Pharisees in the days of Christ; the 72-member Sanhedrin included many Pharisees.

While they manifested a truly missionary spirit over against the Gentiles, as stated by Christ in Matt. 23:15, the Pharisees were still known for their strict observance of the Law. They were steeped in traditionalism. Mould writes about this attitude of the Pharisees:

> But unfortunately their tendency was to stress the outer forms of worship to the neglect of the inner spirit, and so they grew narrow, censorious, self-righteous, and conceited, while their insistence upon tithes and fees laid a heavy burden upon the poorer people.[3]

The scribes of the Pharisees were extremely insistent that the rules, which they developed and passed orally from one generation to another, be observed. They attempted "to set a fence about the Law," lest even accidentally they should violate it. Josephus (*Antiq.* XIII, x,6) says: they "have delivered to the people a great many observances by succession from their fathers, which are not written in the laws of Moses; and for that reason it is that the Sadducees reject them, and say that we are to esteem those observances to be obligatory which are in the written word, but are not to observe what are derived from the tradition of our forefathers." As opposed to the Sadducees, the Pharisees were the upholders of the oral tradition.

The Pharisees accepted the Old Testament Scriptures as the inspired Word of God. They put their traditions on a par with the Old Testament, for which they had an allegorical method of interpretation. They emphasized the doctrine of the resurrection of the dead; they taught that God would bestow upon the righteous a heavenly reward and punish the wicked; their view of the providence of God [Josephus]: "They ascribe all to Providence, that is to say, to God, and yet allow that to act as it is right, or the contrary, is principally in the power of men, although fate or Providence, does cooperate in every action." Gehman says of the Pharisees: "These doctrines distinguished them from the Sadducees, but did not constitute the essence of Pharisaism. Pharisaism is the final and necessary result of that conception of religion which makes religion consist in conformity to the law and promises God's grace only to the doers of the law. Religion becomes external." [4]

The Synoptic Gospels and the Book of Acts often refer to the Pharisees and their clashes with Jesus over interpretations of the Law. From these passages it appears that the Pharisees were noted for their zeal for the Law and the traditions of the elders, which regulated the minutest details of their lives. They observed the Sabbath, made long prayers, paid unnecessary tithes, fasted often, made broad their phylacteries, and observed many ceremonial washings. They were conceited, covetous, loved to be greeted in the market place and be called Rabbi, chose for themselves the chief seats in the synagog and at feasts, and held in contempt all who were not as straitlaced as themselves. They rejected the baptism of John; a few of them became disciples of Jesus: Nicodemus, Paul, and those mentioned in Acts 15.

THE RELIGIOUS SECTS OF JUDAISM

A bitter hostility developed between them and Jesus, because He was not in agreement with their traditions, associated with publicans and sinners, and failed to observe the Sabbath according to their standards. Jesus bitterly denounced the Pharisees in Matthew 23 as hypocrites. Their chief hostility toward Jesus was that He claimed to be the Messiah foretold in the Old Testament.

The Sadducees

They were the second most important religious party among the Jews and are referred to in the New Testament. While they held to the Oral Law, they did not accept the tradition of the scribes and Pharisees. They disagreed with the Pharisees on the resurrection of the body (Luke 20:27-40; Acts 23:8) and denied a future retribution. They repudiated the existence of angels and spirits. Messianic hopes and anticipations, strong among the Pharisees, were not fostered by the Sadducees. Practically all the doctrines treasured by the Pharisees were either treated with indifference or rejected outright by the Sadducees. Gehman wrote about the Sadducees that:

> In opposition to the Pharisees, who laid great stress on the tradition of the elders, the Sadducees limited their creed to the doctrines that they found in the sacred text itself. They held that the word of the written law was alone binding (Joseph. *Antiq.* XIII, 10, 6).[5]

Concerning the origin of the name "Sadducee" different views have been expressed. The Greek Σαδδουκαῖοι is derived from the Hebrew *zaddukim,* which may come from the Hebrew *zaddik,* "righteous." Oesterley rejects this derivation as philologically impossible. Cowley has advanced the theory that "Sadducee" is a corruption of the Persian *Zinkik* (Arab. *Zindikun,* pl. *Zanadiku*), meaning "infidel." [6] He says that this word was in use about 200 B. C. in the sense of "Zoroastrian," and thus would refer to those who favored foreign ideas and did not accept the beliefs generally held by the Jews.

Others derive the name from Zadok, the name of the high priest who in the time of Solomon had supplanted Abiathar in the office.[7] The sons of Zadok were the priestly hierarchy in the time of the captivity (2 Chron. 31:10; Ezek. 40:46; 48:11), and the name was used as a title for the priestly aristocracy. They were comparatively few in number, but they were educated men with influence especially in the social ranks of the nation. Their fortunes varied from time to time. During the last years of John Hyrcanus they were influential — also during the rule of Alexander Jannaeus (103 – 76 B. C.). With Aristobulus II (67 – 63 B. C.) they again became all powerful, but they were persecuted, and their number was reduced by Herod. When the Romans annexed Judea, the Sadducees came to occupy a dominant role as the high priest was regarded as the official representative of the Jews. The high priest between A. D. 60 and 70 was usually a Saducean, which meant that he had considerable influence in public affairs.

Their chief stronghold was the temple; the Pharisees had their adherents in the synagog. The Sadducees numbered considerably less than the Pharisees. Josephus compares the Sadducees with the Epicureans in the Greek world of his day because of their similar religious views and low morals. The Sadducees joined the Pharisees and Herodians in manifesting and organizing opposition to Christ.

The Essenes

The Essenes are not mentioned in the New Testament although many scholars believe that their influence is evident, if one identifies the Essenes with the sectaries of the Qumran community.

Little is known of this religious group as their origin is veiled in obscurity. It is unlikely that they were a survival of the stricter Chasidim of Maccabean days, representing a wing of that original sect more extreme than the Pharisees and modified by influence from Greek and oriental philosophy. The main sources of information concerning the Essenes are Philo Judaeus and Josephus (both first century A. D.). Charles Fritsch in *The Qumran Community* has printed statements from the works of Philo and Josephus relating to the Essenes.[8] In addition there is also an interesting passage about the Essenes in Pliny's *Natural History*. Dio Chrysostom, a first-century pagan writer, is mentioned by Synesius as praising the Essenes "for the happiness of their entire city which is situated near the Dead Sea, in the heart of Palestine, not far from Sodom."

The Essenes are described by Josephus as active in the time of Jonathan the Maccabee (about 150 B. C.), and reference is made particularly to one Judas as an Essene. Josephus, *Antiq.* XIII, 5,9, classified the Essenes together with the Pharisees and Sadducees as philosophers. Ancient writers state that the Essenes were a group of religionists who practiced asceticism and were monastic in character. At the time of Christ their numerical strength was about 4,000. They were to be found in Jerusalem, in several villages of Judea, and at Engedi on the western shore of the Dead Sea. The Dead Sea desert particularly appealed to them. The Essenes separated from the world and had very little communication with human society. Each colony had its own synagog, a common hall for meals and assembly, and provision for daily bathing.

Those desiring to enter into fellowship with the Essenes received three badges: a pickax, an apron, and a white garment. After a year's probation, the candidate was admitted to lustrations. A 2-year probation period followed; at the end the candidate was allowed to participate in the common meal. Before becoming a full-fledged member, he took an oath in which he promised not to reveal any of the doctrines of the order. Children were not admitted as members but were given instruction. The members did not possess property of their own; all goods were held in common. Most of the Essenes were engaged in agriculture, wearing a special garb. With the Pharisees they shared an aversion to allegiance to any king save God. In 21 B. C. Herod the Great excused the Essenes from taking an oath of allegiance to him.

Most of the Essenes practiced celibacy but followed the practice of adopting children, instructing them in the way of the Essenes. One group allowed trial marriages lasting 3 years. The marriage of a couple would be ratified, providing a child was born within the trial period. They did not buy or sell merchandise among themselves but had a common fund administered by a steward. In various cities the Essenes established hostelries for travelers. They helped all people who were in need.

There were no slaves among the Essenes. Anointing with oil was prohibited. Before every meal the members were required to bathe in cold water. They wore linen garments made of vegetable products to prevent defilement through contact with dead animals. They sent gifts to the temple in Jerusalem but did not participate in the temple religious ceremonies. Archaeological evidence from Qumran indicates that they practiced sacrifices, thus refuting the view once held that they did not offer up sacrifices.[9] Their common meals bore the character of sacrificial meals.

In writing about their theological beliefs, Josephus says in Book II of his *The Jewish War:*

> For it is a fixed belief of theirs that the body is corruptible and its constituent matter impermanent, but that the soul is immortal and imperishable. Emanating from the finest ether, these souls become entangled, as it were, in the prison-house of the body, to which they are dragged down by a sort of natural spell; but when once they are released from the bonds of the flesh, then, as though liberated from a long servitude, they rejoice and are born aloft. Sharing the belief of the sons of Greece, they maintain that for virtuous souls there is reserved an abode beyond the ocean, a place which is not oppressed by rain or snow or heat, but is refreshed by the ever gentle breath of the west wind coming from the ocean; while they relegate base souls to a murky and tempestuous dungeon, big with never-ending punishments.[10]

Regarding the origin of certain Essene theological beliefs, Tenney says: "Some of their doctrines seem to have sprung from a contact with Gentile thought, for in their attitudes they resembled the Stoics." [11] Curiously, they are never mentioned in the Gospels.

The Qumran Sectaries

During the Greek period a remarkable community of Jews settled in the barren hills to the west of the northern end of the Dead Sea. This sect flourished here from the 2nd century B. C. till about A. D. 70. Evidence indicates that this religious community lived partly in a monastery whose remains have been excavated and partly in nearby caves. Valuable manuscripts deposited in jars in caves were found and have provided the world with some of the most spectacular archaeological discoveries ever made. Thus far, manuscripts in their entirety or in fragment form have been found in 11 different caves. These manuscripts, together with a description of their contents, are discussed in another chapter of this book.

For further discussion of this sect cf. Ch. XII, *The Literature from Dead Sea Caves.*

At the present time scholarly opinion is divided as to whether this monastic group found at Qumran is to be identified with the Essenes. Because in ancient writings there are many references to messianic and baptizing groups that had their headquarters near the Dead Sea in the Jordan Valley, Bruce believes one should be cautious before identifying the people of the newly found Qumran documents with the Essenes.[12] Fritsch would include the Covenant Community of Qumran under the term Essene in its widest sense.

The Zealots

Josephus traces the Zealots back to A. D. 6, when Judas the Galilean led a revolt against Rome. The Zealots opposed payment to the Roman emperor on the ground that paying the tribute was treason to Israel's God, their true King. Josephus described them as the "fourth philosophy" among the Jews (*Wars,* II, 8.1; *Antiq.* XVIII, 1.1,6). Robert Pfeiffer places the beginnings of the Zealots in pre-Roman times, asserting that "as the Pharisees are the heirs of the Chasidim, so the Zealots are the heirs of the Maccabees."[13] The Jewish historian describes them as robbers and brigands, but it is possible that they were patriots, depending upon from what point of view this group is evaluated.

They were called Zealots because they imitated the example of Mattathias and his sons and those who followed them, who exhibited a zeal for God's law, when Antiochus Epiphanes endeavored to make Hellenes of the Jews and proscribed the worship of the beliefs and practices of Judaism. They believed that they also had Biblical precedent in the example of Phinehas, who showed zeal for Yahweh's cause in the wilderness in a time of apostasy (Num. 25:11; Ps. 106:30 f.). The Zealots are described by Josephus as "sophists," a term which might suggest that within the party there was a planned program of teaching which showed that the program of the Zealots was not merely political in character.

When the revolt of A. D. 6 was crushed by the Romans, members of Judas' family kept the spirit alive. Two of Judas' sons were crucified by procurator Alexander c. A. D. 46 (Jos. *Antiq.* XX, 5.2) and a third, Menahem, tried to seize the leadership of a revolt against Rome in A. D. 66 (Jos. *Wars,* II, 17.8 f). Throughout the war of A. D. 66–73 the Zealots were very active. The movement was crushed with the taking of their last stronghold at Masada, in May A. D. 73, but the spirit of the Zealots continued and was not completely eradicated.

CHAPTER X

Theological Teachings
of the Intertestamental Period

The Doctrine of God

Although the theological doctrines in the Old Testament were taught as essentially set forth in the canonical Scriptures, certain aspects of Old Testament religion underwent modification. This holds true of the doctrine of God. There is a tendency to think of God in terms of His transcendence, of His remoteness from the world. There is also a hesitancy to use the divine name directly, and in its place circumlocutions are employed. In 1 Maccabees the writer conscientiously omits the mention of God's name, but refers, as a rule, to God as "heaven." Thus we read: "Victory in battle standeth not in the multitude of the host, but strength is from heaven." In this period the rabbis allude to God as "the Holy One, blessed be He." For example: "Thou art to give an account and reckoning before the King of Kings, the Holy One, blessed be He (*Pir. Ab.* IV, 29)." It seems that rather than use the name of God the Jewish rabbis preferred to employ words like "heaven," "the Shekinah," or "the Name."

The Doctrine of Angels and Demons

Closely allied with the development of the doctrine of God is that of positing angels between God and the affairs of the world. It is claimed that the employment of angels as intermediaries between God and man is a significant feature of the intertestamental period. In the Old Testament Jehovah is often depicted as a "man of war" fighting Israel's battles. In 2 Maccabees angels fight for the children of Israel. In 1 Maccabees the writer does not describe either God or the angels as fighting for the Jews, but victories are achieved by the good leadership of Judas Maccabeaus. Instead of God having direct contact with creation, the apocryphal writings assign to the angels the responsibility for lightning, snow, rain, clouds, darkness, cold, heat and frost.

A well-developed angelology is to be found in books like 2 Maccabees, Tobit, and 2 Esdras. That men will utilize the resources available in the form of angelic help is taken for granted. In these books the student finds angels with various proper names: Raphael and Uriel in Tobit and Esdras. The belief in demons and their evil effects is clearly demonstrated by the Book of Tobit. In 1 Enoch 9:1 the names of four angels are mentioned as though well known. In 1 Enoch 20:1 ff the names of Uriel, Raphael, Raguel, Michael, Saraqael, Gabriel, and Remiel are referred to as being familiar to the readers in the 2nd and 3rd centuries B. C. The artificiality of the angels' names becomes apparent when reading 1 Enoch 8:3. In nearly every case, the names of the angels are compounded with -el, indicating their subordination to God.

The Old Testament designation "host or hosts of heaven," is frequent in post-Biblical literature as in 1 Enoch 61:10, the prayer of Manasseh 15, and often elsewhere. "Sons of God" as a name for angels is used frequently in 1 Enoch. Another name often used in the post-Biblical literature is "the holy ones," as in Eccl. 42:17; Tob. 11:14; 12:15; 1 Enoch 1:9; 12:2-3; Jub. 31:14; Wisdom 5:5; 10:10. The term "watchers" is noted often in 1 Enoch. (12:2-3; 20:1; 61:12)

An interesting development in angelology was that of the orders into which the angels were divided. Highest in rank were the seven archangels mentioned in Tobit 12:15, "I am Raphael, one of the seven holy angels"; in Enoch 20:1-8 their names are given as Uriel, Raphael, Raguel, Michael, Saraqael, Gabriel, Remiel. It is believed that the prototypes for the seven archangels were the seven planets, all of them Babylonian deities. Among the seven archangels, Michael stands out preeminently as the "prince" or guardian angel of Israel; in 1 Enoch 20:5 he is referred to as "he that is set over the best part of mankind and over Chaos (Tiamat)." Some orders are mentioned in 1 Enoch 61:10: Cherubim, Seraphim, Ophannim, the angels of power, the angels of principalities, and other powers of the earth.

There are passages in the pseudepigraphal literature that describe the appearance of angels. In 1 Enoch 106:2, 5-6, the angel is described ". . . his nature is not like man's nature, and the color of his body is whiter than snow and redder than the bloom of a rose, and the hair of the head is whiter than wool, and his eyes are like the rays of the sun." In 2 Enoch 1:4-5 this description: "And there appeared to me two men very tall, such as I have never seen on the earth. And their faces shone like the sun, and their eyes were like burning lamps and fire came forth from their lips. Their dress had the appearance of feathers; their feet were purple, their rings brighter than gold; their hands whiter than snow." The idea of the great size of angels is also found in early Christian literature (cf. *Gospel of Peter* 40; *Hermas,* Tim. ix, 6, 1 and also *Corpus Hermeticum,* I, 1 [Poimandres]).

Foremost among the functions of the angels was to praise God; thus in 1 Enoch 39:12-13 it is said: "Those who sleep not [i. e. the watchers] bless thee; they stand before thy glory and bless, praise and extol, saying Holy, holy, holy is the Lord of Spirits . . . blessed be thou and blessed be the name of the Lord forever and ever." In Tobit 12:12, the angel says: "And now, when thou didst pray, and Sarah thy daughter-in-law, I did bring the memorial of your prayer before the Holy One." And in verse 15 it is said of the seven holy angels that they present the prayers of the saints, and go in before the glory of the Holy One.

The apocryphal writings often refer to angels as the bearers of God's messages to men. Examples: the angel and Habakkuk in *Bel and the*

Dragon, 33 ff. and the angel-rider spoken of in 2 Maccabees 5:1-3 or Raphael, in the Book of Tobit. Here the Apocrypha are utilizing a truth that the New Testament confirms of the giving of the Law, for as Stephen states in his Apologia (Acts 7:38), an angel served as mediator between Yahweh and Moses.

In the post-Biblical literature of the Jews, angels are spoken of as guardian angels. In Ecclus. 17:17 it is said that "for every nation He appointed a ruler, but Israel is the Lord's portion." In the Targum of pseudo-Jonathan on Gen. 11:7, 8 the writer speaks of every nation as having its own particular guardian angel who pleads the cause of the nation before God. Jub., 35:7 speaks of Michael as the guardian angel of Israel. Angels also appear as the protectors of individuals in the post-Biblical literature. In the *Testament XII Patriarchs*, Jos. 6:6, it is through an angel that the wickedness of Potiphar's wife is made known to Joseph; in the Book of Tobit, Raphael protects and guards Tobit; in 2 Maccabees 11:6 ff the author depicts "a good angel" as coming to help Judas Maccabaeus, and who rode at the head of the army.

The angels play an important role in connection with the eschatological drama. Oesterley wrote concerning this matter: "This is so obvious in the apocalyptic literature that quotations are not needed." [1] An angel of death is mentioned in a number of the pseudepigraphical writings, as the Syriac *Apoc. of Bar.* 21:23; *Test. XII Patr.*, Asher 6:4.

Demonology

The literature of the postcanonical Biblical period has many references to the existence of evil spirits or demons. Concerning the origin of evil spirits, 1 Enoch 15:8 says: "The giants [=the Nephelim of Gen. 6:4; Num. 13:33], who are produced from the spirits and flesh, shall be called evil spirits upon the earth, and on the earth shall be their dwelling. Evil spirits have proceeded from their bodies; because they are born from men, and from the holy watchers is their beginning and primal origin; they shall be evil spirits on earth, and evil spirits they shall be called." The writings of the intertestamental period are replete with references to the evil which evil spirits bring upon the earth. That demons are the offspring of the fallen angels is widely taught in the literature of the period; thus Jub. 5:2; 2 Enoch 18:3-5 give expression to a similar belief. In the Rabbinical literature the demons are believed to be the offspring of Satan and Eve. (*Midrash Bereshith*, Rabba on Gen. 5:1)

The fallen angels have a spirit at their head, who is known under a variety of names. Jubilees refers to him as Masteba, identified with Satan in 10:8, whose activity corresponds with that of Satan in various Old Testament passages. In the apocalyptic writings Mastema heads the demons. In the *Zadokite Fragment from Damascus*, 20:2 there is an allusion to Mastema. The name Sammael is found a few times for the same evil personality in the Greek *Apocalypse of Baruch* 4:8 and in the *Martyrdom of Isaiah* 2:1.

Still another name employed by the head of the evil spirits was Beliar or Belial. It is found in 1 Sam. 2:12 and may at first have been "the angel of death," like Sammael; Beliar occurs in numerous passages in the *Zadokite Fragment from Damascus* and also in the *Martyrdom of Isaiah* 2:4 and elsewhere. In *Test. XII Patr.* the Evil One is mentioned under the name of Beliar and is considered the author of evil.

The prince of evil spirits together with the host of evil spirits or demons is a part of the evil environment surrounding mankind; he is opposed to the "Lord of Spirits," the head of the good spirits. (Mentioned often in 1 Enoch.)

1 Enoch 15:9 speaks of the activity of the evil spirits, who are beings without flesh and blood. According to Tobit 3:8 and 8:3 they have human passions, hunger, and thirst (1 Enoch 15:11), and may be either male or female, with the ability to produce offspring. Not only are the evil spirits responsible for causing physical harm, but they are also depicted as instigators of sin in men. Jub. 7:27 says: "For I see, and behold, the demons have begun their seduction against you and against your children . . ." (10:1 ff; 15:31). In Jub. 11:4-5 is this statement: "Malignant spirits assisted and seduced them into committing transgression and uncleanness. And the prince Mastema exerted himself to do all this, and sent forth other spirits, . . . to do all manner of wrong and sin, and all manner of transgression, to corrupt and destroy, and to shed blood upon the earth." Evil thoughts are also attributed to demons (Jub. 12:20): "Deliver me from the hands of evil spirits who have dominion over the thoughts of men's hearts, and let them not lead me astray from my God."

It was the belief of the Jews in this period that means could be employed to counteract the evil designs of the demons. One of the most effective means was to recite a magic formula; in Jubilees we have a statement that Noah, having received instruction on the subject "wrote down all things in a book as we instructed him, concerning every kind of medicine. Thus the evil spirits were precluded from hurting the sons of Noah." Various methods were used to free a victim of demon influence. Reference: Tobit 8:2-4, where the heart and liver of a fish are placed on the ashes of incense; when the demon smells the smoke, he flees. The demon of Tobit had a proper name, Asmodeus.

The Law

During this period the Law came to be regarded as eternal and of supreme importance. It is in the intertestamental period that full development of the legal religion of the scribes and Pharisees took place. In Jubilees it is asserted that the men of old kept the Law, as did the angels in heaven. According to the Books of Ecclesiasticus and Baruch, the Law is depicted to be the sum total of all wisdom available to men. When Moses revealed the Law at Mount Sinai, it was simply a repromulgation of the Law. For the majority of Jews the term Law also included the oral traditions from the days of Moses down through the prophets and the men of the Great Synagog. Beasley-Murray claims that "this tradition included multitudinous applications of the Law to all possible circumstances [the Mishnah], together with further explanations of these explications [the Gemara], and they both formed the *Talmud,* of which there were two collections, the Jerusalem and the Babylonian." [2]

The rabbis taught that keeping the observances of the Law was the only way to obtain life hereafter. In 2 Esdras, however, the Law is not set forth as vital to salvation. In parts of the "Salathiel Apocalypse" there is found a pessimistic view of human nature which does not include those who live under the Law. (cf. 2 Esdras 8:35). The writer of this portion of 2 Esdras is not particularly inspired by the possession of the Law, believing instead that deliverance from man's evil status can only be effected by God alone. Denton adduces this to indicate that there may have been other people besides St. Paul who were dissatisfied with legalistic Judaism.[3]

Wisdom

The attributes of wisdom, as found in Proverbs 8 were the subject of discussion and comment in the Hellenistic period of Judaism. Thus in the Wisdom of Solomon (cf. 7:25-26), it is said that wisdom is "a breath of the power of God, and a clear effluence of the Almighty . . . For she is an effulgence from everlasting light, and an unspotted mirror of the working of God, and an image of his goodness."

During the intertestamental period it seems that the concept of "the Word of God" became the subject of speculation. In the Wisdom of Solomon 18:15-16: "Thine all powerful word leaped out of the royal throne, a stern warrior, into the midst of the doomed land, bearing as a sharp sword thine unfeigned commandment; and standing it filled all things with death; and while it touched the heaven it strode upon the earth." In chap. 9:1-2 of the same book: "O God of the fathers . . . who madest all things by thy word, and by thy wisdom thou formest man," the Word is made synonymous with wisdom.

In Ecclesiasticus [Sirach] and in the *Pirke Aboth,* the Law and wisdom are identified. Thus Jesus ben Sirach gives a lengthy description of wisdom in chapter 24 and there asserts: "All these things are the Book of the Covenant of the Most High God, even the Law which Moses commanded us . . ." (Ecclus. 24:23). In the *Pirke Aboth,* the Law and the Word are one. "Beloved are Israel in that to them was given the instrument wherewith the world was created . . ." Some students believe that these references are important because they furnish background material against which the prologue of John's Gospel may be understood.

Sin

In the intertestamental period the doctrine of hamartiology was often the topic for discussion. Regarding the origin of sin, different answers were given in various apocryphal writings.[4] Wisdom of Solomon 2:24 attributed it to the devil; Ecclus. 25:24 blamed Eve mostly. 1 Enoch 10:

7-8 makes the evil angels the cause for sin's entrance, while 2 Esdras 7:48 blames Adam. 2 Esdras 3:21-22, 7:48 portrays the world as an evil place in which men go about laden with a heavy guilt of sin inherited from Adam. Dentan contends that 2 Esdras is the first apocryphal writing to give an articulated doctrine of original sin. The writer of 2 Baruch protested the view that the blame for sins was to be placed on the forefathers: "Though Adam first sinned and brought untimely death upon all, yet of those who were born from him, each one of them has prepared for his own soul torment to come, and again each one of them has chosen for himself glories to come . . . Adam is therefore not the cause, save only of his own soul, but each of us has been the Adam of his own soul." (54:15,19). Sacrifices are still the chief means of atonement for sin. Good works are also considered helpful in attaining the same end. Ecclesiasticus says: "He that honoreth his father shall make atonement for his sins," (3:3), and Tobit 12:9 reads: "Alms doth deliver from death, and it shall purge away all sin." In 2 Esdras 8:28-29 the author pleads the merits of those who have "willingly acknowledged that God is to be feared," and in Maccabees the martyrdom of the faithful confessors is suggested as being enough to make satisfaction for sins. (4 Macc. 6:28-29)

Ethics

In the *Pirke Aboth* one rabbi says: "If thou hast practised much Torah, take no credit to thyself, for thereunto wast thou created" (2:9). Eventually the chief end of living was to comprehend what the Law taught and to live according to its precepts. Since the Law was considered the sum total of the revelation of God, some scholars of the intertestamental literature believe that the ethical teaching in the apocrypha is among the finest achievements of this period of Judaism. Frequently the reader of the *Testaments of the Twelve Patriarchs* finds the exhortation, "Love the Lord and your neighbor" (Test. Issachar v. 2) or this teaching concerning forgiveness, as Test. Gad. vi:3-7: "Love ye another from the heart; and if a man sin against thee, speak peaceably to him, and in thy soul hold not guile; and if he repent and confess, forgive him. But if he deny it, do not get into a passion with him, lest catching the poison from thee he take to swearing and so thou sin doubly. And though he deny it and yet have a sense of shame when reproved, give over reproving him. For he who denieth may repent so as not again to wrong thee; yea, he may also honour thee, and be at peace with thee. And if he . . . persist in his wrongdoing even so forgive him from the heart, and leave to God the avenging."

Passages in Ecclesiasticus and Tobit seem to come close to the ethical teachings of the Sermon on the Mount. In Tobit we read: "Watch yourself, my son, in everything you do, and be disciplined in all your conduct. And what you hate, do not do to anyone" (4:14b-15a). This comes about half way between the Old and New Testaments in saying the Golden Rule. However, there is also found in Ecclesiasticus and Tobit a certain superficiality of religious thought which is brought about by the stressing of giving of alms as the most important act of religion. In the 1st Christian century the word "righteousness" had come to be synonymous with "almsgiving," a fact which helps New Testament students to understand the warning of Christ in Matt. 6:2-4.

The Prayer Life

Despite increased emphasis upon God's transcendence in this period, there is a paradoxical development of an increased sense of piety and religious warmth in devotional life. Dentan asserts: "This development . . . of personal devotion is one of the greatest characteristics of the . . . Apocrypha and is especially manifest in the frequency with which private prayer is mentioned, and actual prayers are given in Esther, Three Children, Judith and Tobit." [5]

Eschatology

In eschatology there was a marked development during the intertestamental period. It is here that scholars claim the greatest change took place in the religion of the Jews. The teaching in the Old Testament on the hereafter is limited. Is. 26:17-19 had spoken of the resurrection, and in Job 19:25-27 Job had expressed the conviction that he would rise again. Dan. 12:1-3 asserts clearly a resurrection of the just and unjust on the Last Day. In Psalm 73 the writer looks forward to God's continuing His fellowship.

In comparing the Old Testament teaching on the doctrine of the afterlife with later Judaism, Boussuet says: "The Law of Moses gave man only a preliminary notion of the nature of the soul and of its felicity. . . . The consequences of this doctrine and the marvels of the future life were not then fully developed, and it was only at the time of the Messiah that the great light was to appear in full splendor. . . . One of the characteristics of the new people was to make faith in a future life a foundation of religion, and this was to be the fruit of the coming of the Messiah." [6]

A development concerning the teaching of life after death is found in the apocryphal and pseudepigraphical literature and in the rabbinical writings in the period preceding the Christian era. Jesus ben Sira wrote in Ecclus. 41:4: "Whether it be ten, or a hundred, or a thousand years [that you live], there is no inquisition of life in Sheol." This represents the teaching of the Sadducees, denying a retribution after death. The Book of Enoch (which has parts ranging from 160 to 63 B. C.) knows of Sheol as the rendezvous for the dead, but divine justice is in action there, so that the good are rewarded and the wicked punished. The place for the sojourn of souls in Sheol is divided into four regions: Abel, the type of martyrs, is found in the first; the just are in the second; sinners who were chastised on earth and who are awaiting the time of judgment are in the third; and, in the fourth the wicked will be found who were punished on earth by being put to death. The same book says that the wicked will not

67

participate in the resurrection, since they have already been punished. In other portions of the work, sinners are to be punished on the Last Day, but the righteous or just enter upon their reward as soon as they die.

The eschatological teaching of the Book of Jubilees is to the effect that all the dead descend into Sheol, but when the Messias comes, the souls of the just spirits will experience great joy. According to The Psalms of Solomon the good are preserved from the destruction which will be visited upon the ungodly. When the latter die, they enter Sheol from where they will go forth to be punished on the Day of Judgment, while the righteous will rise to enter eternal life.

The Pharisees or Chasidim are believed to have developed the doctrine of retribution and reward. In 4 Macc. 7:18-19 it is said: "As many as with their whole heart make righteousness their first thought, these alone are able to master the weakness of the flesh, believing that unto God they die not, as our patriarchs Abraham and Isaac and Jacob died not, but that they live unto God."

The literature of the intertestamental period seems to indicate that the closer we approach the first Christian century, the belief in awards and punishments becomes more and more common, namely, that the just begin to enjoy their rewards at once after death; on the other hand, sinners are tortured in Sheol at once.

That the Jews in the first Christian century came to hold the idea of individual recompense at the end of life, may be seen from this statement in the *Pirke Aboth:* "At death, man carries with him neither gold nor silver, neither precious stones nor pearls, but only the Torah and all his good works." (6:10)

The Kingdom of God

Beasley-Murray says that the concept of the kingdom of God in Jewish apocryphal and pseudepigraphical literature may be traced in three separate stages.[7] The well-known passage of Is. 11:1-9 was interpreted by Jews as being earthly and eternally of this world. On the basis of this passage and similar ones, Jewish writers portrayed the kingdom of God in highly sensuous pictures. In 1 Enoch the writer says: "Then shall all the righteous escape, and shall live till they beget thousands of children, and all the days of their youth and their old age shall they complete in peace. And then shall the whole earth be tilled in righteousness, and shall all be planted with trees and be full of blessing. And all desirable trees shall be planted on it, and they shall plant vines on it: and the vine which they plant thereon shall yield wine in abundance, and as for all the seed which is sown thereon each measure [of it] shall bear a thousand, and each measure of olives shall yield ten presses of oil" (10:17-19). It is believed by some scholars that it was from this passage that Papias obtained his description of the millennium.

Another passage in Isaiah which influenced apocalyptical writers of the century before and after the birth of Christ was chap. 65:17-22 (a new heaven and a new earth). According to the apocalypticists, the Messianic kingdom was to be only of brief duration but would then be replaced by an eternal kingdom. The author of 2 Enoch claims that the world is going to last 7,000 years, of which the last thousand will be the time of the millennial kingdom, which in turn will be followed by a new creation (2 Enoch 32:2 – 33:2). To the writer of 2 Enoch the temporary kingdom was of great importance. However, in another apocalyptical writing, 2 Esdras, the temporary kingdom is much less important, because the author holds a pessimistic view of the world. The earthly kingdom will only last 400 years, after which the Messiah and all the living will die. (2 Esdras 7:26 ff)

Beasley-Murray claims that in the later apocalypticists the idea of a temporary kingdom has been completely abandoned.[8] Instead the writer looks only for an eternal kingdom, new in the heavens. The tradition represented by the writer of 2 Baruch was to the effect that assigning a temporal aspect to the kingdom was an unworthy conception. "Whatever is now is nothing, but that which shall be is very great. For everything that is corruptible shall pass away, and everything that dies shall depart, and all the present time shall be forgotten, nor shall there be any remembrance of the present time, which is defiled with evils." (2 Baruch 44:8-9)

In regard to the nature of the coming of the kingdom of God, various views are held by the writers of the intertestamental period. In some writings the coming will be catastrophic, conceived in terms of the description in Daniel 2, as portrayed in Nebuchadnezzar's dream.

Sibylline Oracles III, 669 – 697 contain a lengthy passage about the signs that precede the coming, from which the following may be cited: "From heaven shall fall fiery swords down to earth . . . and earth, the universal mother, shall shake in those days at the hand of the Eternal. . . . and the towering mountain peaks and the hills of the giants shall he rend, and the murky abyss shall be visible to all. . . . the rocks shall flow with blood, and each torrent shall flood the plain. . . . And God shall judge all with war and sword, and with fire and with cataclysms of rain; and there shall be brimstone from heaven, yea, stones and hail incessant and grievous. . . . Wailing and lamenting through the length and breadth of the land shall come with the perishing of men; and all the shameless shall be washed with blood."[9] Other intertestamental writings with similar quotations are 1 Enoch xcix:10-11, c. 1-6; 11 (iv), 4 Ezra V:5-13, vi:13-28; IX:1-6; xiii:16 ff; Syr. Apoc. of Baruch xxv-xxvii, xlvii:30-38; lxx; Assumption of Moses x:3-7. Again, in other writings the coming will be gradual, as in Jubilees 33 and 2 Baruch 73-74. Jubilees teaches that as the Law is more fully studied and known, the kingdom of God is coming to fruition.

The varied conceptions of the kingdom of God affected views concerning immortality. Since the establishment of the kingdom dealt with the lot of people living at the end of time, gradually a view evolved that concerned itself with the lot of the righteous, irrespective of the time they lived. This resulted in a definite belief concerning the resurrection of the body. The resurrection of the dead is clearly taught in Is. 26:19 and Dan. 12:3. However, modification of the doctrine arose in the first pre-Christian century. In the *Sibylline Oracles* 4:179-182 the following description is given of the nature of the resurrection body: "God shall fashion again the bones and the ashes of men and shall raise up mortals once more as they were before." This kind of body was expected where the kingdom of God was to consist of earthly bliss. Where a temporary kingdom is to precede the eternal, the resurrection is to take place at the end of the existence of the earthly kingdom.

Belief in the Messiah

In the intertestamental period the belief in a Messiah became prominent. Along with the belief in the resurrection of the body from the dead there also came the belief in the coming of the Messiah, God's anointed one who would establish the kingdom. While it generally is held that this doctrine was prominent in the pre-Christian centuries, yet there is only one reference to it in the Apocrypha, namely, in 2 Esdras. In chs. 11 – 13 the doctrine appears in a fully developed form, as it must have been understood and believed.

There are more references to this belief in the Messiah in the pseudepigraphical literature. In the apocalypses the Messiah is depicted as coming from the seed of David. However, in the Testaments of the Twelve Patriarchs the reader meets with the puzzling conception that salvation arises from both Levi and Judah. In Test. Reuben vi: 7-12 the Messiah is portrayed as coming solely from Levi, while in Test. Judah xxii and xxiv the Messiah is said to hail from Judah. In general, the view of the Testaments is that the Messiah arises not from just one tribe. This, of course, represents a deviation from the teaching of the Old Testament concerning the human origin of the Messiah.

Another great deviation from the Old Testament picture is the one given in the Similitudes of Enoch (1 Enoch xxxvii-lxxi). In this writing the Messiah is no longer a human figure but is described as a transcendental being who, like John's Logos, was preexistent and exalted above all men. This Messiah was to appear in the last times and would not only rule for God but also establish the kingdom. It is the contention of Charles that the title "Son of Man" employed by Christ in the New Testament, together with such titles as the Righteous One, and the Elect One, had their origin in 1 Enoch (cf. lii, 4; xlv, 1-6). It is therefore held by some scholars that a number of these apocalyptical writings prepare the Jewish people for Christ, who appeared in the fullness of time. For further discussion on the development of the Messianic doctrine in the intertestamental period the reader might consult the chapters on the Messiah in Oesterley's, *The Jews and Judaism during the Greek Period: The Background of Christianity*, chs. x – xi, pp. 137 – 164.

THEOLOGICAL TEACHINGS OF THE PERIOD

The unique century during which Josephus lived witnessed penning and publication of the 27 writings known as the New Testament. All of its writers, with the exception of one, Luke, were Jews. The subject and heart of the religious teaching of the New Testament was a Jew, Jesus, born in Jerusalem and raised in Nazareth, who chose 12 Jewish men as His disciples and missionaries. By the end of the first century the break between Judaism and Christianity was probably complete. Christianity's major source for its beliefs were the 39 books of the Old Testament and the 27 books of the New Testament. Judaism's theology and beliefs, on the contrary, came to be based on the Hebrew Old Testament and the collection of writings known as the Talmud. Rabbinic Judaism may be said to have begun with Ezra and his contemporaries, and to have been handed down by the Pharisees as the staple and official form of religion in the time of Christ and the apostles.

The Talmud grew up between A. D. 100 and A. D. 500 and contains two main divisions: The Mishnah and the Gemarah. The Mishnah ("repetition") was completed by about A. D. 200. Much of its material is of pre-Christian and first century A. D. origin. Of special interest for New Testament students would be the "Eighteen Benedictions" and the "Pirke Aboth," or "Sayings of the Fathers." Both Jewish and Christian scholars are convinced that a study of the Talmud and Midrash could provide great assistance in the understanding of the New Testament. Because of space limitations a chapter on rabbinical writings was not included. However, to completely understand the literature of the intertestamental period, articles on "Midrashic Literature" and "the Talmud" should be consulted by the reader in standard works of reference. New Testament students will also wish to consult a five-volume commentary published between 1922 and 1928 which sets forth materials from the Talmud and Midrash, written by two German scholars, Strack and Billerbeck, who give much illustrative and informative material for a better understanding of the Jewish background and character of the New Testament.

PART THREE

Jewish Literature
of the
Intertestamental Period

CHAPTER XI

The Translation of the
Hebrew Old Testament into Greek

Since the days of Jeremiah a colony of Jews has always been found living in Egypt. Those who fled to Egypt in 587 B. C. and forced Jeremiah to accompany them, may have furnished descendants for the military colony at Jeb or Elephantine. They built a temple sometime before 525 B. C. The most important period of *Greek* colonization in Egypt occurred in 332 B. C. when Alexander the Great founded Alexandria. From then on the Jews played a significant role in this great commercial and cultural center. By the 1st century A. D. there were nearly a million Jews living in Egypt, with two of the five wards of Alexandria known as Jewish districts.

Greek was spoken there by the Jews, who soon forgot Palestinian Aramaic and spoke Greek exclusively. If the Jews were to use the Old Testament, they would need a translation. Just as Aramaic Targums were needed in Palestine and Babylonia when Hebrew ceased to be a living language, so a Greek translation of the Scriptures was necessary for the Jews of Egypt. The Septuagint (LXX), the Greek translation of the Hebrew Old Testament, may be said to be the outstanding product of Hellenistic Jewish literature. The LXX is not the product of one individual's translation activity; it represents the unequal efforts of a number of persons who over a century worked at rendering the 24 books of the Hebrew Old Testament into *Koine* Greek. The internal evidence seems to indicate that the LXX was translated to meet the requirements of the Jewish population, rather than to add a copy of the Hebrew Bible to the famous Alexandrian Library.

The circumstances under which the oldest complete translation of the Old Testament into another language originated are lost in obscurity. Various ancient reports are unanimous that it occurred in Alexandria in the 3rd century B. C. The language of the translation witnesses that the translators were Egyptian Jews and that the quotations of the LXX text of Genesis and Exodus are found in Greek literature before 200 B. C.

The oldest and most romantic story of the origin of the LXX is described in the *Letter of Aristeas* to a certain Philocrates.[1] According to this letter, King Ptolemy II Philadelphus (285 – 246 B. C.), at the suggestion of his librarian, Demetrius Phalerus, made arrangements to obtain for the royal library at Alexandria a copy of the Jewish Torah or Law. At the request of the Egyptian king, Eleazar, the high priest, sent six elders from each tribe, who in 72 days completed their task, each devoting himself to his allotted portion by day; in the evening they compared their efforts and arrived at a rendition agreeable to all. Subsequently Christian writers added embellishments to the story. A later version of the story claims that each of the 72 scribes worked independently in his cell and produced the same translation. Already in Philo's day this part of the legend was circulated.

Modern LXX scholarship has rejected the account of the origin of the Greek translation of the Old Testament as given in the *Letter of Aristeas*. Josephus, the first-century historian, gives a similar version in the *Jewish Antiquities* (XII, 2, 1 – 13) and in *Contra Apionem*, having probably obtained his account from the *Letter of Aristeas*. Written about 125 B. C. the *Letter of Aristeas* is useful despite its unhistorical assertions. The Aristeas romance contains inaccuracies which would have been impossible had the work been written in Philadelphus' time. Demetrius of Phalerum never was chief librarian under Ptolemy Philadelphus II. When the latter ascended the throne, he banished Demetrius to exile because he had supported the wrong person for the Egyptian throne. Another blatant error depicts Menedemus of Eretria as present at the banquet the king gave for the visiting Jewish delegation; but Menedemus had died two years before the end of Ptolemy I's reign.

The Pentateuch was undoubtedly the first part of the Hebrew Old Testament to be translated, because in Jewish eyes the Pentateuch was considered the most important part of the Old Testament.[2] In the synagogue services it was read continuously through on Sabbaths according to a triennial lectionary plan, while only portions of other difficult books were read aloud. At first there was probably more than one translation of the Pentateuch, each differing from the other.

A new translation of the Hebrew Old Testament into Greek was needed for the Jews, and Aquila attempted to supply it. Originally a Christian, he became a proselyte to Judaism; he lived in the first half of the 2nd century A. D. Not only did his translation follow the newly established Hebrew text, but he rendered the Hebrew with slavish literalness so that the product could hardly be called Greek; the individual words were Greek, but they were not arranged according to Greek syntax and composition. An interesting feature of his version was Is. 7:14 where he translated the Hebrew "almah" by the Greek "neanis" — "young woman" and not by "parthenos" — "maiden (virgin)." The LXX translation has parthenos, which was in harmony with the Christian interpretation as found in Matt. 1:23.[3]

Toward the end of the 2nd century A. D. another Jewish proselyte, Theodotion, produced another Greek version of the Old Testament. It is believed that Theodotion did not make a new translation but took a Greek translation from the pre-Christian era and revised it according to the new standard Hebrew text of A. D. 100. Theodotion's version of Daniel was the one translation adopted as the standard text for the Book of Daniel of the Greek Bible. The LXX translation of Daniel has survived in only two manuscripts — cursive 87 (in the Chigi Library of Rome, 9th — 11th century A. D.) and in one of the Chester Beatty Papyri (3rd century A. D.).

After Theodotion another Greek translation of the Hebrew Old Testament was made by Symmachus, a member of the Jewish-Christian sect of the Ebionites. In contrast to Aquila's procedure of translation, Symmachus tried to produce an idiomatic Greek version.

The LXX is considered a valuable translation for the textual study of the Hebrew Old Testament. Pfeiffer claims that in many places the LXX has preserved a more reliable and older text than the Hebrew. However, in utilizing the LXX the lower or textual critic is faced with the absence of early manuscripts containing the LXX text.[4] All surviving manuscripts of the LXX were copied by Christians and prepared for use within the Christian church. Pfeiffer says that strictly speaking, the LXX of pre-Christian and early Christian times is an unknown entity. "It is uncritical to speak of the printed editions of the Greek Bible, or even the Greek text preserved in manuscripts as the LXX, although this practise is well-nigh universal."[5] Roberts puts forth the theory that before the Christian era a text of the LXX became standardized and was used and recopied by the Christians in their educational and missionary programs. As a result of this process eventually other divergent renderings disappeared.[6]

A warning needs to be issued when speaking about the Septuagint. Some modern scholars claim that to insist on or refer to the LXX as a single work is a fiction; they contend that it is a collection of various versions of various books done by many hands independently and that there were independent versions that were not preserved. Whether one adopts the latter position or not, it is certain that the LXX is not the work of one translator. Thus McKenzie writes:

> Certainly there is no compelling reason to assert that the version was made under a single direction. It is altogether probable that the Pnt, as that part of the OT which the Jews venerated most highly, was translated

first, and this may have been done for liturgical use. At least some of the other books appear to be private versions.[7]

A. Vaccari has analyzed the various books of the LXX as a translation from the Hebrew and came to the following conclusions: Song of Solomon and Ecclesiastes are servile in their adherence to the Hebrew. Psalms, Prophets (except Daniel) are literal; the Pentateuch and the historical books are faithful; Job, Proverbs, Daniel, and Esther are paraphrastic or free. Evaluated from the viewpoint of Greek idiom, Proverbs is best; the Pentateuch, Joshua, and Isaiah are mediocre; the others are inferior. In understanding the Hebrew text the Pentateuch is the best; Isaiah, the Minor Prophets and Proverbs are the worst. In Vaccari's analysis the whole LXX translation does not come off very well as a version and is inadequate from any point of view.[8] The work of translation was done by individuals who were without the modern aids used by translators today: dictionaries, grammars, concordances, and scholarly commentaries; they often did not know too much Hebrew and were not skilled in their knowledge of Greek.

The Books of Kings "reflect the work of five distinct translators, each with distinctive characteristics. Their works comprise 1 Samuel; 2 Samuel 1:1-11:1; 11:2 – 1 Kings 2:11; 2:12-21:43; 22:1-11; 22:1-2 Kings." The reader can easily detect differences. The "Greek Job is about a sixth shorter than the Massoretic text, the missing verses" are "supplied from Theodotian in modern editions of the LXX." The Greek text of Proverbs has experienced considerable change when compared with the Hebrew. It appears that "Proverbs . . . has suffered considerable expansion through revisers who felt that the free translations were not sufficiently literal and . . . added doublet renderings. . . . " The text of Ecclesiastes is extremely literal and wooden and seems to show the influence of Aquila's translation.[9] The text of the LXX in Ezekiel is quite literal and gives indications that the Hebrew was not properly understood and often corrupt. The Greek Jeremiah is based on a text that was markedly different from the present Hebrew text in Kittel's *Biblia Hebraica*. There are 2,700 words less in the LXX text, and the order of the chapters is also different. The LXX text of Daniel is at present only available in two manuscripts. For this the early Christians seem to have "substituted an Ur-Theodotian text of Daniel by the beginning of the second century, if not earlier." Some scholars hold that two different texts of the Greek Daniel existed side by side and the one of Theodotian was chosen in preference to the one found in an 11th century Chigi MS and in Chester Beatty 967/8. The Greek Isaiah has been a special subject of study by scholars because of its use in the New Testament and because the book played an important role in Jewish and Christian apologetics. "The translation is very free" and often useless for purposes of textual criticism of the Massoretic text.[10]

McKenzie contends that "the LXX is not only a translation, it is also the first interpretation of the Old Testament." In the centuries before the birth of Christ there was a tendency to remove anthropomorphisms and anthropopathisms, which are found in the earlier books of the Old Testament. Thus "hand" becomes "power" and "rock" becomes "help." [11]

Most LXX scholars hold that the Hebrew text used by the Septuagint as the basis of its translation was not the Massoretic text known today. It is claimed that the differences between the LXX and the Massoretic text are not just due to faulty translations or scribal errors. Gehman asserts: "The LXX represents a pre-Massoretic Hebrew text and accordingly is important for textual and exegetical studies." [12] The LXX accordingly cannot be used in a mechanical manner to emend the Massoretic text.

The character of the Hebrew text used by the Septuagint may be seen from a few manuscripts of Qumran, which contain some fragments of the Hebrew text which belong with the LXX and not with the Massoretic text. Scholars generally hold on the basis of the Qumran MSS that in pre-Christian centuries several different forms of the Hebrew text were in existence in Palestine; one is believed to have been similar to that on which the LXX was based. By far the MSS found at Qumran are to be classified as proto-Massoretic: the precursor of the present Hebrew text printed in Kittel's *Biblia Hebraica*.[13] The Qumran MSS that have the Septuagintal text are a few fragments of portions of the Books of Samuel, written in Hebrew.

The Roman Catholic scholar Fraine cautions against the use of the LXX in textual criticism:

> Great care, of course, must be used in reconstructing the Hebrew text that lies behind the LXX version, and the more slavish this Greek translation is, the more useful it is for this purpose; but that it can be confidently used for this purpose has been amply justified by the find of similar types of Hebrew readings among the Biblical mss. of *Qumran*. It does not follow, of course, that merely because the LXX was made a couple of centuries before the Christian era it necessarily has preserved an older and therefore better text than the MT, which was officially made the standard text only about the beginning of the Christian era.[14]

Fraine is persuaded that the Massoretic text in general is closer to the autographs than is the one on which the LXX is based. Before the discovery of the Qumran MSS Kenyon wrote about the relationship of the LXX to the Hebrew:

> It is maintained by some that they point to a different Hebrew text from that eventually adopted by the Jews; and since the extant manuscripts of the Septuagint are older by several centuries than oldest Hebrew manuscripts, it is argued that the Septuagint is our best evidence for the original Hebrew.[15]

Others, however, have suggested that the translators of the LXX were not good Hebrew scholars—even at times taking liberties with the text. It is at present difficult to know which of the two positions is true in correctly answering the question: Is the LXX of the Massoretic text the best representative of the autographic Hebrew canonical text? In dealing with whether the Massoretic text of the LXX represents the original Old Testament text Orlinsky said:

> It is only reasonable to assume that where the LXX points, or appears to point, to a Hebrew reading which differs from the reading preserved in the Hebrew text currently in use, there may be involved not two variants, of which only one can be original, but only one reading, of which the LXX is simply an interpretation.[16]

The Greek Old Testament differs from the Hebrew Old Testament canon both in contents and arrangement. The Hebrew Bible recognizes three divisions: 1) the Law (the Pentateuch); 2) the Prophets, subdivided into a) the former prophets: Joshua, Judges, Samuel, and Kings, and b) the latter prophets: Isaiah, Jeremiah, Ezekiel, and the 12 minor prophets; 3) the Kethubim or Hagiographa: Psalms, Job, Proverbs, Esther, Ecclesiastes, Lamentations, Ruth, Chronicles, Ezra-Nehemiah and Daniel; altogether 24 books. The Greek Old Testament includes with these a number of our so-called Apocrypha which apparently were read in Alexandria and were published with the 24 books of the Hebrew Bible. These are: 1 Esdras (a different version of part of Chronicles and Ezra-Nehemiah, with an additional passage), 2 Esdras (being the canonical Ezra-Nehemiah), Wisdom, Ecclesiasticus, Judith, Tobit, Baruch and (in some manuscripts) *four* Books of the Maccabees. From the Greek they were translated into Latin, although Jerome, who accepted the Hebrew canon, did not recognize them as a basis for the Vulgate translation he issued.

In his day Luther followed the Hebrew canon; the English translators followed Luther, so that the English Bible, conforming to the Hebrew canon, rejected the Apocrypha.

Some Greek Bibles included books like the Psalms of Solomon, which are found at the end of the Codex Alexandrinus, the Book of Enoch, a book quoted by Jude in the New Testament, and 4 Esdras. These books, however, are generally not considered a part of the Hebrew Bible. In the Greek Bible, the distinction between the three classes of Law, Prophets, and Hagiographa is not observed. There are variations in detail in the early manuscripts, but usually Chronicles, Ezra, and Nehemiah are attached to the four books of the Kingdoms; Lamentations and Baruch, coming after Jeremiah and Daniel (which also includes Susanna, and Bel and the Dragon) are grouped with the three major prophets. The books of the Hagiographa (including Ecclesiasticus, Wisdom, Judith, and Tobit) usually come before the Prophets, as they are in the Vulgate and English Bibles.

The LXX may be considered the Bible of Alexandria, which eventually spread to the Greek speaking world and was adopted by the Greek Christian Church. The Jews continued to use the shorter canon fixed in Palestine and Babylonia. Josephus, the 1-century A. D. historian, follows the canon of the 24 books, as did also the writers of the Greek New Testament, for no quotation from any of the books of the Apocrypha is to be found in the

New Testament, although the New Testament contains references to words as Scriptural that are not found in the Apocrypha or in the canonical Scriptures, as the reference in Jude to the Book of Enoch. (Jude 14-15)

In the course of time the LXX suffered many alterations so that in the 3rd century A. D. Origen decided to undertake a vast critical work on the text of the LXX. In order to emphasize the exact relationship between the original Hebrew and Greek translation, he published a parallel edition of the two texts in the *Hexapla*. It contains six columns: 1. the Hebrew text in Hebrew characters; 2. a transcription of the Hebrew in Greek characters; 3. the version of Aquila; 4. the version of Symmachus; 5. the LXX text; and 6. the version of Theodotion. Origen attempted to revise the LXX in order to restore it to its primitive purity and bring out its relationship to the Hebrew. He adopted the critical signs which the Alexandrian scholars employed in their editions of secular writers. The obelus showed the passages that were not in the Hebrew, and the passages in the Hebrew but not found in the LXX were marked by an asterisk. A metobelus was placed at the end of passages that had an obelus or asterisk to indicate the length of such passages.

It has been estimated that the *Hexapla* of Origen comprised about 6,500 pages. The original of this work was deposited in the library at Caesarea in Palestine. It was consulted by Jerome and seems to have been accessible until the 6th century A. D., but disappeared in the 7th century when the Saracens took possession of the city. The text of Origen is usually called the Hexaplaric Recension and a considerable number of manuscripts have preserved it, if not totally, at least in part.

Two other ancients published a critical edition of the LXX. In the 4th century the Alexandrian scholar Hesychius revised the LXX, and his recension became current in Egypt. At the same time Lucian of Antioch made a similar revision, endeavoring to bring the Greek closer to the original Hebrew. The Lucian Recension was adopted at Antioch and Constantinople.

Many manuscripts containing the entire LXX or parts of it have survived. In 1827 Holmes and Parsons listed over 300 manuscripts which they consulted for their edition. Since then many new manuscripts have been found. The best known are the Codex Alexandrinus (A), 4th—5th century A. D., Vaticanus (B), 4th century A. D., and Sinaiticus (S), 4th century A. D., discovered by Tischendorf between 1844 and 1859.

Besides the manuscripts it is necessary to add the papyri which the sands of Egypt have made available. Most papyri are fragmentary but there are some of considerable length. The Rylands Papyrus 458, which contains fragments of Deuteronomy, has been dated as coming from the middle of the 2nd century A. D. The Chester Beatty Papyri contain, among the 11 papyri codices of this collection, portions of two manuscripts of Genesis; one of Numbers and Deuteronomy; one of Isaiah; one of Jeremiah; one of Ezekiel, Daniel, and Esther; and one of Ecclesiasticus. Chester Beatty Papyri 961 and 962 (second half of the 3rd century A. D.) and Papyrus

911 of Berlin (second half of the 3rd century A. D.) have preserved a more complete text of Genesis than that of Vaticanus and Sinaiticus.

Among the Dead Sea Scrolls, remains of a Greek text of the minor prophets were found written on leather. It was discovered at Khirbet Qumran in 1952. The fragments cover portions of Micah, Jonah, Nahum, Habakkuk, Zephaniah, and Zechariah. C. H. Roberts has dated them between 50 B. C. and 50 A. D.[17] D. Barthelmy has proposed a date near the end of the 1st century and concludes that the version found is a recension rather than an independent text.[18]

The Importance of the Septuagint

The Septuagint is important for a number of reasons. If it is true that the LXX is another version of the original Hebrew Biblical text, then the restoration of the LXX *Vorlage* is important for Old Testament textual criticism. Both the *Revised Standard Version* and the *New English Bible* show how the translators of these two versions have relied heavily upon the LXX text in selecting readings which would never have been accepted by the King James translators.

Another reason for the LXX's importance has been stated by Wevers:

> But the LXX is of importance for its own sake as well. It is a translation document and as such is largely bound by its base, to be sure, but, especially in those books more freely rendered, it constitutes a valuable source for understanding the theological and ethical outlook of Alexandrian Jewry. Many of the attitudes betrayed by the writer of the Aristeas legend are clearly identical with those of some of the LXX translators, notably of Greek Isaiah.[19]

Another point that needs emphasizing is the contribution that the LXX can make to New Testament interpretation. The Greek Old Testament provides the thought world and the vocabulary employed by New Testament writers. The religious vocabulary of the New Testament derives ultimately not from the Greek world but from that of the Hebrew of the Old Testament, transmitted through LXX Greek. The user of Kittel's *Theologisches Woerterbuch zum Neuen Testament* will quickly discover the importance and value of the LXX for New Testament studies.

CHAPTER XII

The Literature
from the Dead Sea Caves

The 28 years between 1947 and the present (1975) have seen the addition of considerable new material to the literature of the intertestamental period. Phenomenal archaeological discoveries of great importance to Judaism and Christianity have been made in caves of wadies entering the western side of the Dead Sea. The manuscripts found at five different places not only throw remarkable light on the community at Qumran itself but also give valuable information about the thinking of those times, the character of the Biblical text, the background to the ferment of Biblical interpretation in which Jesus Christ preached and in which the Christian church was formed, and various aspects of the history of that time.[1] One find in the Judean desert has shed new light on the Persian period of Palestinian history. The Dead Sea caves' finds constitute major discoveries in Palestinian and Near Eastern archaeologies.

The term "Dead Sea Scrolls" is a generic term for various documents found since 1947 in caves of several wadies near the Dead Sea.[2] In 1952 a group of scraps was discovered at Khirbet Mird, the ruins of a Byzantine monastery. The materials were in Greek, Hebrew, Palestinian Aramaic, and Arabic and have their origin between the 5th and 8th centuries of the Christian era.

Another group of materials from the Dead Sea area was found in 1951 in two caves at Murabba'at, a portion of the Wadi Darajah which enters the Dead Sea east of Hebron. They come from the Roman period; most of the documents relate to the Second Jewish Revolt, led by Bar Kochba, A. D. 131–135. The majority of documents were left by Jews who had fled from the armies of the pseudo-Messiah Bar Kochba. Caves 1 and 2 of Murabba'at yielded a number of fragmentary Biblical works of the 1st and 2nd centuries A. D., some legal documents in Hebrew and Aramaic, two letters from the hands of Bar Kochba, and some other miscellaneous items. In 1955 in a small rock cleft near Murabba'at, a well preserved copy of the minor prophets was found, unlike the text of the minor prophets found at Qumran. It is practically identical with the traditional text.

Early in the spring of 1962 rumors reached the Old City of Jerusalem that Arabs had found a cave containing documents in the cliffs of the Jordan fault north of Jericho. The American Schools of Oriental Research excavated this cave which turned out to be the Mugharet Abu Shinjeh, 8 miles north of Jericho. In two campaigns (January 1963 and February 1964) 40 documents were brought from the Taamireh tribesmen.[3] They were papyri brought by the patricians of Samaria who had fled before the Roman soldiers of Alexander the Great in 331 B. C. The groups that took refuge in the cave were massacred there. The dates in these Aramaic papyri range between 375 – 335 B. C. They were composed in Aramaic; two are in Paleo-Hebrew.

These papyri, the earliest found in Palestine, are of great interest to epigraphists and historians of Palestinian history. They shed light upon a period lacking written sources.

Another group of documents was found in 1960 and 1961 by archaeologists from the Hebrew University, who undertook excavations at Nahal Hever (Wadi Khabrah) and Nahal Se'elim (Wadi Seiyal), in the Judean wilderness south of En Gedi. A cave was discovered in the Nahal Se'elim in 1960 which was named "Cave of Scrolls." It gave evidence of occupation in the time of Bar Kochba. In the Nahal Hever another cave, called "Cave of Letters," yielded a Psalm fragment and 15 papyri written by Bar Kochba himself. The following year, 1961, 50 or 60 additional letters were discovered.

A fifth group of materials, from a cave in Wadi Qumran, is often referred to as "The Dead Sea Scrolls." These have no relationship to the previously enumerated finds. Over 40,000 fragments have been found in 11 different caves out of 259 that were examined between 1947 and the present. Scholars date them between 200 B. C. and A. D. 70. The Qumran manuscripts and materials are of leather, papyrus, and copper.

Frank Cross classified the manuscripts from Qumran in three distinct periods: (1) the archaic period, ca. 200 – 150 B. C.; (2) the Hasmonean period, ca. 150 – 130 B. C.; and (3) the Herodian period, ca. 30 B. C. to 70 A. D. According to Cross the majority of manuscripts come from the Hasmonean and Herodian periods.[4] The caves with the Qumran manuscripts were probably sealed between 50 B. C. and 70 A. D. Some caves yielded fragments written in a script not employed on most of the Dead Sea Scrolls, either on the fragments of parchment or papyrus; they are dated by palaeographers as coming from the 3rd or 4th century B. C.

The manuscripts available to students of Judaism and Christianity are partly Biblical and partly intertestamental in character. The mass of written material now available has come particularly from Caves 1, 4, and 11.[5]

Cave 1 yielded the first scrolls. Cave 1 was too narrow for habitation; it served as a storage place where scrolls were wrapped in linen and stored in terra-cotta jars. This cave has yielded seven original manuscripts and fragments of 70 others. Two shepherd boys of the Ta'amireh tribe accidently stumbled on this cave while pursuing lost goats. The important manuscripts from Cave 1 are: two versions of the Book of Isaiah, one complete and the other partial, *Commentary on the Book of Habakkuk,* and the *Rule of the Community.* The latter two together with the complete Isaiah scroll had come into the possession of the metropolitan of the Syriac monastery in Jerusalem and were turned over by him to the American Schools of Oriental Research, which published the manuscripts. Three other manuscripts from this cave, acquired by Dr. Sukenik of Hebrew University, Jerusalem, included a fragmentary copy of Isaiah, a sectarian collection of thanksgiving psalms (*hodayoth* in Hebrew) and a document called the *Order of the War between the Children of Light and the Children of Darkness*, also known as the *War Scroll*. The seventh manuscript from Cave 1 is a work entitled the *Genesis Apocryphon*, first erroneously called the *Apocalypse of Lamech*, an identification based on a preliminary identification of broken scraps of the badly preserved scroll but recognized to be an Aramaic Targum on Genesis; this will help Semitic scholars obtain a better understanding of Palestine Aramaic. These seven scrolls are now in Jerusalem, Israel. From the same cave came 70 fragments dealing with Biblical, apocryphal, liturgical, and apocalyptical subjects. Cave 1 fragments include scraps of Old Testament books: commentaries on Micah, Zephaniah, and the Psalms; of apocryphal books portions of Jubilees, the Testament of Levi, and the Book of Noah. The texts from Qumran are being made available in a series of volumes entitled, *Discoveries in the Judean Desert* (Oxford University Press).

Cave 3 of Qumran has yielded 274 fragments of Biblical materials (Genesis, Psalms, Lamentations) and non-Biblical Hebrew and Aramaic texts. This cave was found by Bedouins in February 1952. News of these clandestine Arab finds caused three Jerusalem archaeological institutions to send out a hunting party which searched the Qumran area, finding and investigating 267 caves or holes in the cliffs. In them artifacts were found in 37, but only 25 gave material that was related to the monastery of the Qumran community. Apparently members of the community lived like anchorites in caves (perhaps also in huts) around the monastery, with common rooms but no individual cells.

On March 14, 1952, Cave 3 produced the most spectacular treasure: the so-called "Copper Scroll." This two-part scroll was cut into strips at the College of Technology, Manchester, England. Its text is in proto-Mishnaic Hebrew, dated about A. D. 100; it describes treasure buried in various places in and around Jerusalem and Jericho. Thus far no connection has been found between this scroll and the Qumran community.

Cave 4, discovered less than 200 yards away from the site of the Qumran community center, eventually produced much written material: over 400 manuscripts, of which roughly one-third are Biblical and represent every canonical book except Esther; Isaiah, Deuteronomy, and the Psalms are found in many copies. A large portion of the manuscripts from Cave 4 were Hebrew or Aramaic documents of apocryphal and pseudepigraphical works. Among these are Tobit, Jubilees, the Psalms of Joshua, pseudo-Jeremianic works, the Testament of Levi and Naphthali, sources of the later Testament of the Twelve Patriarchs, Enoch, and an apocryphal writing of Daniel.

Also among the manuscripts of Cave 4 were works produced by the

Qumranite sect: the *Rule of the Community*, one of the best known writings from Cave 1, and the *Damascus Document*, known before 1947 only from the old Karaite synagogue in Cairo, and various books containing laws, liturgies, prayers, beatitudes, blessings, hymns, and wisdom of the Qumranites (possibly Essenes). Also among the documents of Cave 4 were "commentaries" on various Biblical books such as Micah, Psalms, Hosea, and Nahum. Cave 1 also produced commentaries on Micah, Zephaniah, Psalms, and Habakkuk.

Small and insignificant portions of Biblical and non-Biblical texts have been found in caves 2, 5, and 10 of Qumran. Cave 2 yielded bits of Ecclesiasticus in Hebrew. A fragment of Description of New Jerusalem has been discovered in Caves 2 and 5.

Cave 11 yielded many fragments and some scrolls which are now owned by the Palestinian Archaeological Museum. Among the finds from this cave is a Psalm scroll containing many of the 150 Psalms. Another outstanding text, that of Leviticus, is written in paleo-Hebrew script and has about one sixth of the book.

The Manual of Discipline (Hebrew: Serek Hay-yad)

The Manual of Discipline or *The Rule of the Community* gives students a fairly clear impression of the basic ideas, constitution, and practices of the Qumran community.[6] The text of the *Rule of the Community* is not considered by Burrows, van der Ploeg, and others as being of one piece, but rather that it has parts of diverse origin. It has 11 columns with 26 lines to the column and has been preserved in nearly complete form. Of this work Unger asserted:

> Of special import in this field of research is the so-called *Manual of Discipline* found in the original cache of manuscripts in 1947. This extremely important document, containing the rules of the Jewish sect known as the Essenes, is calculated to play a major role in New Testament criticism.[7]

A number of scholars believe that the *Manual of Discipline* is the work of the Essenes. This group considered itself the true congregation of Israel, convinced that they had to maintain the Law and the Covenant of God at a time when other Jews were guilty of confusion and apostasy. It was their mission to bring men back to the True Way before the coming of the Final Judgment. In order to realize their mission, the Essenes organized themselves as "a church." As an organization they needed a formal set of principles and a constitution, which scholars assert have survived as the *Manual of Discipline* and the *Zadokite Fragment*. The Hebrew title of the *Manual of Discipline* is *Serekh hay-yahad* ("The Order of the Community"). Those who joined the Essene community were indoctrinated in restraining from evil and in walking the path of righteousness. In the *Manual of Discipline* there are blessings for the righteous and curses for the wrongdoers, which are read at the initiation of the novices. They are taken from the following passages of the Pentateuch: Num. 6:22 ff.; Deut.

27:13 ff. and 29:17-19, and some other texts. According to the *Manual of Discipline,* once a year an examination was held for all members of the Qumran brotherhood so that each would know his exact place within the organization. At these annual meetings members would be promoted on the basis of progress made; those who continued to act against the rules of the community were finally expelled.

From a reading of the *Manual of Discipline* it becomes obvious that the Qumran brotherhood adopted a highly organized rigid life, which is described in detail. The community had priests, Levites, and lay members. In all the activities of the community the priests had precedence. The leadership of the community was in the hands of three priests and 12 laymen, all of whom had to be well versed in the Law and its application. In any group of 10 people, one had to be a priest, and the laymen had to sit before him according to their rank.

It appears from the *Manual of Discipline* that women and children had a place in the life of the brotherhood. In the *Manual* there occurs this statement: "When they come they will gather together all the arrivals, women and children, and will recite (in their ears) all the statutes of the Covenant." [8] A boy is not allowed to marry until he is 20, when he is believed to be able to choose between right and wrong.

The executive officers of the brotherhood were also the overseers who regulated the work, kept accounts, and served as chairman at special public meetings. Individuals applying for membership were examined by an inspector *(paqid).* Of those who served as judges of the brotherhood, four were priests and six laymen, all well acquainted with the Book of Hagi (or *Hagu*) and The Law of Moses.

According to the *Manual of Discipline* three stages were specified, for an initiate before becoming a full-fledged member of the society. The initiate was first examined by the inspector as to his motives for desiring affiliation with the Community of the Many. After an unspecified time, the Many debated his case, and either accepted or rejected him. If he was accepted, he was promoted into the Party of the Community, but he was not permitted to touch the Purity of the Many. After a year the initiate was further promoted, if the full-fledged members of the brotherhood did not object. In the last stage, which lasts for a year, the initiate hands over to the overseer all his worldly possessions and wealth, which are credited to his account but not yet added to the common pool. During this stage he is not allowed to participate in the Messianic banquet, but is permitted to the Purity of the Many. If at the end of the last stage he is adjudged worthy of full membership, he is assigned a rank among the brethren, and his wealth is added to the general fund. When solicited, he is allowed to give counsel. He then enters into the Covenant before God, promising "to do all that He has commanded, and to remain constant in following Him even in the face of terror, fright, or ordeal, which may face him during the dominion of Belial." [9]

Those entering the Covenant make a general confession: "We have been perverse (. . .), we have done wickedly, we and our forefathers before us, walking (. . .) truth. But [God] is righteous, (who has executed) His judgments upon us and our fathers; and His faithful mercies he has bestowed upon us from everlasting to everlasting." [10]

The Damascus Zadokite Document

A document related to the *Manual of Discipline* was found in 1897 in a genizah (synagog storeroom) in Old Cairo. President Solomon Schechter of the Jewish Theological Seminary of New York identified certain fragments from the Cairo Genizah as similar in character and content and published them as *Fragments of a Zadokite Work* (Cambridge, 1910). Like the *Manual of Discipline*, the *Damascus Document* appears to be a compilation. Milik says: "On the date of its composition and the milieu from which it came widely divergent hypotheses were put forward, oscillating from the pre-Maccabean period to that of the Qaraites [Karaites] well within the Middle Ages." [11] When the *Manual of Discipline* was published, scholars at once noticed similarities between it and the *Zadokite Fragment*, also known as the *Damascus Document*, because the group described in the Zadokite work had migrated to Damascus. Professor Brownlee in "A Comparison of the Covenanters' Dead Sea Scrolls with Pre-Christian Sects," showed how there were similarities in language and ideas in both writings. [12] Such words as "Teacher of Righteousness," "Man of Lies," "New Covenant," "Community," "sons of Zadok," "men from the Community," are employed in both documents. "The Book of Hagu," unknown elsewhere in the literature produced by the Jews, is mentioned both in the *Damascus Document* and in the *Manual of Discipline*, with the word *"serek,"* employed in the unusual sense of "rule" or "order."

This identification was made certain among the fragments found in the Qumran caves, when they turned out to be parts of the *Damascus Document*. In Cave VI fragments were discovered that are equivalent to the *Damascus Document*, 5:18-6:2, and in Cave IV are fragments of seven documents of Text A of the *Damascus Document*. Among them were large portions of the first part of the *Manual of Discipline*, missing from the scroll from Cave IQ. "The text that the Qumrân exemplars present is substantially that of the *A* recension found in Cairo, but with some noteworthy additions." [13] Some scholars believe that the discovery of parts of the Damascus scroll in Qumran IV indicates that the teachings of the book may have had their origin in the Community of Qumran.

The War of the Sons of Light and Darkness

Closely connected with the two previous documents is the scroll, the *War of the Sons of Light and the Sons of Darkness*, or the *Rule for the Final War*. This MS sets forth in 19 columns and a number of small fragments the war between the combined tribes of Levi, Judah, and Benjamin, who were returning from exile to Jerusalem, and the troops of Edom and Moab, the Ammonites, the Philistines, and the "Kittim" of Assyria. Later on the Sons of Light are to fight against the "Kittim" of Egypt as well as against the descendants of Japheth (who are the Greeks). In this eschatological war first one side, then the other, is portrayed as victorious. The Sons of Light will fight against the Sons of Belial and three times the former will defeat the latter, but at the seventh time, Jehovah causes the Sons of Darkness to be defeated and surrender. The War Rule is a piece of writing in which fantasy and reality are mingled. It is not an apocalypse because it does not recount history in the form of secret revelations.

To the modern reader the description of the warfare appears fanciful and unreal. The Covenanters of Qumran seemed to be convinced that they were living in the final age and that at any time they would be called upon to fight a war such as is described in *The War of the Sons of Light and the Sons of Darkness.*[14]

According to Yadin the weapons and equipment of the armies described are like the Roman armies as equipped in Palestine in the century before the birth of Christ.

Fragments of three different MSS from Cave IV seem to use the same text as the *Rule for the Final War,* but two others seem to differ; the differences in one would indicate the existence of another recension of the text. The differences, however, bear more on the hymnic section of the work and less on the descriptive portion. Yadin has suggested the descriptive part seems to rely on a military manual, based in turn on Roman treatises about the military art. It is proposed that the portrayal of the apocalyptic army utilized a manual prepared for Herod's army. According to Milik: "This strictly military manual was probably adapted into a priest's *vade mecum* for the Holy War, and the latter work was variously expanded, especially in the hymnic sections."[15] In the surviving manuscripts we possess less than two thirds, or possibly even less than half of the original manuscript which has survived.

A short fragment, called the *Two-Column Fragment,* describes the Restored Congregation of Israel. It has excited the interest of scholars because of the description of the protocol to be followed at the banquet to be attended by the Messiah. This text is supposed to be concerned with the future ideal community of Israel. Even if the anointed king himself would attend, the document states, the high priest would be seated first, and it would be his privilege to pronounce grace before the meal.

The Thanksgiving Psalms

The third sectarian writing that came from Qumran Cave I was the *Thanksgiving Hymns,* called by their first editor *Hodayot* (the Hebrew word for thanksgiving).[16] Additional manuscripts having the text of the *Thanksgiving Hymns* were found among the finds of Qumran Cave IV.

It seems that the brotherhood had its own book of hymns, written in the vein of poetic compositions found in the Hebrew psalter. One of the manuscripts from Cave I has 18 columns plus a large number of fragments to be broken up and translated. Gaster claims that there was a space at the end of each hymn, but since the bottom of each manuscript has been corroded, scholars cannot ascertain where one hymn ends and another begins.[17]

Some hymns open with the words, "I give thanks unto thee, O Lord," while others have the formula, "Blessed art Thou." In ancient times there were liturgical compositions that belonged to the categories of "thanksgiving," and "blessing." Accordingly, as Gaster asserts, an appropriate title for these hymns would be: Blessings and Thanksgiving (Hebrew *Beraschoth we Hodayoth*).[18]

Of all the writings of the brotherhood the *Thanksgiving Hymns* are the most original. They resemble the Old Testament in style and terminology. Scholars have difficulty in determining the background and circumstances of the composition of the psalms. Some of the 35 hymns reveal the writer in dire straits of persecution, and he thanks God for having intervened in his behalf. The Teacher of Righteousness has been suggested as the author of certain hymns of thanksgiving.

Midrash on Genesis

Among the seven original manuscripts coming from Qumran Cave I was one which scholars at first called "The Lamech Scroll," because that was the name which scholars could decipher upon the basis of a few scraps broken off the scroll. On November 8, 1956, Professor Maisler of Hebrew University was able to show newspaper men the edition of five columns of the text and their translation. Avigad and Y. Yadin have deciphered and published the Midrash on Genesis under the title *A Genesis Apocryphon: A Scroll from the Wilderness of Judea*.[19] It contains an elaboration of Genesis, written in the style of a midrash; it should contribute considerably to a better understanding of Palestinian Aramaic. The author took as his basis the text of the Hebrew of Genesis and expanded it with the aid of his imagination. What the Hebrew original gives in seven and a half lines, the author of the midrash expands into 30 lines in Aramaic.

The Copper Scrolls

From Qumran Cave III, on March 15, 1952, a spectacular treasure was brought forth in the form of a copper scroll preserved in two oxidized rolls of beaten copper.[20] It took a number of years before science devised a method for unrolling the oxidized beaten copper. By a special technique developed at the Manchester College of Technology the rolls were cut into small strips. On June 1, 1956, the first announcement was made concerning their contents.

Twelve columns of writing were found on the strips of copper. The copper scrolls contain a list of treasures and the places where they were hidden. It has been calculated that the gold and silver and other precious items alluded to amounted to approximately 200 tons of precious metals. There are 60 different treasures listed, together with the places where they are allegedly hidden. Cross wrote about this find: "Both the fabulous amounts of the treasures, and the vague or traditional character of their hiding places are sufficient evidence of the folkloristic character of the document." [21]

Kuhn and Dupont-Sommer do not agree but believe that there must have been a special reason for the use of an expensive roll of pure copper to record the treasure spots. Regarding the riddle of the copper rolls, various solutions have been proposed. "The Copper Scrolls" and materials from the minor caves have been published in the third volume of *Discoveries in the Judean Desert.*

Commentaries from Qumran

The works of the Bible were the most important sources of study for the members of Judaism.[22] Thus it was also with the Essenes, who made a specialty of studying the Old Testament Scriptures. They also believed that the Scriptures could be applied to the events of their own time. For this reason their commentaries on different books contain historical allusions concerning whose exact meaning scholars have differed and for which they have offered various explanations. So far most of these allusions are found in The Commentary to the Prophet Habakkuk, which has in it names like "Teacher of Righteousness," "the Wicked Priest," "the Man of Lies," "the House of Absalom." The fragmentary *Commentary on the Book of Micah* and the *Commentary on the Book of Nahum,* have few historical references.

The Habakkuk Commentary

The Habakkuk Commentary belongs to the first cache of Qumran manuscripts found in 1947. The manuscript measured about 5 feet long and about 7 inches wide before the lower edge was eaten away by insects. The manuscript gives a verse-by-verse interpretation of the prophecy of Habakkuk.[23] The writer of the commentary interpreted everything with reference to the history of the brotherhood. The commentator took the position that the prophecies of Habakkuk were prophecies of historical events of the period in which the commentators lived. All the commentaries found so far reveal what has been called a sectarian type of "interpretation," that is, these commentaries are not truly expositions of Scripture, but rather attempts to read elements of their history back into Scriptures. That this is the case will become apparent to the student if he examines a passage such as the following:

> For the violence done to Lebanon will overwhelm you; the destruction of the beasts will terrify you; for the blood of men of violence to a land, to a city and all who dwelt in it. "Its interpretation: the wicked priest, to repay him for his recompense which he recompensed the poor. For Lebanon is the Council of the Community, and the beasts are the simple ones of Judah, the doer of the Law . . ." I Q1 12:1-5, based on Habbakkuk 2:17.

The Habakkuk Commentary was published by The American Schools of Oriental Research in 1950–51 as *The Dead Sea Scrolls of St. Mark's Monastery, Vol. I, The Isaiah Manuscript and the Habakkuk Commentary*, New Haven, 1950. For a translation of this commentary the student is directed to the translation in the following: Millar Burrows, the *Dead Sea Scrolls*, pp. 365–370.

All that is left of commentaries on Isaiah, Micah, Zephaniah, Hosea, and the Psalms are small fragments. The Teacher of Righteousness and his Opponent are mentioned in the commentaries on Micah and Psalm 37.

The Temple Scroll

During the Six-Day War in June 1967 there came into the possession of the State of Israel the longest yet known Dead Sea Scroll: 8.6 meters or over 28 feet in length as compared with the complete Isaiah which measures 7.3 meters.[24] The beginning of the Temple Scroll has not been preserved and portions of this scroll are missing but altogether 66 columns have been preserved. Yigael Yadin believes that the Temple Scroll was written by a skilled scribe, and he places the date of its composition in the second part of the 1st century B. C. or the beginning of the 1st century of the Christian era. In fact, he claims that there are valid reasons for dating the scroll as early as the end of the 2nd century B. C.

The contents of the scroll are unique. Four features are outstanding as revealed by its contents. 1. It contains numerous *Halakhoth* (religious rules) on a number of subjects referred to in the Pentateuch, and the Torah of Moses is quoted with additions, deletions, and variants. 2. The scroll contains a listing of sacrifices and offerings to be offered at various Jewish festivals. 3. There is a detailed description for the building of a temple. 4. The last part of the Temple Scroll describes the king's bodyguard of 12,000 soldiers – 1,000 per tribe.

The Temple Scroll was written to give the reader the impression that it was given by divine decree to Moses. The rules are given by God and are stated in the first person. Often the author changes the third person of the Pentateuchal text to the first person singular. The sacred name of God, the Tetragrammaton *YHWH*, is always written in the same script as that of the scroll and does not follow the practice of other Qumran scrolls where the name *YHWH* is written in Palaeo-Hebrew. In this scroll, laws that are scattered throughout the Pentateuch are gathered together in one place and give evidence of being sectarian and polemical.

Yadin is convinced that the Scribe was a member of the Qumranite community. He adhered to a special calendar that seems to have been in vogue at Qumran and which was used by the author of the Book of Jubilees.[25] The Temple Scroll contains detailed discussions about the manner in which the Feasts of Tabernacles, Passover, and the Day of Atonement were to be observed. The calendar in vogue at Qumran was organized on the plan that each month had 30 days, with one extra day every three months, and a year of 364 days. The first day of the first month regularly came on a Wednesday.

A good portion of the scroll speaks of a temple that is to be built in the future. Instructions for the construction of a new temple, follow the manner of Exodus 35-40, the chapters that treat of the building of the tabernacle. The specifications given for this future temple do not agree with those of the Herodian temple; this has led Yadin to infer that the Qumranite sectaries did not consider the Jerusalem temple built according to God's instruction. A considerable section in the scroll deals with the rules of cleanness and uncleanness for city itself.

The fourth section treats of the king's bodyguard and outlines plans for mobilization of the army to fight against those who want to exterminate "the land of Israel." Yadin claims that the description of the soldiers and the terminology describing the war reflect political conditions in the middle or late Hasmonean age. The rules for the mobilization and conduct of the war in the Temple Scroll are different from those found in the "War of the Sons of Light with the Sons of Darkness."

Discovery at Masada

Major excavations at Masada in the Judean Desert have produced valuable documents for the years after the fall of Jerusalem in A. D. 70.[26] Under the direction of Yadin of the Hebrew University, in 1963 – 64 and in 1964 – 65 literary finds were discovered from the era of the first Jewish revolt. In A. D. 73 the Herodian fortress held by the Jews fell to the invading Romans. Indications are that rather than suffer enslavement nearly a thousand Jews committed suicide. An important document found at Masada was a Hebrew text of Ecclesiasticus. The manuscript has been dated as coming from 75 B. C. Fragments of Psalms, Leviticus, and Genesis were also discovered. The Biblical text of these fragments is similar to the Murabba'at Biblical manuscripts. One of the most interesting discoveries from Masada was a copy of the "Scroll of the Songs of the Sabbath Sacrifice," a writing found also in Cave IV of Qumran.

The Bar Kochba Revolt

Documents originating in the Judean desert have helped to increase information and knowledge concerning the Bar Kochba revolt of A. D. 132 – 135.[27] From his own letters it is now known that Bar Kochba was called Simeon ben Kosiba. About his antecedents nothing is known. Rabbi Akiba was responsible for proclaiming him Messianic king under the title of Bar Kochba ("Son of a Star"). Not all rabbis favored Akiba's position. In the early stages of the Second Revolt the Romans were driven out of all of Judea. Jerusalem again came under Jewish control; the sacrificial cult of the Temple was restored; Israel was proclaimed a free state, and coins were struck to indicate this fact.

However, in A. D. 133 the Romans under General Julius Severus, with an army of 35,000, counterattacked on behalf of Emperor Hadrian.

The Roman legions first entered Galilee, then invaded the valley of Jezreel, then took the Judean hills, and finally retook Jerusalem. In A. D. 135 Bar Kochba's last stronghold at Bethar was invaded, and gradually every hill and cave stronghold held by the Jews were taken.

Either through Samaritan treachery or lack of water the stronghold of Bethar fell, and Bar Kochba was killed, probably as the result of a snake-bite. Nearly the whole population of Bethar was slaughtered, including school children. According to records 50 fortresses and 985 villages were wiped out; the revolt's casualties were placed at 580,000; in addition many died of disease or hunger. Judea became a desolate land, its population wiped out, and Jerusalem was made into a heathen city, with entrance to the Holy City barred to the Jews.

The Murabba't caves in the Nahal Hever and Nahal Se'elim have furnished letters and documents which enable historians of the Second Jewish Revolt to obtain a better picture of events and personalities of these fateful years. In 1952 in Wadi Murabba't two letters were found addressed by Bar Kochba to Yeshua ben Galgola. The next year a letter was found addressed to Yeshua ben Galgola, in which the latter is warned by Bar Kochba not to mistreat the Galileans. This letter shows that Bar Kochba was in the habit of issuing direct commands to his subcommanders and expected from them absolute obedience.

In March 1960 an expedition of the Hebrew University explored a number of caves of the Nahal Hever. In one of the caves a small package tied with cords was found; it contained 15 letters from Bar Kochba. Nine were in Aramaic, four in Hebrew, and two in Greek. One letter was written on four wooden tablets. All the Hebrew letters are in different hand-writing and do not have Bar Kochba's signature, showing that they were dictated to scribes.

The letters from Bar Kochba have cleared up many obscurities relative to the Second Jewish Revolt. From them scholars have knowledge of different people with whom Bar Kochba had dealings. The impression from Talmudical sources that he was a ruthless leader is confirmed. For the first time the names of villages in Judea that were involved in the revolt of 132–135 are known. Ein Gedi was the economic and military headquarters of Bar Kochba. Bar Kochba described himself as "Prince over all Israel." From the letters it is clear that the rebels were Jews who took Judaism seriously, as is indicated by garments made purely of wool on the skeletons found in the caves and by their preparation for the holiday of Succoth. From the new documents an unknown Jewish figure makes his appearance: Botniya Bar Miasa, who was called *Rabenu,* a title usually only given to Moses and Judah. The new documents also have shown that the Second Revolt was not only political but also religious.

In the various caves in the Judean Desert many household items were found: cooking utensils, textiles, furniture, and clothes, making available new and valuable data on how the Jews lived in Palestine during the years of the Bar Kochba revolt.

CHAPTER XIII

The Apocrypha

The Apocrypha of the Old Testament include 14 writings of varying length, subject matter, and manner of presentation. The order of the apocryphal writings in the various English versions follows the Latin version of the Old Testament, a translation with which the King James translators were familiar. The only exception to the Latin order is the transfer of the two books of Esdras from the last place to the first. In modern versions of the Vulgate these two books are found after the New Testament and the Prayer of Manasseh is not found in the Vulgate.

After listing the 39 books of the Old Testament, the sixth Anglican Article of Religion goes on to say: "And the other Books (as Hierome saith) the Church doth read for example of life and instruction of manners: but yet doth it not apply to them to establish any doctrine: such are these following: The Third Book of Esdras, The Fourth Book of Esdras, The Book of Tobias, The Book of Judith, The rest of the Book of Esther, The Book of Wisdom, Jesus the Son of Sirach, Baruch the Prophet, The Song of the Three Children, The Story of Susanna, Of Bel and the Dragon, The Prayer of Manasses, The First Book of Maccabees, The Second Book of Maccabees."

In these writings a varied assortment of Jewish literature is found, covering the period from 300 B. C. – A. D. 100; none of these books is included in the Hebrew Old Testament, although with few exceptions they are a part of the Greek Old Testament. The statement is frequently made that the Jews had two canons for the Old Testament: a Palestinian (as represented by the Massoretic text of the Bible) and the Alexandrinian (as represented by the Septuagint). However, there is no evidence that Alexandrian Jews regarded any of the apocryphal books as canonical.[1] Greek-speaking Christians gave the Apocrypha canonical status, possibly through the conviction that they had formed a part of the canon of the Old Testament. While it is true that the Jews of Alexandria added the Apocrypha to the 24 canonical books of the Hebrew Old Testament, this is not equivalent to canonizing them. Protestant scholars believe that the addition of these noncanonical writings can be explained on the basis of bibliographical conditions. Thus Bruce writes:

> When each book was a papyrus or parchment-roll, and a number of such rolls were kept together in a box, it was quite likely that uncanonical documents might be kept in a box along with canonical documents, without acquiring canonical status. Obviously the connection between various rolls in a box is much looser than that between various documents which are bound together in a volume.[2]

THE APOCRYPHA

In the Septuagint the apocryphal books (except 2 Esdras) are usually placed alongside the canonical books of the same class. 1 Esdras comes before Ezra and Nehemiah; Judith and Tobit follow Esther; the Additions to Esther and Daniel are found as portions of the canonical books to which they were added; Wisdom and Ecclesiasticus are placed with the canonical Wisdom books (Job, Psalms, Proverbs); Baruch appears after Jeremiah, and The Prayer of Manasseh is included in a collection of psalms and hymns, forming an appendix to the Septuagint.

Different genres of literature are found in the 14 writings of the Apocrypha, as may be seen from the following classification:

1. Historical: 1 Esdras, 1 and 2 Maccabees; 2. Haggadah or Religious Fiction: Tobit, Judith, and Additions to Esther and the Additions to Daniel; 3. Wisdom or Ethical Literature: Ecclesiasticus, Wisdom of Solomon, Baruch, The Prayer of Manasseh; 4. Apocalyptic: 2 Esdras.

None of the Apocrypha are considered canonical by orthodox Jews or Protestants. Jesus and His apostles accepted the Jewish canon and confirmed its authority by the use they made of it, whereas there is no evidence to show that they regarded the apocryphal writings on the same level with the 24 canonical books.

The early Greek-speaking Christians took over the Septuagint from the Hellenistic Jews and made no distinction between canonical and apocryphal. Origen, Athanasius, and others recognized a distinction in theory when they enumerated the books of the Old Testament, but in practice they quoted from the Apocrypha under the same formula as when citing from canonical books. Many of the Latin Fathers, including Augustine, made no distinction; Augustine considered the Old Testament to be comprised of 45 books, including Tobit, Judith, and 1 and 2 Maccabees, Ecclesiasticus, and Wisdom. However, Jerome used the term "apocryphal." The latter term etymologically means "hidden" and may refer to a story in 2 Esdras 14, where Ezra by divine inspiration dictates 94 books of which 24 are to be published and 70 to be kept secret. Jerome did not mean to employ apocryphal in the sense of hidden, but used the name in the sense of ecclesiastical in contradistinction to canonical.

In the days of the Reformation, Protestants and Roman Catholics took divergent attitudes toward the Apocrypha. The Council of Trent, 1545—1563, asserted the canonicity of Tobit, Judith, the Additions to Esther, the Additions to Daniel, Baruch, Ecclesiasticus, Wisdom, and 1 and 2 Maccabees, a position that was reaffirmed by the Vatican Council in 1870. Roman Catholic scholars usually designate these books as "deuterocanonical." Among Protestant Reformers there was a difference of opinion as to the evaluation to be placed on the Apocrypha. The Anglican Church gave them a deuterocanonical status and continued to employ readings from them in their liturgical services. The *Westminster Confession of Faith* (1647) states following about the Apocrypha:

The Books commonly called Apocrypha, not being of divine inspiration, are not part of the canon of Scripture; and therefore are of no authority

93

in the Church of God, nor to be any otherwise approved, or made use of, than other human writings.

Luther did not accept the canonical character of any of the Apocrypha and took the decisive step of gathering out of the body of the Old Testament the books of the Apocrypha and placing them by themselves between the Old Testament and the New Testament. Luther was acting upon a suggestion made by Jerome 1,100 years before. He did this in 1534, the year in which he completed his translation of the Bible into German from Hebrew, Aramaic, and Greek. Luther was not too enthusiastic about the Apocrypha. Miles Coverdale in 1535 followed the pattern of Luther in the first printed English Bible. All Protestant Bibles thereafter adopted this innovation of Luther in gathering the Apocrypha out of the Old Testament: the Matthew's Bible of 1537; the Taverner Bible of 1539; the Great Bible of 1539 (Coverdale) the first Bible with the imprint "appointed to be read in churches"; the Geneva Bible of 1560, produced by the Puritans; the Bishop's Bible (which had ecclesiastical and royal approval) of 1568; and the King James, or Authorized version of 1611. In all these translations the Apocrypha form a separate group following the Old Testament.

This was not the case in earlier translations of the Bible into English. When in the 14th century the Bible was translated into German and English, the translations contained the Apocrypha were scattered throughout the Old Testament, and so they remained in the Latin text (employed by Wyclif and Purvey, 1382 – 88), used by the Roman Catholic translation produced in the days of James I and known as the Douay version, 1610.

The earliest English versions of the Apocrypha had at the beginning of these writings a statement qualifying their value and authority. The Great Bible of 1560 and the Geneva Bible state that they may be read for purposes of edification but are not to be used for confirmation or establishment of doctrine. The removal of the Apocrypha from the Bible is ascribed to Puritan influence, which in some editions of the Geneva Bible caused the Apocrypha to be omitted. In 1629 some of the editions of the King James appeared without the Apocrypha. After 1827 the British and Foreign Bible Societies decided that no funds would be expended in publishing the non-canonical books of the Apocrypha; the result was that while formerly many Protestants were acquainted with these writings of the intertestamental period, thereafter few had knowledge of their contents. The King James translators of 1607 – 11 and the English Revisers of 1870 – 94 neglected the Apocrypha in that they did not put forth the same effort in producing the best possible translation, resting on what was considered in their time the critical text for the Apocrypha. Goodspeed claims that the translation of the Apocrypha has been neglected.[3] In 1535 Miles Coverdale translated the Apocrypha in his Bible from the Latin Vulgate, with the help of the Latin of Paginus and some German translations, especially Luther's. The Coverdale translation of the Apocrypha was followed in all subsequent English versions, and even though revised on the basis of the Greek, it still follows that the translations used before the new translation of Good-speed in *The American Translation* and the new translation of the RSV in 1957 substantially rested ultimately upon the Latin.

Although the Apocrypha are not a part of the inspired canon, they do have great value, whether considered religiously, literarily, or historically. These writings fill the gap between two testaments, when the voice of prophecy and revelation had ceased.

Politically the apocryphal writings aid us in following the history of the Jews through an important period. Especially valuable are the two Books of the Maccabees with a reliable detailed account of struggles by the Jews for religious and political freedom. These two books record one of the most heroic periods of Hebrew history.

The Apocrypha are also important from a religious point of view because of the insight they convey into the spiritual, philosophical, and intellectual life of the Jews in the centuries antedating the birth of Christ. Concerning their great value, Unger writes:

> They supply evidence of the practical disappearance of idolatry, the growth of staunch monotheistic convictions, Messianic hopes, and more and more widespread beliefs in resurrection and future rewards and punishments.[4]

These same documents likewise help students understand the degenerating influences in Judaism which set in during the centuries prior to the coming of the Messiah.

As a group of literary documents the Apocrypha further exercised a considerable influence upon subsequent literature. Many scholars claim that a number of New Testament authors were affected by the writings of the Apocrypha. To what degree the authors of the New Testament had acquaintance with them is a matter of debate. Although the New Testament does not quote the Apocrypha directly nor recognize them as inspired, it does manifest familiarity with them as can be seen from Heb. 11:34-38 where unquestionably there are allusions to the heroes of the Maccabean age.

The person desirous of ascertaining the influence of the entire Bible upon art, literature, and religion cannot dispense with a knowledge of the Apocrypha. They are undoubtedly helpful in understanding the religious world of the New Testament.

CHAPTER XIV

The Individual Books
of the Apocrypha

1 Esdras

The first book of the Apocrypha is known to Protestants as 1 Esdras, from the Greek form of the name Ezra, but to those who use the Vulgate it is known as 3 Esdras. In the Vulgate the canonical books of Ezra and Nehemiah are known respectively as 1 Esdras and 2 Esdras. The Protestant 1 Esdras is one of the books not accepted as deuterocanonical by the Roman Catholic Church. I Esdras is found at the end in the Clementine edition of the Vulgate. I Esdras was probably placed first in the Protestant lists, partly because of the influence of its name and partly because it also seems to constitute a suitable link between the Old Testament canonical books and the Apocrypha. There is no consistency in the scholarly world when referring to the book under consideration. In Kautzsch's German edition of the Apocrypha and in a number of recent German works (including Eissfeldt) the tendency has been to revive the Vulgate terminology of 3 Esdras in place of 1 Esdras. To avoid ambiguity some modern scholars refer to it as the "Greek Esdras."

Contents

1 Esdras presents problems of bewildering perplexity, concerning which much has been written in many languages and by many authorities. I Esdras substantially reproduces the materials of 2 Chron. 35:1 – 36:23, the whole of the canonical books of Ezra and Nehemiah, as the following shows:

1 Esdras 1	= 2 Chron. 35, 36
1 Esdras 2:1-14	= Ezra 1
1 Esdras 2:15-25	= Exra 4:7-24
1 Esdras 3:1 – 5:5	= The original section of the book
1 Esdras 5:7-70	= Ezra 2:1 – 4:5
1 Esdras 6, 7	= Ezra 5, 6
1 Esdras 8:1 – 9:36	= Ezra 7 – 10
1 Esdras 9:37-55	= Neh. 7:73 – 8:13

The portions of 1 Esdras which coincide with the Old Testament were not translated from the Hebrew text we now possess but seem to have been rendered from another form of it.

The Greek of 1 Esdras is in better style than the Septuagint version of Ezra-Nehemiah.

The Contents of 1 Esdras

1:1-24, Josiah's Passover; 25-33, death at Megiddo; 34-58, the reigns of kings to the fall of Jerusalem, 587 B. C.

2:1-15, Cyrus' decree to rebuild Jerusalem, 538 B. C.; 16-30, Samaritan's letter to Artaxerxes, and rebuilding of the temple is halted till the reign of Darius, 520 B. C.

3:1 — 4:46, Zerubbabel's victory in the competition with the other two youths.

4:47 — 5:3, Jews allowed to return and rebuild the temple.

5:4-46, a list of the exiles; 46-65, the rebuilding of the temple; 66-73, the Samaritans cause suspension.

6:1-6, building of the temple begun; 7-34, letter of Sisinnes and the favorable response by Darius.

7:1-15, dedication of temple and the Passover.

8:1 — 9:36, Ezra comes by permission of Artaxerxes, 458 B. C.; brings priests and Levites, and halts mixed marriages.

9:37-55, Ezra reads the law of Moses, 444 B. C.

The above arrangement of materials differs in two respects from the canonical books of Ezra and Nehemiah: (1) by reversing the order of the Persian kings, which in reality was as follows: Cyrus (533 — 529 B. C.), Darius I (522 — 486 B. C.), and Artaxerxes I (465 — 425 B. C.), although 1 Esdras does correctly begin with Cyrus in ch. 2:1 ff., and (2) by ignoring Nehemiah 1:1 — 7:72, thus making the account in Ezra continuous. This means that the events covered by 1 Esdras extend from 621 B. C. to 444 B. C., from the time of the Passover celebrated by Josiah till the reading of the Law in the days of Nehemiah.

In 1 Esdras there are, however, some additions to the events recorded in the canonical Ezra and Nehemiah: 1. The story of the Passover celebration by Josiah and the description of the happenings that followed the destruction of Jerusalem and its temple in 587 B. C., utilizing as its source 2 Chron. 25-26; 2. Chapters 3 — 5:4 (of 1 Esdras) give a completely new version of the rise of Zerubbabel as the leader of the Jews after the restoration by Cyrus in 538 B. C. They relate how he entered into competition with two other youths in expressing wise sayings, when he was a page in the service of the Persian King Darius. The topic concerning which the three vied with each other was: "What is the strongest power in the world?" One youth said that wine is the strongest power; a second asserted that the king was the strongest; Zerubbabel, the third youth, wrote that women are strong but that truth is above all, "it endureth and is always strong; it liveth and conquereth forevermore" (4:38). When the multitude heard this statement, they shouted: "Great is truth, and mighty above all things" (4:41). In Latin it reads: "Magna est veritas, et praevalet." Zerubbabel's answer was deemed the best. As a reward he requested to be sent to Jerusalem so that he might aid in rebuilding the city and the temple. Darius granted the request. Many authorities consider the interesting story of the three guardsmen to be an interpolation just before the opening words of chapter 2 of the canonical Ezra. It is a specimen of a type of literature well known to readers of Arabian Nights.

Because of the resemblances between the apocryphal 1 Esdras and the canonical Ezra-Nehemiah, the question has been raised as to the relationship of these three writings to each other. Josephus had undoubtedly seen 1 Esdras for he uses the material about the rise of Zerubbabel exactly as found in the apocryphal book. The story of the rise of Zerubbabel as related in 1 Esdras stands in contradiction to the version of this episode in the canonical Book of Ezra, according to which Zerubbabel returned to Palestine in the days of Cyrus, while in 1 Esdras he was still in Babylon in 522 B. C. and did not return till 520 B. C. The account of the letter to Artaxerxes, which in Ezra appears in chapter 4, precedes the interpolated material in 1 Esdras (Ezra 4:7-24 equals 1 Esdras 2:16-30).

The Relationship of 1 Esdras to the Canonical Books

The relationship of the three volumes is interpreted differently. Thus A. Robert claims that 1 Esdras (3 Esdras of Vulgate) did not have Esdras-Nehemias as its source. He believes that 1 Esdras is based on an independent Semitic text, full of obscurities and inconsistencies.[1] Oesterley, on the other hand, contends that the sequence of events in the apocryphal Esdras is superior in one matter to that of the canonical books of Ezra-Nehemiah.

Oesterley believes that 1 Esdras, as we have it today, is not the same as when it was first written.[2] That the original form of certain parts of the book is lost is suggested by the fact that both the beginning and the close of the book break off abruptly. According to the apocryphal Esdras, Nehemiah is not cooperative with Ezra in regard to the reading of the Law (9:37-55), as he is in Neh. 8:9.

Scholars are puzzled by the existence of 1 Esdras of the LXX or 3 Esdras of the Vulgate; Dentan calls it "an orphan among books,"[3] which presents a number of mysteries, especially when it is remembered that the Septuagint had a good translation of the two Books of Chronicles, Ezra, and Nehemiah under the names 1 and 2 Paralipomena and Esdras. Metzger claims that there are three ways of explaining the possible relationship between 1 Esdras and the narratives of 1 Chronicles and Ezra and Nehemiah.[4] 1 Esdras may have been the source for the canonical narratives; or Ezra-Nehemiah may have been modified by 1 Esdras; or both may go back to a common original.

Date and Language of the Book

The date of the book is indefinite. It cannot be any later than A. D. 100 for it was used by Josephus, but it is considered to have come from an earlier time, some even assign it to the 3rd century B. C. The original language of the book was either Hebrew or Aramaic.

2 Esdras

Some authorities place 2 Esdras among the Apocrypha, while others place it among the pseudepigrapha. It is found in the English translations of the apocryphal writings, consisting of 16 chapters, and is the only book among the Apocrypha that belongs to the genre of apocalyptic literature. Because of its inclusion among the Apocrypha it is therefore the best known of the noncanonical apocalypses. Some scholars believe that 2 Esdras depicts the spirit of Judaism in a very attractive light. For the modern reader 2 Esdras is probably the most difficult of all the Apocrypha to understand or appreciate.

In the English Apocrypha 1 Esdras represents Esdras A of the LXX or 3 Esdras of the Appendix to the Vulgate; 2 Esdras is mainly the Ezra Apocalypse or 4 Esdras of the Appendix to the Vulgate. Thus in English Protestant usage the name of Esdras is relegated to the Apocrypha.

2 Esdras consists of three parts: the core, 3-14, commonly known as the Ezra Apocalypse, preceded by two chapters and followed by two chapters, which in the opinion of most scholars were not a part of the Apocalypse of Ezra. Even those who defend the unity of the work admit that 2 Esdras contains a medley of ideas. Lagrange claims that the mosaic is found in the ideas, not in the documents. Before the author were certain traditional elements; these he could neither fuse or eliminate those that were incompatible with his main theme.

The message of the book is put into the mouth of Ezra, the scribe, who probably lived about the middle of the 5th century B. C. No part is as old as that; it seems to have reached its present form near the end of the first century of our era.

The Contents of 2 Esdras

Chapters 1 and 2 are considered a Christian introduction, the last two chapters a Jewish invective. The Jewish material revolves around the question of why Israel was forced to suffer so greatly, although it was no worse than other nations and certainly not as bad as Babylon. The problem why so few were being saved is also discussed.

2 Esdras contains seven visions, dated in the 30th year after the fall of Jerusalem (according to our chronology, 557 B. C.). The contents of these visions briefly are as follows:

The First Vision, 3:1—5:13. In the year 558 B. C. Ezra, being in Babylon, complains to God and questions why His chosen people, Israel, are suffering while the pagans flourish. The angel Uriel sets forth the unsearchableness of God's ways: that wickedness has an appointed time, and that the distress of God's people will soon end. The signs that precede the end are described. Ezra then fasts seven days and prepares for a second revelation.

The Second Vision, 5:14—6:34. The teachings in this part are similar to the first. Ezra again complains about the bitter fate of Israel and is rebuked. The angel indicates the signs of the approaching end and shows that there is justification for the ways of God.

The Third Vision, 6:35 — 9:25. The first four visions of 2 Esdras are known as the Salathiel Apocalypse. The climax of the latter is found in the third vision. In it Ezra discusses the problem of Israel's suffering in its final form. If the world was created for Israel, why is Israel being deprived of its inheritance? After a debate has taken place between Ezra and the angel, an announcement is made of the coming of the Messianic kingdom and of the end of the world. This section contains a fragment of 69 verses, which is found in the Revised English Version, but not in the King James nor in the majority of Latin codices; it was recovered by Bensly. It fills a gap between verses 35 and 36 of the Vulgate text and treats of the resurrection and final judgment.

The Fourth Vision, 9:26 — 10:59. Ezra sees a weeping woman who has lost her son. Ezra tells her that instead of mourning for her son she ought to weep for Jerusalem. When the woman disappears, her place is taken by a built city. The angel then informs Ezra that the woman is Zion, the son is the temple of Solomon, and the built city is the New Jerusalem.

The Fifth Vision, 10:60 — 12:39. This has the vision of the eagle with three heads and 12 wings that flew and ruled over the land. The ruling was done successively by each wing and head, but in the end the eagle, who has only two heads left, is set upon by a lion, who predicts the eagle's destruction. As the lion speaks, a fire consumes the body of the eagle. Ezra is told that the eagle is the fourth empire seen by Daniel, the Roman power, which is to be destroyed by the Messiah.

The Sixth Vision, 12:40 — 13:58. In this vision a wondrous man arises from the sea that is storm-tossed. At his look everything trembles; whoever hears this man's voice is destroyed by fire. After he has consumed his enemies, this same man collects to himself a peaceful multitude, some of whom come willingly, others are brought by force. Ezra is informed that the man from the sea is the preexistent Messiah, those who came to fight against him were the Gentiles; the multitudes who rejoiced at the Messiah's coming were the ten tribes of Israel.

The Seventh Vision, chapter 14:1-48. Ezra, warned of his approaching death, is instructed to write the books of wisdom. Accordingly he puts in writing 94 books, of which he is commanded to publish 24, a possible reference to the 24 books of the Hebrew Old Testament canon. Seventy of the 94 books he is to hide, for they were of an esoteric nature. God had five scribes brought for Ezra, and for 40 days God enabled him to write. Ezra completes the commission assigned to him. Waxman claims that the purpose of 4 Ezra is an apology aimed at describing the origin of the apocryphal and pseudepigraphical works.[5]

Chapters 15 and 16 are the least important parts of the book, to which they form an appendix; in them are found denunciations against Babylon, Asia, and Egypt, concluding with an announcement of terrors and tribulations which were to come upon the world. However, the Lord's elect will be saved. The appendix is considered by Oesterley to come from between A. D. 240 and 270.[6]

Original Language of the Book

The book is preserved in Latin and in a number of Oriental versions, the Syriac, Ethiopic, and Armenian. These are derived from the Greek, which, according to a number of authorities, was based on a Hebrew original. Waxman says the book is of pure Hebrew composition and a product of genuine Jewish thinking.[7] An Aramaic original has also been postulated by scholars. The English version is corrupt, being based on the Latin, and contains many interpolations, such as the one in 7:28-29, where references to Jesus are found.

Date of Writing

Various dates are given for the time of origin. Waxman claims the date can be determined almost with precision.[8] The constant reference to the Romans, the destruction of the temple, as well as the acquaintance of the author with the Roman emperors, all point to the close of the first century, the period from A. D. 81 to 96. Canon Box places the editing of chapters 3—14 between A. D. 100 and 135; the date of the Salathiel portion A. D. 100; the date of the Eagle Vision A. D. 81—96 or possibly A. D. 69—79; the date of the Son of Man Vision before A. D. 70; the Ezra legend after 70, and the old Ezra portion before that date.[9] As for the publication of the entire present work, it comes from the same period as 2 Baruch, to which it is very similar.

The Book of Judith

The tale of Judith has come down to modern times in two versions. According to one account Holofernes was commanded by Nebuchadnezzar to punish the rebel vassals of the king of Assyria. With a large army Holofernes conquered Cilicia, Mesopotamia, and the region of Damascus. On his way to northern Palestine he devastated everything in his path. With the help of Jehovah the Jews determined to resist the coming attack of Holofernes on Judean territory. They were terrified by the successes of the general and prepared themselves spiritually by prayer and fasting and physically by the mobilization of their forces.

The story then concentrates on the siege of Bethulia. At the end of 34 days the inhabitants are considering surrendering (1-7) because their water supply had recently been drained. The leaders are blamed by the people for the plight in which they find themselves. One of the elders, Ozear, begs them to hold out five days longer, promising that help will come. At this point in the story (8:1) Judith is introduced, a widow for more than three years and known for her piety and great beauty. When she is told of the plan of the elders to surrender the city, she becomes indignant, exclaiming: "God is not a man, that He can be threatened" (8:16). She announces that she has a plan that will bring about the defeat of the enemy. Chapter 9 contains the prayer she uttered before her journey to the camp of Holofernes. After beautifying herself with all manner of cosmetics, she went with her maid to the enemy camp. She informs the guards of Holofernes that she is a Hebrew woman fleeing from the city about to fall and that she has come to reveal a way in which the city can be taken.

She confirmed an earlier report of Achior that the Jewish city would not fall while the Jews remained faithful to Jehovah. But now they were planning to eat forbidden animals, which would bring God's punishment upon the city (10:14—11:23). Judith was offered refreshments from the general's table, but she requested to be allowed to eat only the food her maid had brought along. She was also granted permission to go outside the camp with her maid to bathe and pray. This Judith did for three nights. Finally the time has come for which Judith has planned. Holofernes arranged a banquet for Judith at which he hoped to enjoy her to the utmost. Again she abstains from eating unclean foods and eats only that which her maid had prepared. Left alone with Holofernes, who is intoxicated, she asks God's help and then takes Holofernes' sword and decapitates him. In the bag she has brought she deposits his head, and as in previous nights, walks past the sentry beyond the camp.

After Judith and her maid arrive at the city of Bethulia, she displays Holofernes' head. In chapter 13 v. 14 she calls upon the people to praise and thank God for the deliverance He effected. The next day the besieged Jews put the enemy to flight. In the epilog the author relates the triumph of Judith and gives her canticle of thanksgiving. (15:9—16:25)

In the other and shorter version, although the story is practically the same, it is placed into a different setting. The place of Nebuchadnezzar is taken by Seleucus, and Jerusalem is the scene of the events, not Bethulia.

The Language of the Book

The original text of Judith no longer exists. A number of scholars believe that certain peculiarities in the Greek version indicate that the book was probably written in Hebrew. Some have suggested an Aramaic original. The Greek version of Judith has survived in a trustworthy recension as found in the codices of Alexandrinus (A), Vaticanus (B), and Sinaiticus (S). The Latin translation in the Vulgate, made by Jerome in one night, reflects the sense of the Aramaic copy from which the translation was made.

Time of Composition

Views differ among scholars regarding the time the book was written. Dates between 175 and 110 B. C. have been proposed. Oesterley has suggested the time of the Maccabean struggle, plainly the time during the years of Jonathan's leadership (160—159 B. C.); also at a time when the temple was in possession of the orthodox party.[10]

The Purpose of the Book

It is quite clear that Judith is not history. Judith was written to encourage the Jews to be faithful to their religion and their law in the face of heathen attacks. The purpose of the book is evident: to arouse the spirit of nationalism and patriotism in a time of great national calamity.

The Book of Tobit

The Book of Tobit is recognized by Roman Catholics as one of the deuterocanonical books of their Old Testament. The Councils of Hippo (A. D. 393) and Carthage (A. D. 419) listed it among the canonical books. The Council of Trent reaffirmed the action taken by earlier church councils. The discovery of one Hebrew MS and two Aramaic MSS in Cave 4 of Qumran seems to show that at the beginning of the Christian era this book was read and valued by Jews.

It was widely circulated in ancient times, as is attested by various translations circulating among Jews and Christians. There are extant three recensions in Greek, two in Latin, two in Syriac, four in Hebrew, and one in Ethiopic.

The Contents of the Book of Tobit

Tobit begins with a summary account of the early life of the devout Tobit (called by some Roman Catholic writers Tobias). This is followed by an account, in a sort of a diptych, of the hard trial which on the same day befell Tobit at Nineveh (2:1–3:6) and Sarah, the daughter of Raguel at Nineveh (3:7-15), prompting both to ask for help from God. God answered their prayers by sending the angel Raphael to aid both of them (3:16 f). At this point the main part of the story begins.

Tobias, the son of Tobit, is asked by his father to go to Rages in Media and collect a large sum of money deposited with a relative, Gabael. Raphael offers his services to Tobias, who needs a guide (5:1-22). In the Tigris River they catch a large fish whose heart, liver, and gall are removed by Tobias at the suggestion of Azariah, alias the angel Raphael. In Ecbatana they call on Raguel, father of Sarah. Tobias meets Sarah and asks for her hand in marriage, but he is told how a demon has killed all her previous suitors and husbands. Since Tobias has been instructed by Azariah how to defeat the demons, Tobias insists on marrying Sarah. On the wedding night Tobias follows instructions and burns the heart and liver of the fish with incense in the bridal chamber and drives the evil spirit to the uttermost parts of Egypt. After this Tobias sends Azariah to Rages to collect the money from his kinsman and then prepares for the wedding feast given by his father-in-law. (Ch. 9)

Upon the return of Tobias and Sarah to Nineveh, the eyesight of Tobit is restored by means of the gall taken from the same fish that has furnished the heart and liver for driving away the demon Asmodeus. Before Sarah reaches Tobit's home, he has regained his sight so that he is able to meet the bride at the gate of the city. Another wedding banquet of seven day's duration is held. Finally, when Tobit and Tobias endeavor to reward Azarias, who was mainly responsible for their happiness, they discover that their benefactor has been the angel Raphael, one of the seven angels who presents the prayers of men before God. The book concludes with a canticle of thanksgiving and the father's last instruction for a happy life for Tobias, who obeys his father's dying wish and lives to hear of Nineveh's destruction.

The Purpose of Tobit

Modern Roman Catholic scholars contend that the purpose of Tobit is to give, not history, but "an edifying story." The historical blunders and chronological distortions, it is believed, indicate that the author was writing a moralizing story, one interrupted with suitable exhortations (4:3-21; 12:6-15; 14:8-11, and others). Tobit's objective is to show religious people the sufferings and trials a good man must endure. However, if he continues to be faithful, ultimately God will bless him with temporal goods (3:17; 4:21; 11:17). With this thesis there are combined instructions on the value of legal observances (1:4-9, 12; 4:6); the importance of prayer (3:1 ff. 11 ff. 24, Vulgate), on chastity (3:16-18), (4:13; 6:16-22, Vulgate); on doing works of mercy (1:15, Vulgate 2:1-2); the excellence of giving alms (4:7-12; 12:8b-9; 19-20), also on manifesting respect for the dead.

The work is written in Biblical language and has many allusions to the Old Testament. Although the original is lost, a number of scholars concur in the theory that either Hebrew or Aramaic is the language in which it was composed. There are differences in the text of the Greek versions. The Codex Sinaiticus (S) has the longest text as contrasted with Codex Vaticanus (B), of which the Alexandrinus is a revision. Jerome made his translation in the Vulgate from an Aramaic text.

Tobit and Pagan Sources

Scholars like Goodspeed, Ferrar, Metzger, and others believe that the author of Tobit made use of pagan sources. Some hold that Tobit was written to counteract an Egyptian work, the *Tractate of Khons*, in which a demon is cast out by a woman with the aid of a Theban deity. The Story of Achikar is also supposed to have influenced the contents of Tobit. Another source allegedly employed was the story of "The Grateful Man."

Scholarly opinion differs as to the extent foreign sources were incorporated by Tobit's author. Some students are convinced that Persian influence is greatly in evidence. The reference to angels and demons is allegedly a new development of Judaism, coming from Zoroastrianism. Asmodeus is supposed to be Aeshma Daeva of Persian demonology. The dog who follows Tobias on his journeys is reminiscent of the dog who in Zoroastrianism attends Sraosha. In Judaism the dog was a despised animal, considered unclean. It must have been a Jew with Greek breath, living under the Ptolemies in Egypt, who incorporated various strands in his fictional story.

Certain Roman Catholic scholars believe that the main source for Tobit was Genesis and its stories of the patriarchs. In Genesis 24 is the story of Eliezer and Isaac's marriage, and Rebecca served as a model for the account of Tobias' journey and wedding to Sarah. Raphael is the angel, who according to Gen. 24:7, 40 was sent by Jehovah to guide Eliezer in finding a wife for Isaac.

Time of Composition

Tobit may be one of the earliest writings of the Apocrypha. Scholars differ as to the time of composition, though it was probably written about 250 – 175 B. C. Metzger says it was composed by a devout Jew about 190 – 170 B. C.[11] Clarke places the date of its composition in the 3rd or early 2nd century B. C.[12] Waxman claims that the book was written before the temple of Herod was built, which was about 20 B. C.[13] The theory has also been advanced that Tobit was composed by a pious Jew in Egypt at the close of the 3rd pre-Christian century.

Additions to the Book of Esther

The Old Testament Book of Esther is a strong nationalistic book, recording that the Jews, at the instigation of Haman, were to be killed. Instead, through the heroism of Esther the Jews were able to defend themselves against their enemies in the Persian Empire and kill 75,000 of them. The canonical Esther does not mention the name of God, which the name of the Persian king is referred to 175 times. Nor is a word said about prayer; in fact the book mentions very little of religion. The apocryphal Esther aims to supplement the canonical book. Besides adding 10 verses to the 10th chapter of Esther, the apocryphal Esther has six more chapters. The new material found in the Additions to Esther, unlike the episode of Bel and the Story of Susanna, adds nothing of intrinsic value to the Biblical book of Esther and contributes nothing to the Biblical story. The Greek Version of Esther, which Jerome used when making the Vulgate translation, had 107 verses not represented in the Hebrew text. Jerome removed them from the body of Esther and arranged them in an appendix and in the order found in the English version where, Clarke says, "they are completely unintelligible."[14]

The new additions to Esther are also calculated to add to the Biblical version a strong religious element; thus Mordecai and Esther speak long prayers; Mordecai explains the word Purim, "lots," by the two lots which God had made, one for the people of God, one for the heathen. It becomes evident that the additions endeavor to clarify what was obscure in the Biblical account. Two long letters of Artaxerxes (Xerxes) are introduced in the decree mentioned in Esther 3:13-15; the other is referred to in 8:13, which abrogates the previous decree.

In the Septuagint these new additions are distributed in seven separate portions throughout the text. To the reign of Artaxerxes are ascribed events that must have occurred before his time. These additions in the English Apocrypha are usually grouped together.

The parts in the Greek Esther missing in the Hebrew Esther are the following:

1. Mordecai's dream; and the episode where the conspiracy against the king is brought to nought. This portion of 17 verses is placed before chapter 1 of the canonical book.

2. The letters sent out by the king of Persia to the effect that all Jews in the Persian Empire are to be killed. It follows chapter 3:13 of the Hebrew text. In the Vulgate it is 13:1-7.

3. The prayers of Mordecai and Esther follow chapter 4 of the Hebrew text. In the Vulgate Mordecai's prayer is 13:8-13 and Esther's is 14:1-19.

4. Esther's audience with the king in the LXX covers 16 verses, whereas the Massoretic text has two. In the Latin Bible this is found in 15:1-16.

5. A copy of the letter of the king of Persia, which gives the Jews permission to defend themselves against their enemies, follows 8:12. In the Vulgate it is 16:1-24.

6. This part contains different subjects. The first consists of an interpretation of Mordecai's dreams. It is climaxed by a discussion of the purpose of the Feast of Purim. This follows the Hebrew text and closes the Greek version of Esther. In the Vulgate it is 10:4-13. The second part of this section, a historical note added to the Greek version, is 11:1 in the Vulgate.

Date of Esther's Composition

The Greek Esther was well known to Josephus around A. D. 90, for he had paraphrased its contents in the *Jewish Antiquities,* XI:6. Clement of Rome, author of one book of the Apostolic Fathers, spoke of Esther as entreating the all-seeing Lord with her fasting and humiliation (55:6, cf. Esth. 15:2 [Vulgate]). Goodspeed believes that this reference to "the all-seeing God nor prayer" is not directed to the canonical Book of Esther.[15] According to Jerome, the Greek Additions to Esther were not accepted by the Jews, but in his Letter to Africanus he states that they are able to edify those who read them.

It is difficult to determine the exact date and place of the origin of the apocryphal Esther. Some authorities believe the Additions to Esther were written somewhere in Egypt between 180 – 145 B. C. According to Waxman, it is feasible that the various additions were written by different men.[16] He calls attention to the superscription in chapter 11, asserting that these letters were explained by Lysimachus, son of Ptolemy of Jerusalem, and were brought to Egypt by a Levite priest named Dositheus in the 4th year of Ptolemy and Cleopatra.[17] However, as there were four different kings named Ptolemy who had wives named Cleopatra, it is difficult to ascertain the exact date.

Ecclesiasticus, or the Wisdom of Jesus, the Son of Sirach

The origin of the name of Ecclesiasticus, which means "the Church Book," is lost in the mist of antiquity. The designation has been in use in the Christian church since the 3rd century and employed also by Jerome. In comparison with other ecclesiastical books, it is the book *par excellence,* if wide usage is a criterion. The book seems to have been utilized in the early church as an instructional manual. It was so popular that it was translated into a number of Oriental languages, including Coptic (Sahidic, Bohairic, and Achmimic [Akhmimic] dialects), the Armenian, the Ethiopic, Georgian, Old Slavonic, and Arabic. Ecclesiasticus is the longest book of the Apocrypha; it is twice as long as the canonical book of Proverbs.

The Contents

Ecclesiasticus is divided into five main parts, unequal in length. After the preface comes the longest section of the work, 1:1 − 42:14, containing the "proverbs of Ben Sirach." It is a collection of proverbs loosely strung together, presenting the author's meditation and lectures on religious and ethical matters. There is a great similarity between the canonical Proverbs and this part of Ecclesiasticus.

The next section, 42:15 − 43:33 is in the nature of a poem of praise; the author lauds the wonderful works of physical nature created by God. Section 44:1-49:16 begins with these famous words: "Let us now praise famous men, and our fathers that begat us!" and contains a recapitulation of the history of the Hebrew people and the accomplishments of its great leaders. This section may have furnished the author of Hebrews with a model for the great roll call of the heroes of faith given in chapter 11.

The last section, 50 − 51 is the nature of an appendix; it contains the best description of the temple services that has survived from ancient times. (50:1-26)

The Author

This is the only apocryphal book of which the author is known. The writer tells his readers that his name is "Jesus, the son of Sirach," the son of Eliezer of Jerusalem (50:27). His grandson 50 years later translated the book into Greek. Nothing further is known about the author nor his grandson. Jesus ben Sirach is described as a resident of Jerusalem, but the text is doubtful. Some scholars believe that Sirach was a student and teacher. He gives evidence of intimate knowledge of the Old Testament. The entire book is replete with ideas taken from the Old Testament and reflects the attitude and training of a person who enjoyed an excellent preparation for the position of scribe. From certain allusions in the book it has been inferred that he was a man of leisure, fond of travel, a man with a philosophical mind, and an adherent of a party which later came to be known as the Sadducees.

The Date

Scholars differ as to the exact time of the book's composition. Eissfeldt believes that Ecclesiasticus was written in Jerusalem around 190 B. C., some years before the outbreak of the Maccabean struggle.[18] Others claim that it was composed as early as 290 and 280 B. C. The translation of Ecclesiasticus was undertaken and completed around 130 B. C. In the preface the grandson states that he had come to Alexandria in Egypt in the 38th year of King Euergetes, or 132 B. C. In the prolog he states what prompted him to undertake the translation.

The Language

The book was written in Hebrew, but the original was lost, and it has come down to modern times in a Greek version. The Hebrew original was preserved many years longer than any other book of the Apocrypha. In 1897 a large portion of the Hebrew original was restored through the efforts of the late Solomon Schechter, discoverer of fragments of Ecclesiasticus in the genizah of the Old Synagog in Cairo. The problem of ascertaining the original text of Ecclesiasticus is complicated and difficult because the extant Greek manuscripts are marred by omissions, interpolations, and transpositions. The reader should be aware of great divergences between the King James Version and the Revised Version. Since the discovery of the Hebrew manuscript at Cairo in 1896, the older translations have become obsolete. Two thirds of the book is now available in a Hebrew text in five parts of five manuscripts. Cave 2 of Qumran yielded additional fragments of the Hebrew Sirach. The evidence points to the Greek text as a translation from the Hebrew.

According to Waxman [19] the book has exercised great influence on later Jewish literature. Although the great Rabbi Akiba prohibited its reading, Talmudic scholars assiduously studied Ecclesiasticus. The leading Tannaitic and Amoraic scholars quote liberally from it. More than 20 proverbs are cited in the Babylonian and Palestinian Talmuds. Some of the quotations in the Talmuds are introduced as if from the Bible: "It is written." In two places Ecclesiasticus is spoken of as belonging to the kethubim, or hagiographa, of the Hebrew Old Testament.

The Wisdom of Solomon

There were many Jews who lived outside of Palestine, especially after the Exile, in the communities known as the Diaspora. One of the largest Jewish settlements was to be found in Egyptian Alexandria, the intellectual and scientific center of the Hellenistic world, with one of the great libraries of the ancient world. In Alexandria Jewish religion and thought came to grips with heathen religion and philosophy. Often the Jews became defenders of their faith because of attacks made upon it and of persecution against them. It is believed that the Wisdom of Solomon was written to encourage the Jews to be faithful to their ancestral religion. This book is classified as belonging to the sapiential genre to which also Ecclesiasticus is assigned. In its religious insight, its religious outlook, and its organization of thought as well as range of ideas, Wisdom is considered superior to Ecclesiasticus.

The Book may be divided into three parts:
1. (1-5) Wisdom brings eternal life to the just and faithful man. Death is the award of the unjust and apostates.
2. (6-9) Wisdom's origin, nature, and activity are explained. Chapter 9 has a beautiful prayer in praise of wisdom.
3. (10-19) This section contains a review of the history of Israel and of its relation to other peoples.
   a. The patriarchs and the exodus (10 – 12).
   b. The Canaanites (12:3-27).
   c. Discussion of idolatry (13:1 – 15:17).
   d. Further considerations of the experiences of the Hebrews and the Egyptians at the exodus (15:18 – 19:22).

The first chapters are a panegyric on righteousness, whose pursuit is depicted as a prerequisite for the acquisition of wisdom, "because wisdom will not enter into a soul that resisteth evil, nor dwell in a body that is held in pledge by sin (1:4, R. V.)." Righteousness is not only concerned with this life but is portrayed as meriting life beyond the grave; therefore whatever a righteous man may suffer at the hands of his enemies in this world, eventual victory nevertheless rests with him.

In chapter 3 the Jews learned that "God made man for immortality." After death, the soul of the just man lived, not in the pale, shadowy reaches of Sheol, but in a life of eternal happiness in the presence of God. Some critical scholars believe that this was the first time in the pre-Christian literature that the doctrine of immortality had been clearly and unequivocably taught.

Chapters 6 to 9 are an appeal to kings and judges to follow wisdom; they contain an account of Solomon's zeal for this quest. Wisdom is personified and comes close to being called a divine spirit. The passage that emphasizes this is explicated in chapter 7:24-26.

The last 10 chapters give illustrations of the power and value of wisdom, taken from the history of the Israelites. The miserable failure of the heathen, who lacked righteousness, is contrasted with the triumph of God's elect. In chapters 11 – 12 there is a prayer directed to God which rises to noble heights in expression. However, with this exception, it is believed that not much would have been lost, if the writer would have condensed the latter part of Wisdom.

Illustrations taken from the lives of the patriarchs and the early history of the nation show that wisdom has always been at the root of success, and the lack of wisdom resulted in failure.

The Purpose of Wisdom

The book is partly polemical and partly apologetic. The opening chapters warn against "the ungodly," by whom most likely are meant the Sadducees. The latter did not believe in future life, and therefore were not deterred by the fear of punishment. Hedonism was a great temptation for the Jews of the Greek-speaking world. One of the purposes of the author of Wisdom was to instruct and keep the Hellenistic Jews faithful to their ancestral religion. The author also addresses himself to the pagans with the idea of attracting them to Judaism. The veiled and mysterious ways in which he alludes to past Jewish history are designed to arouse their curiosity and hold their attention (chs. 10 – 12; 16 – 19). This technique was also employed in the Sybilline Books.

The Author

Nothing is known of the author of the Wisdom of Solomon, except that he was an Alexandrian Jew. St. Augustine believed that Jesus ben Sirach, the author of Ecclesiasticus, was also responsible for penning Wisdom. However, the differences between the two apocryphal books make this view seem unlikely. Jerome claims that "many old writers" of his time regarded Philo as the author, a view that Luther and many Reformation scholars accepted. Some have tried to associate the book with Apollos, because he is considered by some to be the author of the Epistle to the Hebrews. But this conjecture cannot be verified. There are not specifically Christian ideas in Wisdom, which would constitute a serious objection to this theory.

Date of Writing

Authorities are not agreed as to the date. Opinion ranges from 150 B. C. to A. D. 40. The persecution mentioned in 2:10-20 and the oppression referred to in 15:14 may be allusions to the measures taken by Ptolemy Physcon against the Jews who opposed his government. The reference in 15:6 to the worship of absent rulers and elsewhere to persecutions is interpreted as a reference to Emperor Caligula, who in A. D. 40 wished to have himself recognized as God. Other scholars argue that the influence of the Wisdom of Solomon on New Testament books requires a date earlier than A. D. 40, and they place the book back to 100 B. C. or earlier. As in the Books of the Maccabees, so in the Wisdom of Solomon the matter of defection from the Jewish faith was a problem in the 2nd century B. C., when the orthodox Jews were frequently persecuted.

Influence on New Testament

A number of scholars believe that the Wisdom of Solomon has influenced the New Testament. Some claim that there are parallels between it and some of Paul's epistles. Moriarity states that there can be no doubt that both St. John and St. Paul were influenced in their Christological ideas by its teachings.[20] The influence of Wisdom is supposed to be especially evident in the Fourth Gospel where the wisdom concept is supposed to have prepared the way for the Word (Greek: logos) made flesh. There is no direct quotation from Wisdom in the New Testament.

Baruch

The Book of Baruch portrays itself as written by the friend and secretary of Jeremiah, the son of Neraiah (1:1). According to the testimony of the book, it was written in the 5th year after the destruction of Jerusalem, either 592 or 582 B. C. Baruch, the faithful follower of Jeremiah, is among the deported exiles who is sent to his countrymen left behind in Jerusalem. He is entrusted with a sum of money to aid Jewish worship in Jerusalem and with a request that the Jews pray for Nebuchadnezzar and his son Belshazzar. Just how this was to be effected with the temple destroyed and its priesthood scattered is not made clear by the author.

Baruch, the son of Neraiah, came to occupy an important place in Jewish legends. Since he is reported to have rewritten the canonical Book of Jeremiah and also was an eyewitness of the destruction of Jerusalem, it was assumed natural that he should write about events connected with the downfall of the Southern Kingdom.

Content of Book

Baruch falls into three parts: the first, 1:1 – 3:8 contains the letter of Baruch (1:1-14) and a liturgical confession and prayer; second, 3:9 – 4:4 consists of a short chapter on wisdom and is the reason why the book is often grouped with Ecclesiasticus and the Wisdom of Solomon in the category of the wisdom literature. In it the sufferings of the Jews are attributed to the fact that Israel forsook the fountains of wisdom. The third and final section, 4:5 – 5:9, endeavors to encourage the people and promises them the final restoration of Zion. In 4:5-35 the refrain "be of good cheer" or its equivalent (vv. 5, 21, 27, 30) constantly recurs, and in 4:30 – 5:9 there is the regular repetition of "O Jerusalem."

The final lines of the last part of the book end on an optimistic note:

Arise, O Jerusalem, stand up on the height and look toward the east and see your children gathered from east and west, at the word of the Holy One, rejoicing that God has remembered them.

Baruch is a composite work, uneven in quality and not harmonious but incongruous. It consists of two or even three distinct documents. The clearest and sharpest division of the book comes between 3:8 and 3:9. At this point the style changes from prose to poetry; also God is spoken of in different ways. In 1:1 – 3:8 the author uses the following names for God: Lord, 22 times: Lord Almighty, the God of Israel, two times; Lord, our

God, 15 times. Not one of these names for the deity is employed in the second part (3:9 — 5:9). The book was written to persuade the readers to be subservient and obedient to their Babylonian masters (cf. 1:11 — 12), to urge repentance for their sins which had been responsible for the destruction of Jerusalem, and to create faith in God's ultimate purpose of eventually restoring the Jews from captivity.

The Date of Baruch

Scholars are generally agreed that the book is of much later origin, having nothing to do with the time of the Babylonian captivity. What then was the situation that prompted the writing? The answer scholars give is divided: one school of thought places its origin during the persecution of Antiochus Epiphanes, while another school assigns it to a time after the destruction of Jerusalem in A. D. 70. Still others date the origin of the latter portion of the book as late as A. D. 150. Even though the second part may come from the 2nd century A. D., the first part is believed to be quite old.

The Language of Baruch

The original language was probably Hebrew, although a Greek translation has survived. Scholars are divided as to what parts were written in Hebrew and which in Greek. Today the book exists only in Greek and is found in the uncials B A Q V and in a number of cursives; it does not appear in the Sinaitic codex nor in the C codex.

Baruch is found in Syriac in two forms: The Peshitta and the Syro-Hexaplar; the former supposedly is based on the Hebrew original as well as on the Septuagint. The Latin version also exists in two forms; both are translations from the Greek, as are also the other versions: Armenian, Arabic, Ethiopic, and Coptic.

Purpose of Baruch

Goodspeed believes that the book was written to inculcate a loyal attitude toward the empire, which many Jews found difficult to adopt.[21] The Jews are urged to forget the past and not to plan vengeance but to serve the empire faithfully and seek blessings from the emperor. The revolt of Bar Kochba in A. D. 132 — 135 indicated the need for such advice to the Jews of Palestine.

The Letter of Jeremiah

The Letter of Jeremiah was originally a separate writing but subsequently became attached to the Book of Baruch because Baruch and Jeremiah were friends and co-workers. Scholars are certain that the prophet Jeremiah had nothing to do with the authorship of the Letter. Now the Letter of Jeremiah appears as the 6th chapter of the Book of Baruch and is found inserted in different places of various manuscripts of the Apocrypha. In the Vulgate it is attached to the apocryphal book of Baruch.

The source of inspiration for the writing of the alleged Epistle of Jeremiah was verse 11 of chapter 10 of the canonical Jeremiah, the only verse in the entire book that is in Aramaic. "Thus shall ye say unto them, the gods that have not made the heavens and the earth even they shall perish from the earth and from under the heavens." The second person plural, "ye shall say unto them," refers to the men of Israel giving this truth to the Gentiles.

Content and Purpose of the Letter

The opening verse reads: "A copy of the letter which Jeremiah sent to those who were about to be led captive to Babylon by the king of the Babylonians, to instruct them, as he had been commanded by God." Jeremiah 29 portrays the prophet writing a letter to the Jewish exiles in Babylon. With this background it is not difficult to imagine a later Jew writing a letter incorporating the idea of Jeremiah 10:11. The author elaborates on this verse, showing by a variety of arguments the foolishness of the sin of idolatry. Ridicule of the heathen gods is found in Hebrew literature in Is. 44:9-20 and Psalms 115 and 135. Examples of sarcasm are seen in the comparison between Yahweh and the wooden deity being used as a roost for bats, skuas, birds, and cats. The writer says that the food offered the idol by their devotees is sold by the priests, whose wives even salt a portion of it (v. 28). The heathen deities are useless even "as a scarecrow in a cucumber field." If a fire breaks out in the temple, the god burns as does the timber.

The purpose of the book is to show the folly of idol worship. While the author of the Letter refers to "gods," Metzger believes that the author most likely had in mind the god Tammuz. In verse 43 there seems to be a reference to the licentious fertility rites connected with the worship of Tammuz, to whom writers like Herodotus, Strabo, and Lucian allude.

The Language of the Letter

Scholarly opinion is divided about the nature of the original language of the Letter of Jeremiah. Ball has advanced that view that it was written in Hebrew. Torrey, however, contends that Ball has not proven his case and argues for Aramaic, from which the present Greek text was translated. Still others argue for a Greek original.

The Time of Writing

The proponents of Greek as the original language claim the Letter was written in Alexandria as an attack on heathenism; they place the writing around 70 B. C. The advocates of Hebrew as the original language put the time at the end of the 4th century B. C. According to this view the Babylon referred to is the actual Babylon, and the Letter itself was sent to the Jews of Babylon to warn them against assimilation. Other scholars believe that the idolatry referred to was the kind practiced at the temple of Serapis, the most beautiful building in the world except for the Capitol at Rome, and that Vespasian is the Nebuchadnezzar of the letter, and Rome is Babylon.

Together with the stories of Bel and the Dragon, the second part of Wisdom of Solomon, the implications of the Prayer of Manasseh, the Letter of Jeremiah is part of a literature specifically directed against the idolatrous practices of heathenism.

The Prayer of Azariah and the Song of the Three Young Men

The Book of Daniel in the Septuagint, followed also in the Vulgate, has three additional writings not found in the canonical books: The Prayer of Azariah, the Song of the Three Young Men; Susanna; and Bel and the Dragon.

The Prayer of Azariah and the Song of the Three Young Men are found in all Greek MSS of Daniel between verses 23 and 24 of chapter 3. There are two versions of these two Danielic additions: that of the LXX proper and that of Theodotion, which is translated in the English versions. This block of material does not appear in the Aramaic text. In the King James and the Revised Version of 1885 it has the heading: The Song of the Three Holy Children, which follows in the 3rd chapter of Daniel after the assertion that Daniel's three friends fell bound into the burning fiery furnace. (V. 23)

The Prayer of Azariah is linked to the context of the chapter, while the Song of the Three Young Men relates the heating of the furnace, the burning of the attendants, and the descent of the Angel of the Lord.

Some scholars believe that the two are not written by the same author and were not originally together. Azarias, one of the four friends of Daniel, is considered by some scholars to be another Azarias, a hero of the Maccabean struggle.

Azariah's prayer acknowledges that God was just in punishing Jerusalem, bewails the cruelty and wickedness of the enemy, brings to remembrance the promises made to Abraham, Isaac, and Jacob, and describes the forlorn condition of the Jews, who are portrayed as "without prince, or prophet, or leader, or burnt-offering, or sacrifice, or oblation, or incense, or place to offer before Thee to find mercy." The author hopes that the penitence of the people will bring about restoration and judgment on the enemy.

Verses 29-68 contain a blessing of God by the three friends of Daniel, of which the latter part begins: "O all ye works of the Lord, bless ye the Lord." This canticle is used as an alternative to the *Te Deum* in the Morning Prayer in Episcopalian churches.

The Prayer of Azariah is considered a splendid example of Jewish devotional literature. The refrain: "Sing praise to Him and highly exalt Him forever," occurs 32 times throughout the song.

The Time of Writing

Its author is unknown. These two additions to chapter 3 are believed to have been composed during the Maccabean age, probably in the reign of the Seleucid king Antiochus Epiphanes (about 167–163 B. C.). During these years the Jewish people suffered great affliction. In verse 9 the writer laments: "Thou hast given us into the hands of lawless enemies, most hateful apostates, and to an unjust king, the most wicked in all the world." This seems to be references to the renegade Jews in 1 Macc. 1:1-15 and the cruelties of King Antiochus. (See 1 Macc. 1:20-24; 41-64.)

The early Fathers treated these additions as canonical, as does the Roman Catholic Church. The influence of these additions to the canonical *Book of Daniel* has been considerable throughout the Christian church. Not only was it a part of the Latin and Greek versions but these additions were translated into languages like Syriac, Coptic, Ethiopic, Armenian, Georgian, and Arabic. The *Song of the Three Young Men* has also influenced the liturgical history of the medieval church. Roman Catholics, Episcopalians, and Lutherans use it as a canticle. The Benedictus (vv. 35-65) has been employed since Christian antiquity as a hymn of praise. In 1549 it was prescribed in the First Prayer Book as a substitute for the Te Deum during Lent. In the revision of the *American Prayer Book* in 1928 the opening part of the prayer was included in the Morning Prayer under the name of Benedictus.

Susanna

The History of Susanna is found in 20th-century editions of the Septuagint, prefixed to Daniel. In the Vulgate it appears as chapter 13 of Daniel. Miss Dorothy Sayers has placed Bel and the Dragon as the two opening stories of her anthology of mystery stories entitled *Omnibus of Crime* (1939). Metzger regards Susanna as one of "the best short stories in the world's literature." [22]

The Contents of Susanna

The setting of the story is in Babylon and takes place during the exile. Susanna was the beautiful wife of a rich Jew who resided in Babylon. Two Jewish elders were inflamed to passion by her beauty, greatly coveting her. One day the two men met each other as they were spying on Susanna. They confessed to each other their secret lust for Susanna and decided upon a plot designed to make her accept their improper advances. They hid themselves in the garden where she was bathing, and when her attendants left her alone, they surprised her, threatening to accuse her of adultery if she failed to comply with their demands. Susanna refused, and the next day she was brought to trial before the court of Israel. Inasmuch as she was unable to defend herself against the false accusations of the two elders she was condemned to death.

As Susanna was being led away to be killed, suddenly the proceedings were halted by the shout of Daniel, a young man, who asked for the privilege of questioning the witnesses. The young man examined each of the two elders separately and succeeded in showing that their testimony was not in agreement; that they had perjured themselves. Susanna was acquitted, the two elders were executed in her place, and Daniel's fame spread among the people.

Time and Place of Origin of Susanna

The time and place of the origin of this story are not known. Scholars differ as to the original language of the writing: some postulate a Hebrew original, others an Aramaic. There are two puns in the narrative which lead some to infer a Greek origin. The story of Susanna was probably written in Alexandria in the 200 years before the birth of Christ.

The English version is translated from Theodotian's version, not from the LXX. Torrey of Yale claimed that at the time Theodotian made his translation in the middle of the 2nd century, there were still in existence Hebrew-Aramaic manuscripts of Daniel which contained the so-called Additions to Daniel.[23] The Greek translation of Theodotian and the Greek Susanna contain Hebrew idioms that indicate, according to Torrey, that a Hebrew original was utilized by the present Greek version of Susanna.

Motive for the Writing of Susanna

Clarke suggests that possibly the story was inspired by Jer. 29:21-23, "where Ahab and Zedekiah were put to death for misconduct with other men's wives."[24] Clarke believes the story to be a parable, "composed in the later years of Alexander Jannaeus (106 − 79 B. C.), when controversy raged between the Pharisees and Sadducees."[25]

Various opinions have been expressed as to the purpose for this piece of fiction written in the best tradition of story telling. The author of Susanna seems to urge a more rigid examination of witnesses, especially where there is suspicion of collusion. He further recommends that it become a rule to inflict the same punishment on those guilty of perjury as the prescribed punishment for the victims of false testimony.

Susanna has been of interest to the Church Fathers, some of whom gave it an allegorical interpretation. Hippolytus, Bishop of Rome, wrote in the 3rd century as follows: "Susanna is a type prefiguring the Church; Joakim, her husband prefigures the Christ. The garden is the election of the saints, who like trees that bear fruit are planted in the Church. Babylon is the world; the two elders are typical of the two nations that plot against the Church—the one being of the circumcision, and the other from the Gentiles."[26] It was this type of interpretation that seems to have been responsible for the manner in which Susanna is represented in art.

Throughout the ages the story of Susanna has been popular. Many painters have portrayed the story on canvas. The famous statement in the Merchant of Venice, where Shylock addressed Portia as "a Daniel come to judgment," rests on the role of Daniel in the Susanna legend.

Bel and the Dragon

The episode of Bel and the Dragon stands at the end of Daniel in the Septuagint. Bruce Metzger calls it the oldest detective story in the world.[27] In the two stories incorporated in Bel and the Dragon we have an interesting example of the apologetic effort by Judaism to belittle the worship of idols and discredit heathen priestcraft. Ever since the Babylonian Exile, the Jews were attracted to the gods and goddesses of surrounding nations, especially those of the conquerors. Many felt that the victory of the heathen over Israel was achieved because of the superiority of the heathen gods. Furthermore, a majority of the Jews lived in the Diaspora, where since the time of the conquest of Alexander the Great there was a universal tendency to adopt Greek customs and civilization.

In centers like Alexandria and Babylon, where a heavy concentration of heathen existed, great pressures were brought upon the Jews to adjust themselves to their environment by adopting the practices of the land, including the heathen religion. Bel and the Dragon and the Epistle of Jeremy resort to ridicule to demonstrate the folly of trusting in man-made idols.

The Contents of Bel and the Dragon

Bel and the Dragon actually consists of two separate unrelated stories, variations of episodes narrated in the Book of Daniel. The first has as its basis Daniel 3, the episode about the golden image; the second rests on Daniel 6, the story of Daniel in the lions' den. In the first King Cyrus is depicted as coming to the Persian throne. One day he asks his friend Daniel why he does not worship the god Bel who was the chief Babylonian god and consumed each day large quantities of flour and oil and many sheep. Daniel persuades Cyrus to place the usual amount of goods in the temple and thereupon to close and seal it. To prove that the image of Bel does not enter and eat the food, Daniel had wood ashes scattered on the floor to record the footprints of the priests, who with their families and by means of a trapdoor beneath the idol made nocturnal visits and consumed the food and offerings.

In the morning when Daniel and the king return to the temple the food is gone. The king announces triumphantly that Bel is a living god, but Daniel points to the many footprints on the floor made by men, women and children, clearly showing that people had entered by a secret door and consumed the large quantity of food placed there for the idol. For this deception, so the story runs, the priests were killed, and Daniel was given permission to destroy the idols.

The Dragon is a story similar to that of Bel. Here the king is described as worshipping a living serpent — reminiscent of the practice of the Greeks who worshiped serpents at Oriental shrines, such as Aesculapius at

Epidaurus. Daniel, who was summoned to pay homage to it, denied its divinity. He fed it with a concoction of pitch, fat, and hair which caused the serpent to burst asunder. The people became angry at the treatment accorded their god and compelled the king to have Daniel cast into a den of lions, who had been deprived of their food to make them more rapacious. For six days Daniel eats nothing, nor do the lions eat Daniel. On the seventh day the prophet Habakkuk, while carrying food and drink to some reapers in Judea, is suddenly borne aloft by his hair to the lions' den where he deposits food for Daniel. In the twinkling of an eye, the prophet is returned to the field in Judea. On the seventh day the king has Daniel removed from the lions' den, and in his place the enemies are cast, who are devoured immediately.

Goodspeed believes that the name "Dragon" is obtained from the Greek and Latin term *drakon* and *draco* respectively.[28] Attempts have been made to connect the serpent with the Babylonian Tiamat, slain by Marduk according to the Babylonian epic. (Alexander the Great is said to have found veneration of serpents in India.)

Author and Language

Who the author of Bel and the Dragon was remains unknown; neither can it be definitely stated whether it was written in Hebrew or Aramaic. Oesterley believes that the original language was Greek.[29] Like the Book of Daniel, Bel and the Dragon is translated from Theodotian's text.

The Prayer of Manasseh

Some lists of Jewish apocryphal books contain a short work, the Prayer of Manasseh. Actually it was a part of the Septuagint but was included with writings called Songs at the end of the Psalms. In 2 Chron. 33:10-13 it states that Manasseh, son of Hezekiah, became the wickedest king of Judah. He sinned by abandoning the Mosaic law and by introducing foreign cults (2 Kings 21:1-8 and 2 Chron. 33:1-20). The results for Manasseh and Judah were dire because his idolatry ultimately brought upon Judah the destruction of Jerusalem and the temple and forced many Jews into the Babylonian captivity, 2 Kings 23:36 f.; 24:3; Jer. 15:4.

But during his lifetime Manasseh was punished by being taken into captivity by the Assyrians. In prison he experienced a profound change of heart. The Prayer of Manasseh professes to be the king's prayer of repentance which he uttered while in Assyria.

The Contents

The Prayer consists of 15 verses, and includes: invocation to God (1-7), confession of sin (8-10), and plea for forgiveness (11-15). Evaluated from a literary point of view, it is a fine prayer of penitence, reflecting Pharisaic coloring. There is no justification for believing the prayer genuine, but everything points to it as an imaginative composition.

Date, Authorship, and Language of the Prayer

Scholars differ regarding the time of origin of this short apocryphal book. Some believe that an unknown Jew composed this prayer between 150 and 50 B. C. Yale scholar Torrey places it later, arguing for the 2nd or 3rd century of the Christian era.[30] This is based upon the fact that part of the Prayer is written in Greek and is rather late in appearance. Scholars are unable to determine whether it was composed in Hebrew, Aramaic, or Greek. Although there is nothing in the Prayer to indicate its provenance, Metzger seems to favor a Palestinian origin rather than a Hellenistic Alexandrian.[31]

The Prayer of Manasseh is found in most manuscripts of the Septuagint and Vulgate. It has been incorporated in the Ethiopic version of Scripture. It was also rendered into Syriac, being found in the Didascalia, a 3rd-century work translated from the Greek. The Greek text is found for the first time in the *Apostolic Constitutions*, II, 22, a work from the 4th century A. D.

Status of the Book in the Roman Catholic Church

The Prayer of Manasseh is one of the apocryphal books not recognized as deuterocanonical by the Roman Catholic Church as are 10 of the 14 Protestant apocryphal books. By decision of the Council of Trent it was placed as an appendix to the Vulgate, "lest it should be lost." Phrases from the Prayer are employed in several of the responsories of the Roman Breviary.

1 Maccabees

The Historical Importance of the Two Books of Maccabees

The 1 and 2 Maccabees are considered two valuable books of history for the intertestamental period; 1 Maccabees is regarded of greater value than 2 Maccabees. If accuracy in reporting facts is the criterion for the evaluation of an historical writing, then 1 Maccabees would have to be rated very highly. The historiography of the book is characterized by a straightforward presentation and sobriety. The anonymous author of 1 Maccabees avoids references to miracles, attributes no events to supernatural intervention, and does not mention the doctrine of the resurrection. He was a man of conservative religious temper who fits in with the Saddu-cean outlook on life rather than the Pharisaic. And 2 Maccabees is more exciting than 1 Maccabees because it introduces and believes in the supernatural. However, 2 Maccabees does not have the same historical objectivity as does 1 Maccabees.

The Contents of 1 Maccabees

In 1 Maccabees is an account of the Jewish struggle against the persecution of Antiochus Epiphanes, king of Syria, which resulted in the liberation of the Jewish nation in the days of the Hasmoneans. The period

covered by the book is 168 – 136 B. C., from the outbreak of the Maccabean revolt until the death of Simon, the last of the five sons of Mattathias.
The author's plan is that each portion of the book treat one particular
member of the house of Maccabees. Chapter 1 is introductory to the
Maccabean conflict; chapter 2 relates the revolt of Mattathias; chapter
3:1 – 9:22 records the exploits of Judas; and, 9:23 – 12:53 depicts the activities of Jonathan; the last part of the book, 12:53 – 16:23 gives the account
of Simon's career.

The narrative follows a chronological order: 1 Maccabees opens with
a brief account of Alexander the Great's conquests, death, and the division
of the empire. The events of 1 Maccabees begin with Antiochus IV
Epiphanes as king of Syria in 175 B. C. and go to the death of Simon
Maccabaeus in 135 B. C. Included is the formation of a Hellenizing party
in Jerusalem which is willing to adopt the heathen practices in violation
of Judaism. Antiochus Epiphanes, called by the Jews Epimanes ("the Mad-
Man"), embarked upon a plan of forcing Greek culture, civilization, and
religion on the Jews of Palestine. This resulted in violent clashes between
the soldiers of Epiphanes and the Jewish patriots. After the temple in Jerusalem had been desecrated, Mattathias and his sons at Modin killed the
king's officers and fled to the mountains.

In 3:1 – 9:22 Judas Maccabeus is the hero. These chapters describe
him fighting Syrian generals and defeating Appollonius, Seron, Georgias,
Lysias, and Nicanor. Within three years after the desecration of the temple,
Judas and his brothers were able to rededicate its altar and have the traditional worship resumed. Judas sent ambassadors to Rome to conclude a
treaty with the Romans. The political aspirations of Judas led the Chasidim,
who later became the Pharisees, to break with him. In 160 B. C. Judas was
defeated and killed in battle with the Syrian commander Bacchides.

Jonathan, Judas' youngest brother, succeeded him as leader of the
Jews (160 – 142 B. C.). Chapters 9:23 – 12:53 treat of his reign. Although
Jonathan was powerless for a long time, he finally prevailed over the
Syrian general Bacchides. As a result Judah enjoyed peace. Jonathan
exploited the rivalry between Demetrius II and Alexander Balas, receiving
from the latter the title of high priest. Jonathan also showed great adroitness
in exploiting the rivalries between Demetrius II and Antiochus VI, playing
one against the other. Like his brother Judas, Jonathan was murdered at
a banquet near Jericho. John Hyrcanus, his son, succeeded Jonathan in the
position of high priest and combined in one office the civil, military, and
religious leadership of the Jewish nation.

Next an older Maccabean brother Simon (chapters 13 – 16), (leader
from 142 – 135 B. C.), led the resistance of the Jews to Syria. He drove the
Syrian garrison out of Jerusalem and made alliance with Demetrius II
and other foreign powers. The Sadducean dream of the political independence of Judah was recognized by Syria, and Simon was made general,
ethnarch, and high priest. During his 7-year rule the country enjoyed peace
and prosperity. Simon together with his two sons was assassinated by his

son-in-law, Ptolemy. John Hyrcanus, the third son of Simon, became the latter's successor.

The Author of 1 Maccabees

The author of 1 Maccabees was a good historian and perhaps an eye-witness of some of the happenings; he undoubtedly had many opportunities to secure firsthand information about the events and personalities he reported in his book. As a social psychologist he grasped the deeper significance of the deadly battle his countrymen were waging against great odds. As a participant in various campaigns, he obtained an excellent knowledge of the topography and geography of Palestine. The book does full justice to its traditional name, for it obviously aims at the glorification of the Maccabean family, who are depicted as liberators of Judaism. Furthermore, 1 Maccabees is anti-Greek, portraying not only the Syrians as the enemies of God's people, but including with the latter the apostate Jews who were trying to adjust to Hellenism.

Some scholars believe it strange that 1 Maccabees does not refer to the immortality of the soul or to the resurrection of the dead in such places where reference to these matters would have been in place. This has caused scholars to infer that 1 Maccabees was written by a Sadducean because they were known to reject these doctrines.[32] Waxmann, however, cautions against acceptance of this conclusion, for omission of these doctrines may have been for other reasons; the author of 1 Maccabees may not have been interested in stating doctrines but merely in giving events.[33]

Outstanding Characteristics of 1 Maccabees

Goodspeed calls attention to the fact that the name of God does not occur once in 1 Maccabees.[34] This absence has been explained as extreme reverence for the divine name as the author certainly was not irreligious. The reader senses the belief that God was guiding the destinies of the Jewish nation.

The religious interest of the writer is also shown in his concern for the temple and priesthood, and for the Law rather than for the refinements connected with it. The author continues his history after religious liberation has been effected and relates how political freedom was also achieved.

Preserved in 1 Maccabees are about a dozen state papers, decrees, proclamations, and some letters to Rome and Sparta. If they are genuine, so argues Goodspeed, they belong to a later date than is ascribed to them in the book.[35] The decrees of the Syrian kings, considered by most scholars as interpolations, may have been inserted in the history of the Hasmoneans by some other writer who obtained them from the history of Jason of Cyrene, mentioned in 2 Macc. 2:23. Some scholars believe that chapters 14—16 were not originally a part of the book. This deduction is based on the fact that Josephus, who in *The Antiquities* follows 1 Maccabees very closely, does not go beyond chapter 13; after that he employs some other source of reference. However, H. W. Ettelson's *The Integrity of 1 Maccabees* has shown that chapters 14 – 16 are a part of 1 Maccabees.

The Original Language of 1 Maccabees

Jerome in his Prologus Galeatus makes the assertion that he had seen a copy of 1 Maccabees in Hebrew. Some also postulate an Aramaic original. Neither of these two possible Semitic versions has been found thus far. In the Septuagint, 1 Maccabees has survived in a text represented by Codex Sinaiticus, Codex Venetus, and some other MSS. The translation in the Vulgate is regarded as a revision of the Old Latin text.

1 Maccabees and the Old Testament Canon

Clement of Alexandria, Hippolytus of Rome, Origen, and Eusebius all refer to it as being a part of Scripture. In Egypt it is found together with 2 Maccabees in the Clermont list of the books of Scripture. From the LXX, 1 Maccabees passed into the Vulgate and was considered a part of the Old Testament canon throughout the Middle Ages.

The Date of the Book

The First Book of Maccabees seems to have been written between 100 and 90 B. C., probably after the death of John Hyrcanus in 105 B. C.

2 Maccabees

2 Maccabees is not a sequel to 1 Maccabees. Luther said: "It was a second book of the Maccabees' struggle, not *the* second book." Some scholars hold that a man dissatisfied with the Sadducean point of view found in 1 Maccabees, set about to write a history of the Hasmonean uprisings according to the Pharisaic point of view. The story of the Maccabees is retold in Pharisaic vocabulary, rectifying what the anonymous author felt were the weaknesses of 1 Maccabees.

The Content of 2 Maccabees

The style and emphasis of 2 Maccabees are considerably different from that of 1 Maccabees. The question is still disputed among scholars whether or not the author of 2 Maccabees was acquainted with the contents of 1 Maccabees. While 1 Maccabees rests upon the personal experiences of the writer, 2 Maccabees does not represent the efforts of historical research but is merely an abridgment of a longer history of Jason of Cyrene (2:23). The scope of 2 Maccabees is limited in comparison with 1 Maccabees. Portrayal of the Hasmonean heroes is confined to Judas; the careers of Jonathan and Simon are ignored. In order to have his book end on a happy note, the author concludes his account with the victory of Judas over Nicanor.

The following is an outline of the book:

    1. Introductory letters, 1:1 – 2:18.
    2. Author's preface, 2:19-32.

3. History up to the time of the rising, 3:1 – 6:11.
4. The two martyrdoms, 6:12 – 7:42.
5. The story of the rising to the death of Nicanor, 8:1 – 15:36.
6. The epilogue, 15:37-39.[36]

At the beginning of the book there are inserted two letters sent from Jerusalem to the Egyptian Jews, calling upon them to commemorate the feast of dedication of Hanukkah (1:1 – 2:16). The second of the two letters tells a legend about the altar in Jerusalem, and a strange story about the prophet Jeremiah. In the author's preface which follows he announces that his narrative of the Maccabean Wars is only an abridgment (2:20-23). The narrative is divided into two sections. The first part covers events of the reign of Antiochus Epiphanes (3:1 – 10:8), including the struggles for the office of high priest, the attempt of Antiochus Epiphanes to Hellenize the Jews, the desecration of the temple, the defeat of the Syrians, the death of Antiochus Epiphanes, and the purification of the temple. The celebration of a feast commemorating the cleansing of the temple was to be an annual observance.

The second part (10:9 – 5:37) deals with events that happened during the reigns of Antiochus V Eupator, and Demetrius I: the struggle against neighboring peoples, the Syrians, and particularly against Nicanor. When the latter was defeated by the Jews, it led to the institution of a feast called the Day of Nicanor. The conclusion of the book (15:38-39) is reminiscent of the preamble (2:20-23).

Regarding the purpose of the volume, the author himself asserts:

> Now I urge those who read this book not to be depressed by such calamities, but to recognize that these punishments were designed not to destroy but to discipline our people. In fact, not to let the impious alone for long, but to punish them immediately, is a sign of great kindness. For in the case of the other nations the Lord waits patiently to punish them until they have reached the full measure of their sins; but He does not deal in this way with us, in order that He may not take vengeance on us afterward when our sins have reached their height. Therefore He never withdraws His mercy from us. Though He disciplines us with calamities, He does not forsake His own people. Let what we have said serve as a reminder; we must go on briefly with the story (6:12-20). RSV

The Date of the Book

2 Maccabees was probably written in Alexandria about 125 B. C. The work was known to Philo, who died A. D. 40. Clarke says that the date of composition is unknown, save that it must be earlier than the capture of Jerusalem by Pompey in 63 B. C.[37] Some scholars wish to find traces of influence in the New Testament Book of Hebrews (where the reference in 11:35 seems to refer to 2 Maccabees 6 – 7).

The Language of the Book

Most modern scholars dealing with the intertestamental literature are convinced that on the basis of style, 2 Maccabees was written in

Greek. The two letters introduced in the work were also composed in Greek, although the letters are said to bear the stamp of Hebrew genius.

Religious Value of the Book

With great warmth and energy the author endeavored to admonish his readers, the Alexandrian Jews, to be conscious of their Jewish race and religion which they had in common with their Palestinian brethren. The author continues his admonitions by vividly portraying the courage of the martyrs and of those who defended their nation and faith. He also explains the reasons for celebrating the Feast of Lights and the Day of Nicanor.[38]

If 1 Maccabees may be said to represent the Sadducean standpoint, 2 Maccabees is certainly written from a Pharisaic point of view. There is no reserve or reticence on the part of the author of 2 Maccabees. He never misses an opportunity to point out the moral of the story. The most interesting feature of the theology of this book is its teaching regarding the resurrection of the dead. In fact the doctrines of the immortality of the soul and the resurrection of the dead are nowhere so clearly taught in the intertestamental literature as it is here, save in Wisdom of Solomon, where there are passages from which it may be inferred (4:20 – 5:14).[39] In 2 Maccabees, doctrines covering rewards and punishment after death (6:26; 7:36; 12:45), prayer for the dead (12:43, 44, 45), and the intercession of the saints are taught.

CHAPTER XV

Introduction
to the Pseudepigraphical Literature

Contemporaneously with the Apocrypha there came into existence a group of writings which are generally known as the pseudepigrapha. These writings are believed to have originated between 200 B. C. and 200 A. D. Roman Catholic Biblical scholars usually refer to the Apocrypha as the "deutero-canonical" books of Scripture and reserve the term "apocryphal" for the group of writings designated by Protestant and Jewish scholars as "pseudepigraphical."

Professor Torrey has objected to the use of the terms "apocryphal" and "pseudepigraphical" as unsatisfactory, and proposed a return to two classes of books: those that were recognized by the church as canonical, and those books which were not included in the canon, called in the early church "the outside books." In his book *The Apocryphal Literature*, Torrey treats the books of the Apocrypha and pseudepigrapha under the designation "outside books." However, inasmuch as the majority of books on the intertestamental period follow the designation of "apocryphal" and "pseudepigraphical," it will be used in this volume also.

The pseudepigrapha are writings which were falsely ascribed to Biblical characters of the ancient past and assigned to Biblical times, and are therefore, false or spurious writings. They were never accepted as canonical by the ancient church. H. S. Miller says of the pseudepigrapha:

> Whether these writings were intended to deceive or not is not certainly known, but the writers were doubtless men of piety who saw, in those dark days when Judaism was struggling either with or under foreign powers, the need of teaching or exhortation or denunciation, and who thought they could better command attention and accomplish their purposes by using the name of some eminent person or by reference to some noted event in early Jewish history.[1]

Various literary genres are represented among the pseudepigrapha: apocalyptical books, legendary books, poetical, and didactic writings. The most famous of the pseudepigrapha are those that emphasize apocalypticism. The following books have been classified as belonging to this class: (1) The Book of Enoch, (2) The Secrets of Enoch, (3) The Apocalypse of Baruch, (4) The Rest of the Words of Baruch, (5) The Assumption of Moses, (6) A Revelation of Moses, (7) Prophecy of Jeremiah, (8) Ascension of Isaiah, (9) Apocalypse of Elijah, (10) Apocalypse of Zephaniah, (11) Apocalypse of Esdra, (12) Sibylline Oracles. These are supposed to have been written in Hebrew and Aramaic, but those that have survived are in Greek, Syriac, Coptic, Ethiopic, Latin, and Slavonic translations.

Apocalyptics belong to a special genre that developed especially among the Jews in the two centuries before the Christian era. It is not altogether a new type of literature, because portions of certain Old Testament books are apocalyptic in character such as Joel (2:28-32), Isaiah (24–27, 34–35, 65–66), Ezekiel (38–39, 40–48), Zechariah (1–6) and Daniel. The last book of the New Testament, Revelation or the Apocalypse also belongs to this class of literature and is the only representative of this type of literature in the New Testament.

The name "apocalypse" is the Greek designation for revelation, and constitutes a form of prophecy. The authors of these writings were not supposed to utter their own thoughts, but only what was revealed to them either by direct vision, that is, by communion with the Spirit of God or through the medium of an angel, or sometimes only through the medium of an angel—sometimes through both.

The Book of Daniel, it is believed, was the great model followed by all subsequent apocalypticists. Apocalypses are said to have come into existence to comfort Jewish people in days of trouble and to show them that ultimately God's purposes for His own people would triumph. The persecution of Antiochus Epiphanes (175 – 164 B. C.) set this type of writing in motion. Although the Maccabean victories had given some relief, they did not endure. The Roman and Herodian oppressions were discouraging, the inspired prophecies had not been realized, and the future appeared inauspicious. Therefore, the outstanding purpose of the pseud-epigrapha was to revive hope. In the apocalyptic literature there are many visions concerning a bright future, the coming of the Messiah, and the establishment of the Messianic kingdom.

The doctrine of eschatology is prominent in the pseudepigraphic writings: emphasis on the immortality of the soul of the individual, the day of judgment, and the new world which will follow the destruction of the present one. A dominant note in the apocalyptic literature is the problem of suffering in its double aspect: individual and national. In the apocalyptical writings the concern is especially with the problem of the national Job. Due to the times the people were asking, why does God's chosen people suffer, who are more righteous than the heathen surrounding them, while the wicked nations prosper? How long will this situation continue? In the Old Testament prophets a solution was promised, for the Messiah is predicted as a king coming to rule His people with justice, conquer the nations, and bestow prosperity. This promise, however, was not being fulfilled. When the coming of the Messiah was delayed, the apocalyptical writers changed the concept of the Messiah, portraying Him as a superhuman being, whose coming would be ushered in by an entirely new age. The present world with its iniquity and lawlessness could not be redeemed, but a new one must replace it. Thus the Messiah and the Messianic age were given embellishments and glamour.

The apocalyptic writers despaired of the world as evil and unredeemable; they saw no hope for it; the only result was destruction. They therefore logically centered their hope on a world to come, where the righteous would come into their own and where evil would not exist.

The apocalyptical writings have a strong supernatural coloring and numerous statements in them strike the modern reader as bizarre, but this should not deter the modern reader from appreciating their teachings. In justifying this characteristic, Charles writes:

> Mental visions are not always easily expressed in words; the seer who in a vision has received a message in some fantastic guise necessarily has the impress upon his mind of what he has seen, when giving his message; and when he describes his vision, the picture he presents is, in the nature of the case, more fantastic to the ear of the hearer than to the eye of him who saw it. Allowance should be made for this; especially by us Westerners who are so lacking in the rich imaginativeness of the Oriental.[2]

To evaluate the apocalypses it is necessary to bear in mind that they were written for Oriental readers.

An examination of this literature will reveal to the discerning student frequent inconsistencies in the teachings and theology they present. This is to be explained by the theory that, although the writers were saturated with the teachings of the prophets, the apocalyptists were also absorbing the newer conceptions of the age. They did not always succeed in harmonizing the old with the new. The result was often a compromise which the modern reader finds illogical and contradictory.

Another fact the student of apocalypses must know, to appreciate them fully, is the presence of a rigid predestinarianism which was a general characteristic of these writings. The apocalyptists believed that the growth, decline, and history of nations were predetermined by Almighty God from the beginning. The writers spend much time and energy in making calculations, based upon prophecy, as to the exact time when history would reach its consummation. These facts were known only to God, but He allowed God-fearing men to look into the hidden things and to make them known to their contemporaries.

Although there is considerable mysticism of a rather fantastic nature in the apocalypses, with frequent references to supra-mundane visions, yet the writers were cognizant of the need to emphasize practical religion. They stressed keeping the Law as a religious necessity, but in contrast to the Pharisees, the apocalypticists emphasized the spirit rather than the letter of the Law. In the literature under consideration there is a wholehearted veneration for the Law; it is looked upon as a real guide to life, with punishment awaiting those who fail to keep it.

In general the apocalyptic writings advocate a universalistic attitude which is different from that of the Pharisees, whose outlook was characterized by nationalistic narrowness. While the apocalypticists are not always consistent, they usually include Gentiles with individuals from other nations in the scheme of salvation; likewise, among the wicked who are excluded from eternal happiness there are not only Gentiles but also Jews.

Besides apocalypses there are books that are ascribed to famous Biblical characters and thus may be labeled "legendary." The following belong to this class: (1) The Testament of Adam, (2) The Book of Jubilees, or "The Little Genesis," (3) Testaments of Abraham, Isaac, and Jacob, (4) Apocalypse of Abraham, (5) Testaments of Twelve Patriarchs, (6) Life of Asenath (wife of Joseph), (7) Testament of Job, (8) Testament of Solomon, (9) The Book of Noah, (10) Penitence of Jannes and Jambres.

Another type of apocalyptical literature is poetical in nature; outstanding in this class are the (1) The Psalms of Solomon; (2) Additions to the Psalter; Psalm 151; (3) apocryphal psalms in Syriac.

A fourth type has been called didactic and comprises (1) The Magical Books of Moses, (2) The Story of Achiacharus, cupbearer to Esarhaddon, king of Assyria.

There is at present no recognized list of books known as the pseudepigrapha. Thus R. H. Charles has added to the usual list comprising the pseudepigrapha: The Sayings of the Fathers *(Pirke Aboth),* The Story of Ahikar, and Fragments of a Zadokite Work;[3] while Charles Cutler Torrey omits these three works, but adds the Lives of the Prophets and The Testament of Job.[4] Waxman gives the following list as "The Jewish Apocalyptic" books: (1) The Book of Enoch; (2) The Book of Jubilees; (3) Testaments of the Twelve Patriarchs; (4) Psalms of Solomon; (5) Apocalypse of Baruch; (6) Assumption of Moses; (7) 2 or 4 Ezra; (8) Book of Adam and Eve; (9) Slavonic Enoch; and (10) Sibylline Oracles.[5]

Professor Gehman lists the following writings as belonging to the pseudepigrapha: (1) The Letter of Aristeas; (2) The Book of Jubilees; (3) The Martyrdom and Ascension of Isaiah; (4) The Psalms of Solomon; (5) The Sibylline Oracles; (6) The Book of Enoch; (7) The Slavonic Book of Enoch; (8) The Assumption of Moses; (9) The Syriac Apocalypse of Baruch; (10) The Greek Apocalypse of Baruch; (11) The Testaments of the 12 Patriarchs; (12) The Life of Adam and Eve.[6]

The pseudepigrapha which have survived are actually only a part of a much larger literature which once existed in the early centuries, as can be seen from references in patristic literature, for which the reader is referred to M. R. James, *The Lost Apocrypha of the Old Testament: Their Titles and Fragments.*

Although the surviving pseudepigrapha are the works of Jewish authors, they seem to have exercised little influence on subsequent Jewish thought. Many of them are quoted by the Christian Fathers, some of them possibly by New Testament writers. These writings have been preserved to the modern world by Christians: a large number because they were taken up into the canon of the Ethiopic church; a considerable number were preserved by the Ambrosian Library at Milan, where many were discovered in the last 200 years.

CHAPTER XVI

The Individual Pseudepigrapha

The Testaments of the Twelve Patriarchs

This book seems to have belonged to a type of literature that was popular at the beginning of the 1st century A. D. In this category fall such books as the Legends of Moses, the Book of Adam and Eve, the Ascension of Isaiah, the Apocalypse of Abraham, and the Lives of the Prophets. Old legends of patriarchs and prophets were assembled and new ones composed. In some Christian lists these writings appear among the canonical and apocryphal books.

The Value of the Book

The value of the Testaments of the Twelve Patriarchs is not to be found in its apocalyptic nature but rather in its ethical character, because it contains mostly exhortations and encouragements to follow the God-fearing way and gives warnings to eschew sin. The name of the book is derived from the 12 sons of Jacob, who are depicted as speaking with their father Jacob before his death and who, in turn, receive from him a moral testament and ethical injunctions. Even though the work is undoubtedly Jewish and was penned in Hebrew, yet there are many Christian interpolations which contain references to an incarnated Messiah. The Testaments of the Twelve Patriarchs is a collection of 12 little books, one for each patriarch, probably written by one person as is evidenced by the uniformity of format.

The Pattern of the Book

The general pattern for this work was given by Genesis 49 — where Jacob faced by death called his sons to the bedside and foretold the future of each; possibly also by Deuteronomy 33, where Moses blesses the 12 tribes, one by one, and assures them of ultimate triumph. However, in the Testaments of the Patriarchs prediction plays only a minor part.

In each of the testaments to the 12 patriarchs three distinct elements can be noticed. First the patriarch gives the history of his own life, telling of the sins he has committed and also the virtues he has demonstrated. These stories were interesting and came to constitute the early *Agada*, the folk embellishments of the lives of Bible heroes. Next, the writer draws for his readers a practical lesson from the material related, warning them against the sins of the heroes in the story; on the other hand, they are encouraged to emulate the virtues related. Ethical instruction was a prominent feature of this work. Finally, the patriarch enters the field of the apocalyptic, and informs his sons of future happenings. This feature does not occupy a prominent place in the writing. In the prognostications apostasies of the tribes are often predicted, their exile described, and the destruction of the temple announced. There are also numerous prophecies of the coming of the Messiah.

The Messianic Predictions of the Book

In regard to the Messianic predictions, it has been noted that instead of the Messiah coming from Judah, He would descend from the tribe of Levi. The descent from Levi has been explained by the fact that the greatest part of the Testaments of the Patriarchs was composed during the reign of John Hyrcanus while he was still a Pharisee. At first the author looked upon Hyrcanus as the chosen Messiah and promised him a glorious future. Therefore, the Messiah had to come from Levi, for John Hyrcanus was a priest. But when he broke with the Pharisees and their descendants, and the Maccabeans were far from being the ideal rulers the Jews were looking for, later additions to the Testaments of the Patriarchs announced that the Messiah would come from the tribe of Judah.

The Ethical Teaching of the Book

The ethical teachings are considered by scholars to be very important. Reuben warns against unchastity (Gen. 35:22; 49:4); Simeon berates his sin of jealousy against Joseph and his anger toward Judah. Levi in 6:7 admits undue violence in the case of the city of Shechem (Genesis 34) but in general is glorified for his past history and is the object of favorable prediction. Judah foretells the coming of the Messiah from his offspring and also warns his progeny against greed, wine, and women. Issachar is boastful of his accomplishments on the field. Zebulun calls upon his descendants to imitate his example of being sympathetic, compassionate, and full of pity. He claims credit for being a renowned fisherman and for planning the first mast and sail for his boat (5:5 – 6:3). Dan stresses avoidance of the sins of enmity and falsehood and illustrates his warning by a reference to his conduct over against Joseph. Naphthali calls upon his tribe to strive for harmony. Gad admonishes his descendants to love their brothers and kinsmen and not to imitate his example of hating Joseph. Asher advises his followers to be honest in all dealings and not be guilty of double-facedness. Joseph relates in detail his temptation in Egypt and enjoins upon his son to be chaste above all things. Benjamin urges his followers to pureness in mind, to flight from all temptation to do wrong, and to a life above reproach.

The Time of Origin of the Book

According to Pfeiffer the Testaments of the Patriarchs was written in Hebrew about 140 – 110 B. C., probably in the days of John Hyrcanus (135 – 104 B. C.).[1] Charles believes the author to have been a Pharisee who wrote in the early part of the reign of John Hyrcanus.[2] J. E. H. Thomson disagrees with Charles and others and argues for a dependence of the book on the New Testament and not vice versa.[3] This would mean that it is a product of the last part of the first century A. D.

The Book of Jubilees or "The Little Genesis"

The Book of Jubilees, also known by the title "The Little Genesis," is an interesting book. The usual name of this work is derived from the type of chronology it follows, namely that of a system of jubilees. Each jubilee consists of 49 years, which in turn is divided into seven weeks, each year representing a day of the week. The second name was given Jubilees because it mainly supplements the facts recorded in the canonical book of Genesis.

INDIVIDUAL PSEUDEPIGRAPHA

The Contents of Jubilees

The materials of Jubilees are supposed to have been dictated by an angel of the Presence to Moses, after the latter had ascended Mount Sinai and been told of the destinies that awaited Israel. Jubilees is a book of religious fiction, in which the author has reworked the story of the history of Israel from the creation of the world up to the time of the giving of the Law at Mount Sinai; by comparison with the canonical Genesis that covers the same territory this must be said to supplement the Biblical stories. This additional information is conjectured to have been handed down orally from father to son. Beginning at chapter 2, Jubilees parallels the account of the Hebrew Bible from Gen. 1:1 to Ex. 14:31, with frequent insertions of midrashic material. The author of Jubilees has omitted incidents and features of the canonical book. What has been added might be labeled additions and expansions. It would seem that the material omitted was done for apologetic reasons. For example, the act of deception by Abraham in Egypt, when he gave Pharaoh the false impression that Sarah was only his sister, or when Isaac was guilty of a similar act toward Abimelech. No doubt it was felt that it would be difficult to justify these events. The episode where Simeon and Levi trapped the people at Shechem into being circumcised and then murdered them when they were helpless, is omitted. The devices employed by Jacob to increase his flocks at the expense of Laban are not recorded. Likewise Genesis 49, referring to the blessings by Jacob, is not in Jubilees, because the blessings pronounced on Simeon and Levi do not agree with earlier denunciations by their father. Other additions have an apologetic tendency, as when Dinah is said to have been raped at the age of 12, or when Jacob is depicted as giving his parents presents four times a year. The longer additions of Jubilees were mostly concerned with the ceremonial. The warfare of the Amorites (34:1-9), and the war of Esau (37 and 38) are treated at length.

Types of Literary Genre in Jubilees

Jubilees consists of two types of literature, homiletic and apocalyptic, of which the homiletical material predominates. Some scholars claim that in Jubilees the reader will find the first attempt at systematizing the various Agadic legends and stories which began to crystallize in early times around the personages of the patriarchs, heroes, and events related to the Bible. There is a considerable apocalyptic element in Jubilees; angels and demons are mentioned constantly. Jubilees records the fall of the evil angels and their influence on men. The future is depicted in a manner reminiscent of other apocalyptic books. The Messiah will come to Judah, but supernatural characteristics are not ascribed to Him, as is usually the case in other apocalyptic books. When the Messianic era comes, it will be characterized by physical and ethical transformations. Men will live without pain and sin for 1,000 years, after which death will pass into immortality.

The Purpose of the Writing

The purpose of the work is to show that the Judaism of the writer was as normative as that which existed from the beginning of human history. The author also desired to demonstrate that the sacred number seven played a more important part in history than is generally realized by most people.

Time of Writing of Jubilees

Authorities are not agreed as to the time of the composition of Jubilees. Such formidable scholars as Charles [4] and Littmann [5] favor an early date—one before the quarrel of John Hyrcanus with the Pharisees. Thomson disagrees and claims that in view of its apologetic tone and hatred of Edom, the work must have been written during the Herodian period when the Romans controlled Palestine and when "Greeks and Graeculi were frequent, when those who, being Jews and knowing Hebrew, yet had imbibed the Hellenic culture, and really saw the points where assault might be made on their faith and its sacred literature." [6] This date would explain the hatred of Edom. Thus the time of composition is placed around 4 B. C. when Herod the Great died. Robert Pfeiffer places the writing of the book near the end of the reign of John Hyrcanus (135 — 104 B. C.)—not too long after the Testaments of the Twelve Patriarchs. [7]

Torrey believes that such names as Beliar and Mastema can be used in determining the time of composition. In the Sibylline Oracles, the Ascension of Isaiah, the Testaments of the Twelve Patriarchs, and the Lives of the Prophets the name Beliar occurs. [8] Therefore, Torrey claims that the origin of Jubilees could not be earlier than the 1st century A. D. He further claims that the author was a priest who took pride in the institution of the Hasmonean priesthood.

The Original Language of Jubilees

The Book of Jubilees has survived only in an Ethiopic version, which was based upon a Greek translation. Most scholars are convinced that the original language was either Aramaic or Hebrew.

The Ascension of Isaiah

This book belongs to the apocalyptic literature of the intertestamental period. However, it differs from many other apocalypses of this period, since it contains a large admixture of Christian materials. Present knowledge of the ascension of Isaiah is dependent upon the Ethiopic version found by Archbishop Laurence in a London bookstall. Some fragments in Greek and Latin have also been discovered.

The work is composed of three parts: the Martyrdom of Isaiah (1:1 — 3:13; 5:2-14), generally considered a Jewish writing; the Testament of Hezekiah (3:13 — 5:1); and the Vision of Isaiah (6 — 11). The Martyrdom of Isaiah agrees with the account of the death of Isaiah as given in the Talmud, according to which Isaiah was killed in Jerusalem. It is Ferrar's conviction that the Greek version of the Martyrdom of Isaiah is the translation of the account in the Talmud.[9] The same story of the Martyrdom of Isaiah is also found in the Lives of the Prophets, a collection of Jewish legends from about the 1st century A. D. Heb. 11:37 appears to have a reference to the martyrdom of Isaiah in the words: "They were sawn asunder."

The Martyrdom and the Ascension of Isaiah are often referred to by early Christian Fathers, especially by Origen. The latter mentions the Ascension of Isaiah as "The Apocryphon of Isaiah." Justin Martyr speaks of the death of Isaiah in such language as to indicate that he had an acquaintance with the Ascension of Isaiah.

The Contents of the Book

Chapters 1 – 5, which comprises the Martyrdom of Isaiah, are mainly the narrative in which the prophet Isaiah prophesies to Hezekiah that Manasseh would worship Beliar in place of Jehovah and that Isaiah would be sawn in half. After Hezekiah's death, Manasseh commits all manner of evil, necessitating all true believers, including Isaiah, to flee to the wilderness. A man of Samaria, Bechira by name, accused Isaiah of prophesying against King Manasseh, resulting in the prophet's arrest and martyrdom. (5:1b-14). In 3:13 – 5:1a, considered a Christian interpolation, Beliar is portrayed as hating Isaiah because the prophet predicted redemption through Christ.

The second part of the work, the Vision of Isaiah (6:1 – 11:40), was written by a Christian. In this portion, in the 20th year of the reign of Hezekiah, Isaiah had a vision which he related to the king. In the seventh heaven he saw the saints, beginning with Adam and God Himself. After hearing God announce His plan to send His Son to the earth, Isaiah returned from the seventh heaven. Again by means of a vision all the events from the birth of Jesus to His return were shown Isaiah. It was because of this vision that Satan caused Manasseh to have Isaiah cut in sunder.

The Date of the Work

According to Robert Pfeiffer the Christian portion of the Martyrdom of Isaiah probably dates from the 2nd century A. D.[10] Some scholars believe that the Jewish Martyrdom was written in Aramaic and may be of 2nd century A. D. provenance.

Charles has connected the story of the martyrdom with a Persian legend of King Djemid, for whom God caused a tree to open to hide him from his opponent, but by the assistance of Iblis he was found, and the tree containing Djemid sawn asunder.[11]

An interesting characteristic of this work is the designation of the Messiah as "the Beloved," although scholars are not agreed whether to accept this title as a part of the original or a later Christian insertion.

The Paralipomena of Jeremiah

This writing has survived in a Greek text which has been edited by James Rendel Harris as *The Rest of the Words of Baruch: A Christian Apocalypse of the Year 136 A.D.* A reference to Agrippa, who may be either Agrippa I (died A. D. 44) or Agrippa II (died A. D. 110) necessitates dating the book after A. D. 50. The first eight chapters of the book may be of Jewish origin; this would mean that it was written in Aramaic and then translated into Greek. From the latter Ethiopic, Armenian, and Slavic translations were made.

The Contents of the Book

In the first part (chapters 1 – 4) Jeremiah is told by Jehovah that the Chaldeans will destroy Jerusalem and that he should bury the sacred vessels from the temple. After that he is to go into the Babylonian captivity. Before the destruction of Jerusalem, Jeremiah sends Abimelech, a eunuch, to obtain figs from the orchard of Agrippa. The eunuch falls asleep in the orchard and awakes 66 years later. It is an old man who informs him what has transpired (ch. 5). Jeremiah receives a letter from Baruch, who was instructed by God to tell Jeremiah that the Jews in Babylonia were to remove all foreigners from the midst of God's people, otherwise Jehovah would not bring His people back to Jerusalem. Baruch's letter, together with figs that were fresh though plucked 66 years before, was conveyed to Babylonia by an eagle (ch. 6). The eagle then did some remarkable things in raising a dead man to life and in persuading Jeremiah to bring the children of Judah back. Those Jews, however, who would not permanently separate from their heathen wives, were not allowed to return to Zion, but instead they founded the city of Samaria and the sect of the Samaritans (ch. 7 – 8). The last part of the Paralipomena of Jeremiah records that Jeremiah fainted while offering sacrifices in Jerusalem but after three days became alive again, proceeding to praise God for the redemption made possible through Jesus Christ. It was only after Jeremiah had given the Jewish populace permission, that they were able to stone the prophet to death. (Ch. 9)

Some scholars believe that the entire work may be of Christian origin, although the Paralipomena emphasize the duty of Jews to keep apart from the heathen, particularly to avoid heathen women. (6:13-14; 8:2)

The Lives of the Prophets

The Lives of the Prophets consists of a series of biographical sketches written, probably in Hebrew, during the 1st century A. D. From Hebrew it was translated into Greek, Latin, Syriac, and Ethiopic. Torrey has published a critical edition of the Greek text together with an English translation.[12] All surviving translations have been made from the Greek version. In 1883 Hamaker endeavored to prove that the original language of this work was Hebrew. In Torrey's opinion the Greek version clearly contains translation Greek – a fact he claims should become obvious to anyone capable of reading Greek.[13]

The Contents of the Book

The Lives of the Prophets is an account of the Hebrew prophets, each of whom is portrayed as telling where he was born, to what tribe he belonged, and where he was buried. The Biblical materials about the prophet's life are not repeated but supplemented. Many legendary stories have been added. This holds true in the biographies of Isaiah, Jeremiah, Ezekiel, Daniel, Jonah, and Habakkuk, while those of other prophets are short and as a rule contain extra-Biblical material.

A comparison of the various recensions reveals considerable diversity regarding the order in which the lives of the prophets are presented. The most commonly followed order is that given in Swete's *Old Testament in Greek.*

According to the Lives of the Prophets, Jeremiah was held in great honor by the Egyptians, because he drove out dangerous reptiles (vipers and crocodiles) from the Nile in Egypt. Subsequently Alexander the Great transferred Jeremiah's bones to Alexandria, which resulted in the extermination of the crocodiles from that region. Jeremiah is supposed to have introduced *argolai*, snake-fighting creatures, in his work.

Ezekiel was killed by a tribesman of Dan and Gad in Babylonia, because Ezekiel had rebuked him for idolatry. At one time, when the people were starving, Ezekiel fed them with fish from the Chebar Canal, which under the influence of the prophet were caught in shoals. Other miracles were also attributed to Ezekiel.

The chief interest in the life of Daniel, covering three fourths of the story, is the transformation of Nebuchadnezzar. He was changed into an animal of composite form, having parts of a bull and the legs and hinder parts of a lion. Finally, through the prayer of Daniel, Nebuchadnezzar's sanity was restored after he had confessed his sin.

Amos was killed with a cudgel by the son of Amaziah. Jonah, as the legend has it, was the son of Zarephath, at whose house Elijah had lived according to 1 Kings 17:8-24. Jonah was the boy whom Elisha had restored to life. Jonah's later years were spent among the heathen populace of Tyre, doing penance for his false prophecy against Nineveh.

The life of Habakkuk contains a story that is also found in Bel and the Dragon. Habakkuk, a native of Beth-Zechariah, of the tribe of Simeon, predicted the destruction of Jerusalem and the captivity of Judah. The prophet fled to Egypt when the armies of Nebuchadnezzar destroyed Jerusalem. Later, one day as he was performing the duties of a farmer, when he was about to bring food to the reapers, he said to his family, "I am off for a far country, but I will return at once." As he finished speaking he was in Babylon, presenting Daniel in the lion's den with food. Quickly he was back in Palestine attending to the feeding of the reapers there without any introduction.

In the material dealing with the life of Nathan, the reader is informed in a dream that David was to commit a great sin. Upon receiving this information, Nathan set out to warn the king, but Beliar prepared a trap for Nathan by which he was prevented from warning David in time.

Torrey believes that stories of Elijah and Elisha did not originally belong to the Lives of the Prophets because they do not supplement the Biblical data but simply copy the biographical material of Kings.[14] Some manuscripts of this work have included the stories about Zechariah, (Luke 1:5 ff), Simeon (Luke 2:35 ff), and John the Baptist. In a number of biographies in the Lives of the Prophets Christian elements appear, in which there are predictions about the coming of the Messiah. Torrey is convinced that they are interpolations.

The Testament of Job

This is a writing which until the 18th century was generally unknown by scholars, although it belongs to a type of literature represented in several of the so-called pseudepigraphical writings. Today it is only extant in a Greek text, first published by Cardinal Mai, in Vol. VII of his *Scriptorum Nova Collectio*, Rome, 1833. In 1897 Kaufmann Kohler reprinted the Greek text and gave a translation of Mai's text, together with an introduction and notes.

While the Testament of Job was practically unknown at the beginning of this century, it seems to have been known in ancient times, for it is referred to in the Decree of Galasius (Bishop of Rome in A. D. 492 – 496) in a long list of apocryphal writings. The book is of interest to the modern scholar because of its relation to the Book of Job in the Septuagint. M. R. James, who in his *Apocrypha Anecdota* issued a slightly different text than that represented by the Mai text, claimed that the LXX borrowed the profuse speech of Job's wife from the Testament of Job.

The Contents of the Book

In this book Job's wife Sitidos plays a more important role than she does in the Biblical Book of Job. She defends her husband, though he is reduced to wretched poverty and near starvation. She lives to see her husband vindicated by God but dies before his health and riches are restored. Sitidos departs this life in comfort and peace after she sees her children in heaven.

The three friends and Elihu are assigned prominent parts in the book. Because of their attempts to rebuke Job, God threatens them with death, but they are forgiven through Job's intercession on their behalf. After the death of Job's first wife, Job marries Dinah (the name also given her in the Targum), who becomes the mother of three daughters that are inspired and chant hymns. Nahor, the brother of Job, continues the narrative by relating how at the end of three days he saw Job's spirit being taken away by shining chariots. The book ends with Nahor, Job's seven sons, and others singing a brief dirge.

In the Paris text the Greek translator supplied Job's sons with names; in the original Hebrew their names are not given. Two sons bear the name Tersichoros; two others that of Nicephoros, and another two were assigned the two parts of the name Iphiphrouron [Torrey].

The structure of the book seems to indicate that in chapters 1−45 Job is the speaker. According to Thomson the last two chapters are definitely additions; the new gifts to the daughters are inexplicable.[15]

The Original Language of the Writing

Torrey claims that the Testament of Job is translated from a Semitic language which most likely was Aramaic.[16] Instead of the Greek *diabolos*, the Greek word for devil, the Aramaic form *stana* is everywhere employed. R. Pfeiffer agrees that Aramaic was the original language.[17]

The Date of Composition

James has expressed the opinion that the book was written in the 2nd and 3rd century A. D. by a Jew by birth, but a Christian by religion.[18] According to James this individual translated the Testament of Job into Greek from a Hebrew Midrash on Job, in connection with which he utilized the Greek version of Job, and employed some familiar New Testament expressions when he paraphrased his work.

On the other hand, Kohler, in his article on "The Testament of Job," in the *Jewish Encyclopedia*, VII, 200−202 claims that the work is Jewish throughout, without any Christian element in it. In view of the many Mishnaic parallels, Kohler designates it as coming from the pre-Christian period of Jewish literary history.

The Book of Adam and Eve

This book is known by several titles, the most common of which is found in the Latin version by the name "The Book [or Life] of Adam and Eve," while the Greek version carries the title "Apocalypse of Moses." The Book of Adam and Eve belongs to the Haggadic literature of the Jews. The work has been translated into other languages and made available in Armenian and Slavonic. Torrey says that all these texts may go back to a Jewish or Semitic archetype.[19] The work is characterized by numerous insertions and additions most likely made by Christians. Information not found in the canonical Genesis concerning Adam and Eve is supposedly supplied in this pseudepigraphical writing.[20]

The Contents of the Book

The northern and eastern parts of Eden were assigned to Adam, and the southern and western parts to Eve. When their two guardian angels were absent, the devil tempted Eve, and as a result of her succumbing, she at once recognized her nakedness. When she attempted to make a girdle, all the trees refused to have their leaves used except the fig tree.

After Adam and Eve had been expelled from Eden, they went hungry for days because they were unable to eat grass (4:1 f). To overcome this difficulty, Adam decides to do penance by standing for 40 days on a stone in the Jordan River in water up to his neck; Eve does the same in the Tigris for 37 days.

The book then relates the circumstances attending the birth of Cain. This is followed by an account of the murder of Abel and the birth of Seth. Adam narrates to Seth his flight from Paradise. Surrounding Eden there were great rivers, but Michael froze the waters around paradise and brought Adam back to earth. Adam then predicted to Seth the history of the Jews up to the Last Day. When Adam became very sick, Eve and Seth set out for Eden to secure a drop of oil from the tree of mercy (36:2), which would cure Adam. Wild beasts attack them on the way and Seth is bitten. Upon arrival at the gate of Paradise, Seth and Eve are informed that the oil can only be had at the end of the present age, and that Adam would die in six days.

In the Greek version of "The Apocalypse of Moses," Eve gathers her offspring and gives them a detailed account of transgressions and their immediate consequences, stressing particularly the pronouncement and judgment upon Adam and Eve by Jehovah. As Michael blows the trumpet, the hosts of heaven assemble. Then God enters Eden on His chariot of cherubim and as angels sing, all the trees in Paradise shoot forth blossoms. Following this is a paraphrase of Gen. 3:9-19. With the death and burial of Adam and Eve the book ends.

Time and Place of Composition

It is believed that the work was composed before A. D. 70 because there is no knowledge of or any reference to the destruction of Jerusalem in the little Apocalypse, 29:4-10, which brings events down to the author's time. It is difficult to ascertain where this book originated.

The Assumption of Moses

The Assumption of Moses appears to be only a fragment of a much larger work to which references are found in ancient writings. It was discovered by Ceriani in the library of Milan in 1861. The allusion in Jude 9 to the fight between the archangel Michael and Satan for the body of Moses is assumed by many scholars to be a reference from the Ascension of Moses. The fragment known by the name of the Assumption of Moses exists only in Latin. The present Latin translation, made from a Greek text, does not have a reference to the assumption of Moses, but is an apocalypse which Moses before his death is said to have revealed to Joshua. In early lists of apocryphal books, mention is made of two

writings: the Testament of Moses and the Assumption of Moses. What
has survived of the Assumption of Moses characterizes the book as rather
a testament of Moses. It does not contain an account of Moses being taken
into heaven; in fact, it seems to exclude the idea of an assumption of Moses.

The Contents of the Book

The book purports to give an address delivered by Moses to Joshua.
In it there is a description of how Moses, when he is about to die, delivers
to Joshua the sacred writings. Moses reveals to his successor prophecies
which he is instructed to record but to hide until the appointed time concerning the Hebrew nation. A panorama of the history of the Jews up to
the author's time is described. He tells how one tribe shall say to another:
"Lo, is not this that which Moses did once declare unto us in prophecies?
Yea, he declared and called heaven and earth to witness against us that
we should not transgress the commandments of the Lord, of which he
was the mediator to us." There are references to the destruction of Jerusalem in 587 B. C., the persecution of Antiochus, the rule of the Hasmoneans,
the divisions between Pharisees and Sadducees, and the reign of Herod.
The book ends on an optimistic note, for the promise of a happy future
is given.

The Date of the Book

The date may be fixed within narrow limits. The Assumption takes
the reader up to the death of Herod, in 4 B. C., and it is most likely that
it was written before the destruction of Jerusalem A. D. 70. The writer
speaks of Herod's sons in a way which would seem to imply that the book
was penned before the end of their reign. Thus the time of composition
may be placed between A. D. 1 and 30.

The Original Language of the Work

Torrey has determined the original language of the Assumption from
the cryptic name "Taxo," which according to him is a cryptogram for "the
Hasmonean," referring to Mattathias and his sons.[21] Thus Torrey claims
that the numerical value of the letters in "Taxo" correspond to "the Hasmonean" in Aramaic, but not in Hebrew. This would demand that the
book was written in Aramaic. Not all scholars, however, are convinced
that the book was written in Aramaic and believe that Torrey's arguments
are artificial and therefore doubtful from the fact that "Taxo" had seven
sons, while Mattathias had only five.

The Religious Teaching of the Book

The chief interest of the book lies in its general viewpoint rather than
in its teaching about Jewish theology. The important question raised by
this book is: What ought to be the attitude of a religious Jew over against
persecution? The zealots advocated the use of force, of answering violence
with violence. They admired the example of Judas Maccabeus who resorted

to force rather than submit to the Syrian oppressors. The Assumption of Moses is opposed to this view. It contains polemics against the Maccabees and advocated nonresistance. Eleazer, the great martyr of the Maccabean era, is held up as example to imitate. The Messianic age will be ushered in by martyrdom and not by violence. The Assumption of Moses, therefore, is a document proclaiming Jewish quietism.

Value of the Book for New Testament Study

Scholars are convinced that the Assumption has value for the New Testament student in that it sheds light on several phrases found in the Epistle of Jude and in Stephen's speech in Acts 7. Also the writer's description of the ruling classes in Palestine (the Sadducees) shows that others besides Jesus keenly felt the degradation into which the government of that day had fallen.

The Apocalypse of Baruch (2 Baruch)

This is commonly known as "The Syriac Apocalypse of Baruch," because the complete book is preserved in a Syriac version, and was made from the Greek, a rendering believed to rest on an Aramaic original. Among the writings that are ascribed to Baruch is also one apocalypse. The book is a comparatively recent discovery made in the Milan Library and was published in a Latin translation in 1866 by an Italian scholar named Ceriani.

Contents of the Book

The book is supposed to be Baruch's account of what happened to him at the time that Jerusalem was destroyed. The seer received divine revelations beginning in "the 25th year of Jehoiachin, king of Judah" (1:1). If this were true, it would mean that the divine revelation occurred in 590 B. C. From 6:1 the reader learns that on the day before receiving the visions, the Babylonian armies arrived and surrounded Jerusalem; this would place the prediction in the tenth month of 587 B. C. The deportation of Zedekiah to Jerusalem is referred to in 8:5. Scholars are unable to harmonize these dates. Dating the book in the 25th year of Jehoiachin was a blunder, for the Israelite king ruled only three months. The truth of the matter is that the author was speaking of the destruction of Jerusalem in A. D. 70, and instead of using contemporary figures and names, he clothes the account in imagery of ancient Biblical history.

The book divides itself into seven sections. It begins after the model of prophecy: "The word of the Lord came to Baruch, the son of Neraiah, saying." In the first section the fall of Jerusalem is announced, but Baruch is comforted by the promise that the overthrow of Israel will only be "for a season." In the second section Baruch has a vision in which he is told to fast for seven days after which he is permitted to pour out his complaint before the Lord. Baruch is informed of the judgments which will come over the Gentiles and of the glory of the world to come, which is to exist especially for the righteous. The destruction of Jerusalem is described as the work of angels instead of the Chaldeans. In the third section Baruch raises the problem of the nature of evil, which is also the theme of 2 Esdras. In the fourth section the reader is assured that the future world is made for the righteous. In the fifth section Baruch complains about the delay of God's kingdom and is assured that first the number of the elect must be fulfilled. When this has happened, the Messiah will come. Section six gives the vision of the cedar and the vine, which symbolizes the Roman Empire and the triumph of the Messiah. Baruch asks who will share in the glory to come and is told, "Those that believe." The six "black waters" described represent six evil periods in world history, and the "six clear waters" denote the number of good periods. It is in this section that the doctrine of the resurrection of the body is set forth by the author.

The Date of the Book

The Apocalypse of Baruch is a composite writing, a fact seen from the diversity of tone and outlook that characterizes certain parts of the book. R. H. Pfeiffer places the date of origin shortly after 2 Esdras, between A. D. 90 and 100.[22] Bentzen claims that it was written somewhere between 4 Ezra and the Epistle of Barnabas, sometime before 130 A. D.[23] By contrast, Thomson sets the time of composition sometime before A. D. 70, asserting that there are three lines of evidence that point to A. D. 59 or 60.[24]

If the book were written between A. D. 70 and A. D. 100, it would be a literary work contemporaneous with the great mass of New Testament literature and have value for New Testament students. The book records Jewish doctrines and beliefs that prevailed in the latter half of the 1st century and which were defended and upheld by its leaders at a time when Christianity was making an aggressive attack upon Judaism.

The Religious Teachings of 2 Baruch

The teaching of the Apocalypse of Baruch is considered very interesting and possesses a number of points worthy of notice. Its Messianic conception is different in that it teaches a double Messianic time, a temporary restoration of Zion, followed by a great war, and then only the real Messiah would make his appearance. After this the permanent Messianic time would begin. This was a view later adopted by the Talmud wherein it was taught that all Jews would be gathered by a Messiah ben Joseph, and Gog and Magog would come to make war on Israel. In the ensuing battle the Messiah would be killed, and after that the Messiah of the house of David would appear.

The teachings of Christ and St. Paul are elucidated by contrast. The orthodox Pharisee's view about keeping the oral law and written law is demonstrated by the following statement: "Shepherds, lamps, and fountains come from the Law, and though we depart yet the Law abideth."

A careful reading of the Apocalypse of Baruch will show that the writer believed salvation depended on good works which provide a treasury of merit that can benefit others. The problems of sin, free will, and predestination are all wrestled with in 2 Baruch. Instructive along these lines are these statements: "Each one of us hath been the Adam of his own soul" (54:19); and "O Adam, what hast thou done to all those who are born of thee?" Here is expressed an antithesis which the author cannot resolve.

The Book of Enoch

The Book of Enoch, next to Daniel, is considered the most important apocalyptic work in this class of literature. It is a collection of writings of various dates from the first two pre-Christian centuries, written by different authors at different times. In it is found a diversity of religious ideas not always in harmony with one another but bound together by a unity of tone and outlook. Parts of ten Aramaic manuscripts of Enoch were found in Cave 4 of Qumran. 1 Enoch is composed of five parts — not arranged in any logical order whatsoever. The choice of Enoch as the supposed author of these heterogeneous writings is to be explained by the fact that the interpretation of the words in Gen. 5:24: "And Enoch walked with God, and he was not, for God took him," means that Enoch was translated into heaven during his lifetime, a belief current among the Jewish people at an early time. The visions in the book are portrayed as having been received by the patriarch Enoch. While the book is mainly eschatological in nature, there is a fine section, 91 — 104, which contains excellent examples of the wisdom literature of the Jews. In the opening part of the book, Enoch saw the vision of the Holy One in the heavens, "which the angels showed me, and from them I understood as I saw, but not for this generation, but for a remote one which is for me to come."

Composite Character of Enoch

Charles divides the 1 Book of Enoch into the following parts: chapters 1 — 36 (before 170 B. C.); chapters 37 — 71 (94 — 64 B. C.); chapters 72 — 82 (about 110 B. C.); chapters 83 — 90 (166 — 161 B. C.); chapters 91 — 105 (104 — 95 B. C.).[25]

In contradistinction to Charles, Rowley places the earliest parts of the book in the Maccabean, not pre-Maccabean age, shortly after Daniel.[26] Other chapters are placed after the Maccabean period but before the Roman conquest of Palestine in 63 B. C. (85 — 90; 91 — 105), exclusive of the Apocalypse of Weeks: 37 — 71; 1 — 5; 83 — 84 and 108), 12 — 36; 81 — 182; and 72 — 82 are dated before 150 B. C. These passages it is assumed were known by Jubilees 4:17-19.

The Contents of the Book

The book was arranged by its last editor in five sections, as in the Psalms and other Jewish Books.

Section I (1 − 36) is mainly concerned with pronouncing God's judgment by Enoch on the angels, or watchers who fell through their love for the daughters of men (Gen. 6:1-4), and Enoch's intercession for them. A weird description of Hades is found in this portion of 1 Enoch.

Section II (37 − 71) has three "parables," or apocalyptic revelations, together with the story of Enoch's translation into heaven.

Section III (72 − 87) is primarily concerned with furnishing a treatise on astronomy, the secrets of the movement of the stars as revealed to Enoch, who sees with his own eyes their very course, even the portals through which they enter and issue forth, for the purpose of transmitting the information to future generations.

Section IV runs along lines laid down in the first two portions dealing with the problem of sin and suffering of Israel. Enoch relates to Methuselah his visions of the deluge, the fall of the angels, and their punishment in the underworld, the deliverance of Noah, the Exodus, the giving of the Law, the conquest of Canaan, the time of the judges, the establishment of the united kingdom, the building of the temple, the story of the two kingdoms, the fall of the Northern Kingdom, and the Exile. This is followed by four periods of angelic rule up to the time of the Maccabean Revolt, the last assault of the Gentiles, and the great Judgment. The last part of Section IV contains the prediction of the foundation of the new Jerusalem, the conversion of the Gentiles, the resurrection of the righteous, and the coming of the Messiah.

Section V is without any account of the origin of sin but seems to be mainly devoted to the problem of suffering of the righteous and the prosperity of the oppressing sinners. It denounces evil and utters woes on sinners and promises blessings to the righteous. Within Section V is an older work "The Apocalypse of Weeks" (93:1-10; 91:12-19). It concludes (105): "In those days the Lord bade to summon and testify to the children of earth concerning their wisdom: show (it) unto them; for ye are their guides, and a recompense over the world. For I and My Son will be united with them forever in the paths of uprightness and in their lives; and ye shall have peace; rejoice, ye children of uprightness. Amen."

Several passages (37 − 71; 72 − 82; cf. 108) are probably independent books, partly furnished with superscriptions. Some passages which were originally independent (6 − 11; 39:12a; 54:7 − 55:2; 60; 65:1-69; 25; 106 − 107) are not Enoch passages but treat of the traditions of Noah and perhaps may be identical with a Book of Noah referred to in Jubilees 10:13 and 21:10.

Authorship and Original Language

The authentic authors of the book are thought to belong to Pharisaic circles, although some think that should not be taken in too narrow a sense. The fact that in 82:2 the celibate is praised, has been taken to be evidence of Essene influence, but the rejection of marriage is not a fundamental doctrine of the Essenes.

The original language of the book was Hebrew, and only a small part of it was written in Aramaic. Later a translation was made into Greek by Alexandrian Jews; and from Greek into Ethiopic, the only language in which the book has survived.[27] The 8th century A. D. chronographer George Synellus had made extensive extracts from the Book of Enoch and with the exception of these fragments, European scholars had no knowledge of this writing. In the last quarter of the 18th century, Bruce, the Abyssinian traveler, brought to Europe three copies of the Ethiopian version. In the Abyssinian Church the Book of Enoch was regarded as canonical and consequently preserved.

The Psalms of Solomon

The Psalms of Solomon are a collection of 18 Psalms which possess great interest for the student desirous of understanding the soul of the pious Jew during times of great religious ferment. Somebody has named them, "The Psalms of the Pharisee." Some of the early church lists of the books of the Bible designate 18 "Psalms of Solomon." They are written in a style and form reminiscent of the poems of the Psalter. Many of them, like the canonical psalms, have superscriptions. The word "selah" is found twice in them and indicates their liturgical use. R. H. Pfeiffer warns against confusing these with the five Christian odes to be found in the Gnostic work, The Pistis Sophia.[28] The Greek and English texts of The Psalms of Solomon were published by H. E. Ryle and M. R. James.[29] The famous Codex Alexandrinus originally contained this work. Several early catalogues listed it as an authoritative religious writing. The Psalms of Solomon was one of the pseudepigrapha that hovered on the border of deutercanonicity. Like other Jewish and Christian books it sank into oblivion during the Middle Ages. Hoeschel noticed it in a MSS in the library at Augsburg in the early part of the 17th century, and della Cerda published it in 1626. Since that time, four additional Greek MSS of the same work have been found and served as the basis for a printed text.

The Purpose of the Psalms

The purpose of the writings was to denounce the last of the Maccabean princes for "despising the Law" and allying themselves with the Sadducees. These poems speak of a strange man from a strange land, not of the Jewish race, who struck a mighty blow at the Jews. Scholars believe that this historical reference is an allusion to Pompey, for in Psalm 2 the reader is told that the dragon which had conquered Jerusalem was itself put to death by the seashore in Egypt.

The Contents of the Psalms

The Psalms are closely modeled after the pattern supplied by the canonical psalter. The first psalm announces the declaration of war, but is mainly concerned with the denunciation of hypocrites. The second portrays the siege of Jerusalem and admits that the hardships and punishments encountered were well deserved, but concludes with a description of the conqueror's death on the sands of Egypt. The third psalm is a poem of thanksgiving by the God-fearing. In the fourth we find a denunciation of hypocrites in language strongly reminiscent of that used by Christ against His enemies. Psalm 5 is a prayer for mercy to God. The sixth psalm is primarily occupied with a description of the blessedness of righteousness. In the seventh there is a prayer of Israel in a time of distress, asking God not to remove His tabernacle from their midst. The eighth psalm describes the siege of Jerusalem and denounces its sins. In the ninth, Israel as captive petitions Jehovah for forgiveness. The tenth psalm shows how the man who takes the chastening of the Lord is blessed. The next psalm speaks of the return of the captives. The 12th psalm is not unlike a stanza of Psalm 120 of the inspired psalter. The 13th has as its theme the blessedness of the righteous. The following one has a similar sentiment. The 15th begins with the assertion: "When I was in trouble I called upon the Lord." The 16th is experimental in the sense of the old Puritans. The first 16 psalms have no allusion to the Messiah, but discourse on the Messianic kingdom. Psalm 17 contains, however, what is believed to be one of the chief Messianic passages in the post-Biblical literature of Judaism.

The main interest of Psalm 18 is in its Christology. The Messiah is portrayed as of the seed of the House of David, who would come to overthrow the Romans after the downfall of the Hasmoneans. The rule of the Messiah is to be wise, holy, just, and spiritual. There is also a reference to the doctrine of the resurrection of the righteous, who do not arise to enjoy material blessings of the Messianic kingdom, but for eternal life in the spirit. Pfeiffer claims that the teachings of the Psalms of Solomon are in the spirit of Pharisaic theology.[29a] The people in the Psalter are divided into the righteous that fear the Lord, and the sinners or transgressors, identified with the Hasmoneans and the Sadducean aristocracy. According to Pfeiffer, the following would be a summary of the teaching of the early Pharisees:

> Our works are subject to our own choice and power. To do right or wrong by the works of our hands; And in thy righteousness thou visitest human beings. He who does righteousness lays up life for himself with the Lord; And he who does wrongly forfeits his life to destruction (9: 7-9).[30]

The Original Language of the Psalms

The original language of Psalms of Solomon was Hebrew, but like other writings it is lost. Today the text is available only in Greek (in several MSS). There is some evidence that the Greek version was rendered into Latin. In 1909 J. Rennel Harris published a Syriac translation in his *Odes and Psalms of Solomon*.

The Date of Composition

Inasmuch as the Psalms of Solomon contain references to the coming of Pompey and his death in Egypt in 48 B. C. and to other events prior to the conquest of Palestine in 63 B. C., a date in the last quarter of the 1st century B. C. is assigned as the time of the origin of these poems. They were probably written between 63 and 40 B. C. Pfeiffer is inclined to believe that the uniformity of style indicates that all 18 poems were written by the same man.[30a]

The Sibylline Oracles

Before the beginning of the Christian era there were a number of collections of Sibylline Oracles. Both Greek and Roman writers disseminated the belief in sibyls. The word "sibyl" means "the counsel of God." A sibyl in classical antiquity, however, was a woman residing in a cave who, supposedly under the influence of divine inspiration, gave forth prophetic utterances. The *sibylla* among the Greeks was a figure of fiction from pre-Homeric times who was made the daughter-in-law of Noah. The Sibylline Oracles received their typical form especially in Greek surroundings.

Women claiming to possess this prophetic gift lived in different places, anywhere from Italy to Babylonia. Erythrae in Asia Minor is alleged to have been the home of the original sibyl. In early Roman history the Cumaean sibyl played a very important role. Her oracles, eagerly sought by Roman decemvirs, were destroyed in the temple of Jupiter in 83 B. C. In Ionia a new book of oracles came into existence, but it too was destroyed. When the famous Sibylline books were destroyed with the burning of the Capitol, Sulla searched in Italy and Greece for oracles to replace the contents of the burned books. A half century later Augustine revived the search for the Sibylline Oracles.

In Egypt another collection of Sibylline Oracles sprang into existence and at first were under the influence of the Roman oracles. By the 3rd century B. C. many Jews had become familiar with the Sibylline Oracles. Jews in Alexandria took a nucleus of heathen oracles and through interpolations and insertions of Mosaic ordinances introduced Mosaic monotheism into these pagan writings. About 150 B. C. a Jew in Alexandria published a volume of Sibylline Oracles in hexameter lines, and in the epic dialect of the poems of Hesiod and Homer, in order to advance the cause of Judaism among non-Jews. These oracles were purported to be authentic utterances of the ancient sibyl of Erythrae. The Gentiles would willingly listen to hexameters, which contains allusions to their own histories as well as references to their mythology.

Purpose of the Oracles

The Sibylline Oracles were written by Jews for propaganda purposes. In these poems Judaism is glorified, and the fortunes and vicissitudes of the

Jews are foretold. How successful the Jewish Sibylline writings were in effecting conversions to Judaism cannot be known, but it is believed that they exerted a considerable influence.

The Sibylline books begun by the Alexandrian Jews were continued by the Christians. It is believed the entire Sibylline Oracles were comprised of 15 books, of which Books 9, 10, and 15 are still nonexistent. A portion of Book 3 was composed in the 2nd century B. C. Books 4 and 5 have Christian interpolations, although written by Jewish authors. Of all the 15 Sibylline books, Books 2, 4, and 5 contain materials related to the Old Testament apocrypha. The present edition contains books made up of fragments from different ages. Book 3 is best suited to give the reader an understanding of the manner in which Alexandrian Jews utilized pagan oracles for propaganda purposes of the Jewish faith. Besides containing a glorification of Jewish history, Book 3 also has predictions about the times of the Messiah.

Contents of the Book

Book 1 begins with creation and relates the history of the human race till the exit of Noah from the ark. This is followed by the history of the life of Christ, a portrayal of His miracle of the loaves, His crucifixion, and the destruction of the Jews. In this book, Hades is derived from Adam [Thomson]. Like the Book of Enoch, it has an allusion to the holy watchers and an arithmograph which seems to be fulfilled in *Theos Soter*. Book 2 is patterned after the eschatological discourses of Jesus Christ, and there appear to be echoes of them in this book. As also in Enoch, four archangels are introduced: Michael, Gabriel, Raphael, and Uriel. Book 3 is by far the largest; it contains a mass of confused material. It has a number of historical allusions, for example, the building of the tower of Babel, the establishment of the Solomonic kingdom, as well as events of historical importance to other nations. There is an early reference to the conquest of Egypt by Rome, the siege of Troy, the conquests of Alexander the Great, a sketch of the history of the Jews up to the time of Cyrus, and a series of oracles predicting judgment against Babylon, Egypt, Gog, Magog, Troy, and Lybia for their sins of idolatry. It also has prophecies directed against Antiochus Epiphanes, Phrygia, Cyprus, and the Hellenes, and predictions about the coming judgment on a wicked world, terminating in the coming of the Messiah. In the prophecies the Jews are lauded as a people who are faithful to the law of God, and conversely, the paganism of other peoples is denounced, and the heathen are exhorted to embrace Judaism.

Book 4 is Jewish throughout. It contains a sketch of the history of great empires, beginning with that of Assyria and ending with Alexander the Great. The fifth book tells the story of the successive emperors from Julius Caesar to the Antonines. The sixth has only 26 lines in which the Cross is praised. The next, 7, is fragmentary. The eighth book has an arithmogram and acrostic: IESOUS CHRISTOS THEOU HUIOS SOTER STAUROS.

Date of the Sibylline Oracles

The dates of the various books of the Sibylline Oracles can be determined from their contents. Various books come from different times. Book 3 is the oldest and was composed about 140 B. C. Book 4 comes from about 80 B. C. and Book 5 from about 130 B. C. These were all written in Greek and comprise the strongest and boldest polemic of the Jews against paganism. The Christian parts are from a later date and extend to the 5th century A. D.; the complete present text was edited in the 6th century A. D.

3 Maccabees

The two books called 3 and 4 Maccabees, which are found in editions of the pseudepigrapha, have no connection whatsoever with 1 and 2 Maccabees. There are, however, copies of the Septuagint which have preserved 3 and 4 Maccabees as part of the Apocrypha. And 3 Maccabees has no relation to the Maccabee family. It is of a fictional nature, based on unascertainable historical facts, and primarily treats of the attempt by Ptolemy IV of Egypt (221–203 B. C.) to kill the Jews of Alexandria and of his desire to enter the temple. He is entreated by the Jews to refrain from desecrating the temple by his presence, but he enters nevertheless and is struck by the hand of God.

Upon his return to Egypt after the Battle of Raphia, Ptolemy IV (Philopater) decided to wreak vengeance upon the Jews. He ordered all Jews to worship the Ptolemaic patron god Dionysius, threatening to deprive them of all privileges unless they complied with the imperial order. Those Jews who failed to obey the decree were imprisoned in the Hippodrome in Alexandria where they were to be trampled to death by intoxicated elephants, but by angelic intervention the elephants turned against the Egyptian persecutors. This episode convinced Ptolemy IV that the Jews were protected by God, and he ordered the captive Jews released, henceforth bestowing favors on them.

How authentic these facts are, scholars do not know. It may be based on an account told by Josephus (*Against Apion*, II, 5) about Ptolemy VII (145–117 B. C.), who determined to punish the Jews in a similar manner but was frustrated in his attempt. R. Pfeiffer calls the story in Josephus and its parallel in 3 Maccabees fiction, and he is convinced that the occasion for its being written was some unsuccessful attempt to persecute the Jews.[31]

The motive that prompted the writing of 3 Maccabees was similar to that found in Esther—glorification of the Jewish race and their religion for stiffening the moral fibre of the Jews by reminding them how in the past God had protected them when they remained faithful to Him.

Time of Composition

Waxman says there is a possibility that the story was written around A. D. 30, when the first persecution took place against the Jews under

Caligula.[32] There is, however, no evidence to corroborate this theory, because 3 Maccabees contains no references to Caligula. Ferrar places its origin around 100 B. C., at the same time that The Letter of Aristeas and 2 Maccabees originated, with both seemingly linked by literary similarity.[33] Hadas would have the book originate in the year 25–24 B. C., when the privileges of the Alexandrian Jews were in danger of being lost.[34]

The Language of the Book

The original language of 3 Maccabees was Greek. Its author had at his command an unusually large vocabulary and considerable resources of rhetoric. The faults of style of 2 Maccabees and of the Alexandrian School are also found in this writing. Torrey describes this style as "bombastic and inflated to the last degree . . . . This is not Greek that can be read with pleasure." [35] With this judgment, Eissfeldt is in agreement.[36]

The Author of 3 Maccabees

The writer was an Alexandrian Jew, whose name is unknown. The work cites the Book of Daniel with its apocryphal additions and seems to have known of 2 Maccabees. While the book is considered historical, it is still deemed valuable because of the interesting light it throws on the feelings of the Jews at this period toward their Egyptian conquerors, and also of the anti-Semitic attitudes in Egypt in the 3rd and 2nd centuries B. C.

4 Maccabees

The Relationship to the Other Maccabee Books

The title of this book gives the impression that it contains a narrative similar to that found in the three other Books of the Maccabees. However, 4 Maccabees belongs to the class of philosophic and didactic literature.[37] In form it is a discourse or diatribe of the Greek pattern or a tract "on the rule of reason over the passions." The author of 4 Maccabees has secured most of its illustrative material from the story of the Jewish martyrs told in 2 Maccabees 6:18–7:42. In the opening sentence the writer states his intention of demonstrating that pious reason is absolute ruler over motives and passions. He contends that not only can man control his passions but even his emotions—despite possible contradiction of justice. The book appeared early with the title "On the Supreme Power of Reason" (thus named in Jerome and Eusebius). Among the works of Josephus it appears under the name "On the Supremacy of Reason." [38] However, the name 4 Maccabees is also found at an early time.

The purpose of the writing seems to be to stiffen the spirits of Jewish hearers by recalling the heroism of the martyrs of the Jewish nation in the days of Antiochus Epiphanes.[39]

The Contents of the Book

In a brief introductory paragraph, the author indicated the scope of the question which he proposes to discuss (1:1-11) and the method he will use in the course of his presentation. The book has two main divisions: 1) A philosophical discussion on the main proposition (1:13 – 3:18); 2) The story of the martyrs and the lessons to be learned from it (3:19 – to the end). Chapters 3-7 of 2 Maccabees furnishes the basic material for the second part of the book.

Because the book is in the form of a discourse or sermon and seems to be largely addressed to an apparent audience (1:17; 2:4; 13:10; 18:4), Freudenthal and others believe that in 4 Maccabees we have an example of a Jewish sermon delivered as written.

The sufferings and triumph of Jewish martyr are discussed beginning with the 5th chapter and covering three fourths of the book. It is an expanded version of 2 Maccabees 6:18 – 7:42. In this portion of the book the following divisions can be made: 1) Story of the trial and torture of Eliezar, the aged priest (5:1 – 6:30). 2) Applications deduced from this narrative in 6:31 – 7:23. 3) Description of the torture of the seven youths (8:1 – 12:19). 4) Comments on the bravery of the youths (8:1 – 12:19). 5) Reflections on the sufferings and constancy of the mother (14:1 – 17:6). 6) Conclusion (17:7 – 18:23).

The Philosophical Viewpoint of 4 Maccabees

The philosophical standpoint of the writer is that of Stoicism, for 4 Maccabees emphasizes the Stoic principle that reason must dominate passion.[40] The author appears as a champion of philosophy (1:1), and it becomes clear to the discerning reader that he wishes to make prominent the philosophical side of his presentation, although he is more concerned about giving religious instruction. His doctrine of the four cardinal virtues: providence, temperance, justice, and fortitude is derived from Stoicism. His all-dominating reason is that which is guided by the divinely revealed law, the same Law for which the Jewish martyrs died. According to 1:15-18 the four cardinal virtues are but forms of that true wisdom. In opposition to Stoicism the passions are not to be annihilated but merely regulated (1:16; 3:5), inasmuch as God has planted them in man. The author of 4 Maccabees is saner and more human than the Stoics.

In illustration of his thesis that man is to attain balance of character by the attainment of the right measure of the four Stoic virtues, he refers to the lives of Joseph, Jacob, Moses, and David, and then at length describes the martyrdom by Antiochus of Eleazar, the seven brothers, and their mother. The author recites the tragic conversations between Antiochus and his victims – the old man, the seven brothers and their noble mother, all of whom are cited as examples of the power of reason to make people remain true to their convictions. The seven brothers are praised for their adherence to the ceremonial law. The doctrine of the resurrection, assuring eternal and blessed life in heaven, is emphasized, although it varies somewhat from the normal doctrine of the intertestamental period. In this book the idea is also found that the martyrdom of the righteous serves as an atonement for the sins of the generation, an idea which was later adopted in the Talmud.

The Author of the Work

According to Jerome and other early Christian writers, Josephus is the author of 4 Maccabees. In Greek editions of the works of Josephus, it constitutes the last chapter of his writings, having the title: "The Discourse of Flavius Josephus: or Concerning the Supreme Power of Reason." However, this position is completely contradicted by the dissimilarity of style and manner of Josephus' works.

Many believe that the author was an Alexandrian Jew belonging to the Pharisaic party (see 4:7), who was also a Hellenist as he clearly shows the influence of Greek philosophy. The earliest references to 4 Maccabees occur in writings that are of Alexandrian origin, and the author of 4 Maccabees makes considerable use of 2 Maccabees which had its origin in Alexandria.

The Language of the Book

The book was written originally in Greek and has many Greek philosophical terms. It bears the general characteristics of Greek as it was spoken in Alexandria. 4 Maccabees occurs in the chief MSS: S, A, V, and was found in the Peshitta text of Codex Ambrosius. No old Latin translation has survived.

The Letter of Aristeas to Philocrates

The Letter of Aristeas claims to be the work of a courtier of Ptolemy Philadelphus (285 – 247 B. C.), Aristeas by name, who describes to his brother Philocrates events that are supposedly contemporaneous with the writer's time. The letter purports to give a description of the origin of the Greek version of the Pentateuch. Modern scholarship, however, has rejected the authenticity of the letter and established it as an anonymous or spurious writing. The Letter of Aristeas is classified by R. H. Pfeiffer as belonging to the Alexandrinian propaganda literature; he says that "the story is merely a pretext for the glorification of the Jews and their religion; the events narrated are legendary or fictitious, although there is no reason to doubt that the Pentateuch was translated into Greek about 250 B. C." [41]

Modern scholars are agreed that although the letter attributes its writing to a Gentile, its purpose is that of promoting the cause of Judaism among the Gentiles, to portray its religion in a favorable light. The Letter of Aristeas has been compared to a modern novel that is written with a purpose. One reason for the writing addressed to Philocrates was political, to praise the generous action of Ptolemy who had released the political prisoners of the Jews. The other purpose was religious and was achieved by the description of the translation of the Hebrew scriptures by 72 translators, together with 72 questions put by King Ptolemy, which were designed to praise and exalt the Jewish religion in the eyes of the Gentiles.

Critics are agreed that the author of the Letter of Aristeas did take advantage of an event that was a real landmark in the history of Judaism, namely, the rendering into Koine Greek· of the Hebrew Old Testament Pentateuch. For Jewish proselytism the Septuagint afforded a wonderful means for winning converts in a world which was characterized by decay.

The Contents of the Letter

The Letter of Aristeas is dedicated to Philocrates, brother of the author of the letter, in this way: "My brother in character no less than in blood, but one with me as well as in the pursuit of goodness." It begins by telling how King Ptolemy Philadelphus (285 – 247 B. C.) was advised by his librarian to have the laws of the Jews translated for his library of 200,000 volumes which had no translation of the sacred scriptures of the Jews (vv. 1-8). Ptolemy selects Aristeas to go on an embassy to the high priest Eliezer with the request to send a body of scholars to translate their sacred scriptures into Greek. Aristeas takes the opportunity to suggest to Ptolemy the freeing of the 30,000 men whom his father had brought from Palestine as garrisons for the country districts (vv. 17-27). The king agrees to free the Jews and also pays their owners 20 drachmae per head, the total being 660 talents. (Vv. 28-40)

Eleazer answers Ptolemy's request favorably (vv. 41-50). The king then sends a gift of 100 talents of silver to Eliezer for the temple sacrifices: a sacred table (vv. 51-72), gold and silver bowls (vv. 73-78), and golden vials. (Vv. 79-82)

A most interesting account of the temple, city, and country is then given (vv. 107-120), which is believed to be from a lost work of Hecate. The translators selected by the high priest leave for Egypt (vv. 121-127). This is followed by a disquisition on the enactment of laws that treat of food, which are justified by means of the allegorical method (vv. 128-171). Ptolemy accords the Jewish elders great deference (vv. 172-186), entertains them at a banquet for seven successive days, and is delighted with the answers to the 72 questions given by the leaders from Palestine. (Vv. 187-300)

At the end of the week the elders are installed on the island of Pharos, where they work every day and complete their translation in 72 days (vv. 201-311). The translation is read before the Jewish population and recognized by the latter to be accurate (vv. 312-317). Any person who tampers with it in the future is to be subject to a curse. The king receives the scrolls with great satisfaction and dismisses the translators, who return to Jerusalem with costly gifts. (Vv. 318-322)

Critical Evaluation of the Letter

This account, which in the course of time was subject to marvelous additions, was accepted by Josephus in its original form. The account in the Letter of Aristeas was accepted for generations by the Jews as a true account, hence the name of the translation Septuagint, i. e. the translation of the 70, as the two additional men were only the leaders of the delegation, and were not included in the number.

The first known scholar critically to evaluate the Letter of Aristeas was Humphrey Hody, Regius professor of Greek at Oxford during the 18th century, who claimed that the LXX was produced in response to popular need rather than royal mandate, as stated in Aristeas' Letter.[42] Toward the end of the 19th century, scholars came to definitely regard the alleged writing of Aristeas as a pseudonymous work that originated between 150 – 100 B. C. Recently H. G. Meecham has taken a more favorable attitude toward it.[43] Decipherment of papyri has led to a modification of the criticism of Hody concerning the spuriousness of the Letter of Aristeas, in which the writer demonstrates a knowledge of Alexandrian customs. Meecham claims the letter is a piece of Jewish apologetics of the late Ptolomaic era. Moses Hadas contends that there is nothing in the linguistic usage of the writing that would require a date below 150 B. C.[44]

The Date of Composition

The date of the composition of the Letter of Aristeas has been placed somewhere between 200 B. C. and A. D. 33. Thus Schürer assigns the letter to around 200 B. C., one of the earliest dates given by authorities, while some German scholars believe that it was composed as late as A. D. 33. Dr. Wendland, publisher of one of the standard text editions of the Letter of Aristeas, claims it originated between 96 – 93 B. C.[45] Charles sees the bulk of writing coming from the time period between the years 170 – 130 B. C., with the material being enlarged and edited somewhat later.[46] Bentzen says that on philological grounds the letter can be dated with certainty as harking back to the period between 145 – 100 B. C.[47]

CHAPTER **XVII**

Philo and His Writings

The Life of Philo

One of the outstanding Jewish philosophers of all time, a representative of Hellenism, was Philo. To distinguish him from other Philos of antiquity, he is usually referred to as Philo Judaeus (the Jew) or Philo of Alexandria. He is generally regarded as the greatest and most influential writer of the Alexandrian school. Students of Hellenistic Judaism are greatly aided by

Philo's writings in ascertaining the character of Judaism in the Dispersion.

Some historians place the birth of Philo around the year 13 B. C. in Alexandria, Egypt; others put it around 20 B. C. or even 30 B. C. His death is believed to have occurred in the closing years of the reign of Claudius, 41 – 54 A. D. He appears to have spent most of his life in Alexandria. Thus Philo was a contemporary of Jesus and St. Paul. Philo belonged to a relationship that was reputed to have been wealthy and prominent, possibly a family of sacerdotal Jews. He was a true-blooded Jew of Aaronic descent. His brother, Alexander Lysimachus, was alabarch or arabarch (that is, probably chief farmer of taxes on the Arabic side of the Nile). One of Philo's nephews was the husband of King Agrippa I's daughter. Another nephew, Tiberius Julius Alexander, was Roman procurator of Judea, prefect of Egypt; he later accompanied one of the generals that participated in the war against the Jews.

Philo was the recipient of an excellent Jewish education and received training in grammar, rhetoric, philosophy, geometry, poetry, music, and Gentile learning. With this preparation he continued the study of philosophy in its three branches of physics, ethics, and logic, and as his writings show, he acquired an extensive rather than a profound grasp of Greek philosophical learning. Inasmuch as the Alexandrian Jewish community exercised a great influence on the Roman Empire, it may be seen how the relationship to which Philo belonged affected the Dispersion. In A. D. 39-40, Philo was sent as spokesman on a deputation to Rome to register strong objection to the imposition of emperor worship upon the Jews throughout the Roman Empire. Of this embassy Philo has left a full account in *De legatione ad Gaium*. This date is the only one in Philo's life which scholarship has been able thus far to ascertain definitely. Success did not crown the mission of Philo and his two colleagues; Emperor Caligula was indifferent to the protest of the deputation regarding emperor worship and treated Philo in a humiliating manner; a crowd mobbed his embassy. Scholem Asch has given an account of this mission in *The Apostle*. Philo did not concern himself with political activity, and as far as is known, did not further participate in any form of it. However, despite his interest in philosophy and his zeal in applying Hellenistic concepts to Judaism, he was a loyal Jew faithful to the ideals of his nation. In A. D. 50 Philo undertook another trip to Rome. These few facts constitute all that is known about the personal life of Philo.

The time of world history during which Philo lived coincided with an important epoch in Jewish and world history. Of it Wenley wrote:

> For it witnesses, not only the foundation of the Roman imperial system, but also the beginning of the end of ancient classical civilization in its dominant ideas, and the plantation of Christianity. Preeminently an era of transition, it was marked by significant displacements in culture, the effects of which continue to sway mankind even yet.[1]

This era was characterized by an attempt to revive the religions of pagan antiquity, the appearance of Christianity, and the syncretistic movement which eventuated in Gnosticism and Neo-Platonism. At Philo's time in the Roman Empire Roman authorities tolerated what historians have called "universalism," that is, the allowance within the political framework of different religious and philosophical systems and ideas. A number of contemporary currents met and fused in the person of Philo.

The Writings of Philo

Philo probably wrote before his first trip to Rome. He attempts to reconcile Greek philosophical ideas with the history, usages, and beliefs of Judaism. Most of his writing was done before A. D. 38. His language was formed on the best classical models, especially Plato. Citations from Greek poets are frequent in his writings, but Greek philosophy was his ·chief study. Although he was primarily a philosopher, most of his 38 works are either parts of a running commentary on the Pentateuch or essays on selected topics taken from the Five Books of Moses, which means that Philo treats Biblical history down to the time of Moses. Two voluminous books that have survived the 1st century are commentaries on the Penta-teuch and the Mosaic law. These works were not so much intended for the trained initiate as for the instruction of the educated Hellenists.

The writings of Philo may be divided into four classes: 1) a small, probably early, group of purely philosophical books (*De aeternitate mundi; Quod omnis probus liber sit, De providentia, De Alexandra* 2) expository writings on the Pentateuch: *De opificio mundi, De Abrahamo, De Josepho, De decalogo, De specialibus legibus, De virtutibus, De praemiis et poenis;* 3) historical and apologetical: *In Flaccum, De legatione ad Gaium, De vita contemplativa, Apologia pro Iudaeis, De vita Mosis;* 4) an allegorical commentary on Genesis — considered by scholars as Philo's most important work.

In his biography of Moses Philo presents the former as the wisest of legislators. The Biblical history set forth in the *De vita Mosis* and other works is colored by his philosophical outlook. In the *De vita contemplativa,* Philo gives a description of the sect of the Therapeutae, a group of ascetic hermits devoted to the contemplative life; they employed an allegorical interpretation of the law of Moses.

The work *On Virtues,* which has only partially survived, is important for understanding the political history of the 1st century A. D. Eusebius in his *Ecclesiastical History* gives a brief summary of it. (II, 5,1; the sequel, 5,6 — 6:3). Of the five original books *On Virtues,* only the third, *Against Flaccus,* and the fourth, *Embassy to Caligula,* survive. The main topic of *On Virtues* deals with the miserable end of the chief persecutors of the Jews, namely, Sejanus, Flaccus, Caligula, and probably Pilate. The idea of divine vengeance was also stressed in earlier Jewish histories, 2 Kings 19:36 f. and 2 Macc. 3:22-40; 5:6-10, 13:4-8; 15:28-35.

The Task of Philo

Philo represents a strange fusion. By nature and upbringing he was a Jew; by residence in Alexandria a mystic; by higher education a Greek humanist, by contact and social position an ally of the Roman aristocracy. Philo attempted to achieve a twofold purpose by his writing: 1) He endeavored to justify the Jewish religion to the cultured people of Graeco-Roman society. In view of the deterioration of pagon society and religion, he had a splendid opportunity to portray the Jewish faith as fulfilling "the desire of all nations." On the other hand, he tried to show and persuade his strict coreligionists that Greek philosophy and learning were not actually hostile and opposed to the tenets of the Hebrew religion but that each stood for practically identical principles. Philo thus adopted an eclectic viewpoint, one in which he blended Old Testament theological concepts with Greek philosophical principles. Katz claims that "Philo witnesses to a development in which philosophy turned religious and religion philosophic." [2] While Philo spoke philosophically with the intention of bringing home dogmatic and ethical truths, in so doing it involved on his part a dilution of the religious substance of divine revelation. Likewise his religious convictions were modified by philosophical inheritance.

An examination of the writings and views of Philo will reveal that he was not a true Jew in the same sense as were the Scribes and Pharisees, although Philo claimed faithfulness to the teachings of Judaism. It was his purpose to amalgamate heathen philosophy and Jewish theological teachings. Strangely, he considered both heathen philosophy and the Jewish Torah to be in possession of the truth, which explains his attempt at amalgamation. Philo wove the divergent views of philosophers like Pythagorus, Plato, Aristotle, and the Stoics into one system which seemed to be harmonious. Plato was for Philo "the greatest of the great," but at the same time he held that there was nothing more sacred than Israel, and also that Moses "was the greatest of the great." It was the conviction of Philo that the great sages of the ages had acquired their wisdom from Moses, the Prophets, and the Old Testament; especially in the Pentateuch all truth was to be found. At the same time he also believed that the Greeks had "truth." Philo set out to prove that between sound philosophy and revealed religion there was complete agreement and that they were simply two aspects of the same truth. Moore says of Philo: "If we had to give his own philosophy a name, we should label it a Stoicizing Platonism with a penchant for Pythagorean number-jugglery. But we should have to add that adaptability to Jewish theology enters as a factor of choice into his personal eclecticism." [3]

Philo's Method

To harmonize Greek philosophy with Jewish religion necessitated adoption of a hermeneutics which differed from that previously used by his coreligionists. Historians of interpretation call his the "allegorical method." Philo was convinced that truth was to be found in all the letters of the Bible. While in a limited sense the allegorical method had been used by the Jewish rabbis, Philo went further than any other Jewish interpreter in that he perfected, systematized, and formulated the rules for this type of interpretation. The tendency to fusion had been evident for some 300 years before Philo's time. The Hellenic Greek philosophers, particularly the Stoics, applied this method to the myths of Hesiod and Homer. The advantage of this method, according to Wenley, was that it rendered interpretation "malleable" and allowed for adjusting interpretation to what was judged to be "the intellectual necessities" of the time. In his philosophical-theological writings, Philo employed certain basic methods. He ascribed literal inspiration to the Greek translation of the Bible as he did to the Hebrew text. Furthermore, he taught that the Old Testament was literally and historically true on the one hand, and philosophically and allegorically acceptable on the other. The allegorical method was used to bring the truths of Scripture into relationship with physiological, psychic, moral, and mystical doctrines. Philo allowed for mythological tendencies even in his beloved Pentateuch, and he argued with great power against anthropomorphisms. He does, however, stress the fact that the literal meaning of Scripture is not to be ignored in favor of the allegorical meaning.

A sample of Philo's allegorical interpretation (from the *Sacred Allegories*, I, 39) is illustrated in the following:

> For the mind imparts to the irrational part of the soul . . . a share of that which it has received from God, so that the mind is besouled by God, while the irrational part [is besouled] by the mind . . . just as Scripture does not hesitate to speak of Moses as a God to Pharaoh.

Philo was of the opinion that when he was at his best in the process of interpretation, he became a vehicle of divine possession. "He says: 'Through the influence of Divine inspiration I have become excited profoundly . . . then I have been conscious of a richness of interpretation, an enjoyment of light, a most penetrating sight, a most manifest energy in all that was to be done.' Again, 'I am irradiated with the light of wisdom,' and 'all intellect is a Divine inspiration.' Little wonder, then that we have a strange mixture of philosophy and religion, of rationalism and piety, of clear Greek intellectualism with hazy oriental mysticism." [4]

"The literal sense must be wholly set aside, when it implied . . . anything unmeaning, impossible, or contrary to reason. Manifestly, this canon, if strictly applied, would do away not only with all anthropomorphisms, but cut the knot wherever difficulties seemed insuperable." [5] According to Katz, Philo's exegetical method consisted in transforming "the clear-cut figures of biblical history into psychological tendencies by means of an allegory which more often than not is guided by the most far fetched etymologies of biblical names." [6]

Subjects of Inquiry

Philo concentrated upon three main subjects of inquiry: 1) the conception of God; 2) God's relation to the world; 3) human nature.

Conception of God

Like the neo-Platonic school, whose teachings Philo accepted, he was "thoroughly dualistic" (Wenley). He asserted that God's existence was necessary for the governing of the world, just as a soul is required in a human body to keep it alive. Again, as the soul of man remains unchanged throughout all the bodily changes of a lifetime, so behind the changing world there must be a changeless Being. However, human analogies could not extend to God's being. For Philo, God was void of all human qualities, nothing finite could be predicated to Him. Anthropomorphisms were to be avoided when describing God.

Philo once stated that God existed, but what He is, no one can say. Adopting the Platonic concept of a perfect God, Philo taught that God did not concern himself with the world but dealt with the world through divine or mediating forces. Philo wrote: "For He is unchangeable, requiring nothing else at all, so that all things belong to Him, but He, speaking strictly, belongs to nothing" (as in Wenley). This doctrine of the transcendence of God was an important tenet of Platonic philosophy. Since God expels all imperfection, He is the Being for which all men have been yearning. While men stand in a necessary relation to this Being, He, on the other hand, does not stand in any relation whatever to men. "Yet, men must return to God, but He abides so remote, in the realm of pure contemplation and completion, that He cannot approach them." (Wenley)

God's Relation to the World

Since God is so remotely transcendent from the world, He is incomprehensible and immaterial. There is no direct connection between God and the world. This was a Platonic position in opposition to Stoic philosophy which identified God and the world. According to Philo, God created and sustains the world by *intermediate* powers, or ideas *(logoi)*. These agencies were adapted from Plato's ideas. Philo personalized these intermediate powers and included them in his doctrine of the Logos. (Wenley)

It was easy to identify the *logoi* issuing from God with the Biblical *bene-Elohim*, or "Sons of God." There is a certain fluidity of thought in Philo's philosophy in regard to the exact relation of these *logoi* to God. The term *logos* was used in place of the Platonic term *idea*, being suggested to Philo by the Scriptural phrase the "Word of God." (Higher critical New Testament scholars believe that the writer of the Gospel of John borrowed the Logos concept in 1:1-14 from Philo.)

Concerning Philo's concept of the Logos, Rehwinkel asserted: "Philo's logos was not the Logos of the Targums, neither the Platonic conception of the Logos as the 'Archetypal idea,' nor that of the Stoics as the 'world-reason' pervading all matter. But Philo's Logos was one his own mind had conceived, drawing a little material from here and there. His Logos was not a concrete personality, but the simple reflection of God; it is not a Person, but a shadowy unreal Voice of the Mind of God." [7]

Bentwich asserted about the relation of Philo's Logos and that of the opening chapter of the Gospel of John: "In the first we have a thought which might well have been written by Philo himself: 'In the beginning was the Word, and the Word was with God, and the Word was God.' But in the fourteenth verse there is a manifest sharp cleavage: 'and the Word was made flesh, and dwelt among us, and we beheld His glory, the glory as of the Only Begotten of the Father, full of grace and truth.' [8] There may be a fine spiritual thought beneath the word here, but the concept of the Incarnation is not Jewish nor philosophical, nor Philonic."

In his doctrine of the Logos, Philo tried to preserve the transcendence of God as well as His immanence. In the past history of philosophy and religion, Philo noted that men were so impressed with the mystery of the Divine Being that they either banished God from the world or mingled the finite particulars with the Deity. Philo sought to avoid the extremes of pantheism or dualism by combining the two tendencies. In his portrayal of God, he depicted a Being that would be worthy of veneration and adoration (this is the Jew in Philo), but at the same time he wanted a definite relationship to exist between God and His creation (this is the Oriental influence). To connect God and His creation, a mediator was necessary. Wenley also says about this attempt of Philo: "But Philo could not surmount one difficulty peculiar to contemporary thought. He was unable to connect God directly with creation *and* preserve His purity unsullied. Hence the obscurity which surrounds his conception of the Logos, likewise his vacillation with respect to its personality." [9] The result was that past philosophical heritage influenced his interpretation. Sometimes the Platonic theory of ideas controls Philo's thinking; at other times he seems to favor Stoicism, with its immanent world-reason. Then again Philo's rabbinical love prompted him to bestow upon the Logos a priestly or an atoning function. For the Alexandrian Jew, the Logos became the intermediary between God and man, the great agent of God in the moral and material worlds, and the only form in which God made himself known to man. It is also through, by, and in the Logos that men are enabled to feel after God and raise themselves toward Him.

The Logos is portrayed as the Mediator between God and men, the High Priest and Intercessor for the world. He is also man, par excellence, made in the image of God. But Philo never identified the Logos with the Messias. Philo remained undecided concerning the relationship between the Logos and God. Thus Philo wrote: "It is not unbegotten, like God, nor begotten, like ourselves, but stands midway between these two extremes" (as quoted in Guignebert). Philo's conception vacillated in a manner which indicates that his conception of the Logos was "vague and fluid." (Wenley)

In regard to sin Philo had some definite ideas. Evil does not come from God but from matter or from inferior powers, the imperfect *logoi* who work upon matter at the order of God. Into matter, which is coeternal with God, although formless and inert, the *logoi* have introduced the spirit of life (νοῦς) to bring about creation.

Doctrine of Man

In his anthropology Philo shows the influence of Platonism and Stoicism. He thinks of man in terms of Greek dualism and distinguishes the soul from the body, stating that one might exist without the other. Souls fill the space between the world and God and it is only when they approach the earth that they take on corporeality, and at the same time sin enters them together with the imperfection of matter. Human souls are unable by their own power to escape the consequences of this fall, and it is only through the grace *(charis)* of God that they are able to do any good deeds.

Philo differed radically from the Stoics in his doctrine of salvation. According to Stoic philosophy, man had to save himself. Philo's doctrine of soteriology maintained that all the efforts of man should be concentrated on the liberation of the soul from the shackles of matter and be directed to the attaining of the original purity by rising again to its source in the Godhead. Guignebert says: "Thus the aim and science of life is 'the good life,' by which is meant the attainment of *askesis* (ἄσκησις), or detachment from matter, leading in turn to *ecstasy* or full understanding of the divine, apprehended directly and by evidence (ἐναργείᾳ)." [10] Man must gain the state of ecstasy in which he beholds the vision of the Deity and keeps himself free from the attachments of the body. To achieve this result, the spirit of God dwells in man and stirs him like the strings of a harp. "Man must renounce all sensuousness and achieve the extirpation of desire and of the passions." Escape is the only hope for the soul. Here Philo differs radically from the Jewish Apocrypha, which taught the resurrection of the unglorified body.

Philo's dialectical edifice was a mixture of Biblical texts and philosophical teachings, blended together by a philosophical method which would be unacceptable to philosophers today. Guignebert: "Today, Philo's dialectical edifice, reared upon a foundation of purely verbal dexterity, seems to us wholly arbitrary. But it satisfied him, and his methods were in keeping with the spirit of his environment and of his age." [11]

According to Guignebert, the metaphysical thought of Philo had a number of interesting consequences: 1) The Bible as interpreted by Philo became more intelligent to the non-Jews of the Roman world. 2) Philo, who became international-minded, taught that bliss is the destiny of all righteous people who keep the Law — irrespective of race." 3) The Jews of the Diaspora gave ritualism a much smaller place in religion than did the Palestinian rabbis. 4) The followers of Philo "did not reject the Messianic ideas of Palestine but they diluted them." The Philonians "were more interested in the destiny of the soul" than in the realization of the Messianic kingdom. [12]

To evaluate the lasting results of Philo's work, Marshall quotes Emil Schuerer as saying *(The Jews in the Time of Jesus)* that "Philo struggled in behalf of a cause that was doomed to failure." [13] With the fall of Jerusalem in A. D. 70 Hellenism grew weak and waned among the Jews. Rabbinic Judaism supplanted it. The preservation of the Jewish-Hellenistic writings was not due to the Jews but to the Christians. The energetic propaganda conducted by the Jews was checked by the destruction of Jerusalem by Titus and was soon supplanted by the missionary aggressiveness of the Christians. Both developments were hostile to the survival of the philosophy of Philo.

F. H. Heinemann claims that Philo exercised a great influence on Christian theology through his method of exegesis and the main elements of his religious philosophy. His influence on Neoplatonism was much greater than is usually conceded. While Philo did not create a system, he introduced certain new ideas and principles which were different from those held in Greek thought. He proposed a world-scheme that was new as far as European thought was concerned. Philo began with the first principle of revelation, which he did not endeavor to prove but accepted on the authority of revelation.

Philo anticipated medieval philosophy by deducing from the Old Testament the following doctrines: 1) God exists; 2) There is only one God; 3) The world is created by Him; 4) There is only one world; 5) God is the Providence of the universe.

It is generally agreed that Philo exerted no influence on the New Testament, nor in turn was he influenced by the teachings of New Testament writers. He did, however, affect the thinking of the Alexandrian fathers of the church, and through Clement and Origen of Alexandria, much of subsequent Christian theology was indebted to Philo for his fusion of theology and philosophy. The early church adopted much of Philo's method. Though the early writers considerably changed his teachings, still a study of Philo helps one to understand better many patristic writings.[14]

CHAPTER **XVIII**

Josephus and His Writings

Flavius Josephus, a younger contemporary of Jesus and the apostles, was probably the one Hellenistic Jewish writer in ancient times most widely read by both Jews and Gentiles. One reason for the popularity of Josephus was that his writings were the only source for the greater part of Jewish history in Palestine and the Diaspora during the century before the birth of Jesus and the 1st century of the Christian era. Josephus has given us a consecutive and complete history covering a period of over 2,000 years. His works are also valuable because they have preserved various events of Graeco-Roman history.

For the life of Josephus, students of the intertestamental period are mostly dependent on the historian's own autobiographical references, found partly in his own incomplete biography and in scattered notices in his *Jewish Wars*. The Great War (A. D. 66 – 70) divides the life of Josephus into two nearly equal parts. The first comprises 33 stormy years in Palestine as a priest, patriot, general, and prisoner; the second consists of the years that he lived as a citizen and writer in Rome, the capital of the Roman Empire.

Flavius Josephus was born A. D. 37 – 38, the year of the accession of Gaius Caligula, and died early in the 2nd century. Pontius Pilate had been called back from Judea in the previous year; Herod Agrippa I had just received his liberty together with a kingdom from the new emperor. Josephus' father's name was Matthias, a priest, and his mother was of princely blood, being a descendant of the Hasmonean leader Jonathan. Both of his parents belonged to families that were of priestly aristocracy. With this background it is not surprising that Josephus received an excellent education and that at an early age he was introduced to Jewish and Hellenistic learning and culture. His parents had intended for him to become a priest and had him introduced to Jewish law and literature when he was quite young. Because of his precocious talents, learned rabbis came to consult him. At the age of 16 he attended the meetings of the leading sect of Jews, the Pharisees, also the Sadducees and the Essenes, and acquired knowledge from all three, with the intent of joining one of them. He also spent some time with a hermit named Banus, who was a resident of the desert. After showing precocity in the study of the Law, at 19 he became a member of the Pharisees. In A. D. 64 at the age of 26 or 27 he made a journey to Rome and succeeded in securing the release of a number of priests who had been deported to Rome because of participation in a plot of the Essenes against Roman rule. A famous Jewish actor and the Empress Poppea, wife of Nero, aided Josephus in accomplishing his mission. In Rome he learned to fear and respect the Roman powers and culture and was greatly impressed by Roman might and invincibility. Not long after Josephus' return to Palestine, the Jews took up arms against the Roman forces of Palestine. Josephus was not in favor of this Jewish rebellion because of his conviction that the Jews could not possibly win. The turbulent condition of the country quickly brought Cestius Gallus, Governor of Syria, to the scene. Gallus nearly conquered Jerusalem, but for some unaccountable reason withdrew his troops. Then in the defiles of Bethhoron, the Roman legions in the autumn of A. D. 66 were subjected to a disastrous defeat which resulted in Rome taking steps to crush the revolt. Still, for reasons not apparent to scholars, Josephus was made commander of the Jewish troops in Galilee.

At the age of 29 Josephus the priest was also appointed governor over Galilee, a province it was believed would be the first to be attacked by the Romans. The opening scenes of the Galilean campaign, A. D. 66—68, are not easily followed for we have two accounts of the period. In the pages of the *Life*, Josephus has given a discussion of the policies and aims of himself and of the Jerusalem leaders, which is far from clear. In the *Life* we have his defense against a rival Jewish historian, who had accused Josephus of being responsible for a revolt. In the *Jewish War* we have a shorter account of the same event written under Roman patronage. Josephus himself tells us that he was sent by the Sanhedrin with two other priests to persuade the people of Galilee to lay down their arms. Although unqualified for the position of governor, through the influence of his friends Josephus was nevertheless appointed to this position. The Zealots were dissatisfied with his leadership and were convinced that he did not make adequate preparations to protect Galilee. They endeavored to have him removed from the position but without success.

Marcus asserts about this period of Josephus' life: "We cannot be certain just what his attitude and status were, since he left us contradictory accounts of his military career." [1] Despite his misgivings he sincerely attempted to defend the province of Galilee against the Romans.

Josephus and his army fled to a place near the Sea of Galilee, where at Jotapata the Romans besieged them in 67 B. C. After 47 days the Roman General Titus was successful in storming the stronghold and massacring the defenders. Josephus and a group escaped through a cave, where Josephus adroitly succeeded in obviating a joint pact of suicide. Hailed before the Roman comander-in-chief, Vespasian, Josephus succeeded in ingratiating himself with the Roman general by predicting that the latter would become emperor. Vespasian took Josephus to Alexandria and later to Rome, where he enjoyed the favor and patronage of the imperial family.

During the Great War (A. D. 66—70) Josephus acted as mediator between the Romans and the Jews. His coreligionists hated him, while Titus was suspicious of his dealings, and whenever the Romans would suffer reverses, they suspected him of treachery. When Titus staged his triumphal procession in Rome, Josephus accompanied the Roman general.

Josephus lived over 30 years in Rome; of this there is little to report. He was favored by Flavius, who also commissioned him to write a history of the Roman's triumph over the Jews. Josephus was given the right of Roman citizenship, received lodging in the former palace of Vespasian, and was awarded a pension from the same emperor. While living in Rome, Josephus witnessed a number of triumphal processions. Besides seeing the new Rome arise from the ashes of a fire started by Nero, for which the Christians had paid dearly in persecutions and crucifixions, Josephus also saw the building and completion of the Colosseum, the Forum of Vespasian and Titus, and the Temple of Peace.

The tranquility of his life in Rome was broken by the accusations of his enemies that he had subsidized a Jewish revolt in Cyrene. He was slandered by his son's tutor. Justus of Tiberius, a rival historian, published a work, appearing toward the end of the 1st century A. D., in which Josephus was accused of being responsible for the Jewish war against the Romans, or at least of causing his native city, Tiberius, to revolt against Rome. These attacks threatened to stop the sale of Josephus' books. The autobiography is an attempt by Josephus to refute these attacks by Justus of Tiberius.

The death of Titus in A. D. 79 deprived Josephus of his patron and forced him to change his literary activity. From this time on he became an apologist for his nation. However, his own countrymen would not forgive Josephus for having been a renegade. Eusebius, the Christian historian, reports that it was the Romans, not the Jews, who perpetuated his memory by erecting a statue in Rome and having his books placed in the public library. Josephus was a court favorite during the reigns of three emperors, Vespasian, Titus, and Domitian. Domestically Josephus had considerable matrimonial trouble. Three times he was married; one wife deserted him, and Josephus divorced another.

From A. D. 71 till the time of his death, Josephus began and pursued his literary career. His objective was to give the Greeks and Romans a better understanding of the history and religion of the Jews. He wrote in Greek, which he had most likely learned in Palestine, but in order to avoid defects in style he consulted experienced writers. Josephus also seems to have had a knowledge of Latin, for in one passage he quotes from the writings of Livy.

During the Roman period of his life, Josephus produced four works which have survived.

I. *The Jewish War*

Thackeray believes that the first draft of this work was done in Aramaic and sent to the inhabitants of Upper (or inland Syria) Galilee. This edition is lost, but Thackeray is convinced that two conjectures may be made about it. The Aramaic version was shorter than the Greek. Second, the Jewish readers did not need the unusually long historical introduction which carries the account back more than 200 years before the Great War and covers nearly two books in the Greek.

The Greek edition that has survived was done under imperial patronage. Although Josephus states that *The Jewish War* is a translation from the Greek, there is an absence of any Semitic parentage. In *Contra Apionem* Josephus states that he "employed certain collaborators for the sake of the Greek style (1:50)." To these Greek assistants credit may be given for the style and for producing what is tantamount to a new edition. *The Jewish War* was published in parts and was the subject of a long correspondence between Josephus and Herod Agrippa II. The completed work appeared toward the end of the reign of Vespasian, A. D. 75—79, and copies were at once given to the imperial patrons. The Emperor Titus gave his imprimatur. According to Josephus, Titus was anxious that *The*

Jewish War should be the official version from which the facts of the Great War were to be ascertained.

This work was comprised of seven books: I. The period from Antiochus Epiphanes (175 B. C.) to Herod the Great (4 B. C.); II. The period from 4 B. C. to A. D. 66, covering the early events of the war with the Romans; III. The occurrences in Galilee in A. D. 67; IV. The course of the war till the siege of Jerusalem; VI. The investment and fall of Jerusalem; VII. The aftermath of the rebellion.

Josephus had a splendid opportunity to secure reliable information in the conduct of the war of the Romans against the Jews. At first as commander of the Jewish forces in Galilee and later behind the Roman lines throughout the siege of Jerusalem, Josephus was enabled to secure exceptionally reliable information. Deserters from Jerusalem kept him informed about events in Jerusalem while he was in the Roman camp. In addition to his notes and recollections, the imperial *Memoirs* were at the disposal of Josephus.

Wilhelm Weber believes that the Jewish historian also had access to the Latin *Memoirs*, an official record based on the field notes of Vespasian. The famous passage on the organization of the Roman army, it is believed, was obtained from this source. Thackeray asserts about the general reliability of *The Jewish War:* "Yet, with access to these first-hand sources, with the weighty authority both of his imperial patrons and of King Herod behind him, and with the further (possibly more questionable) advantages of good literary assistants, we cannot, I think, but accept the *general* trustworthiness of the narrative of Josephus." [2]

In evaluating the historical worthiness of *The Jewish War*, it must not be forgotten that the *Memoirs* are written from a Roman point of view. Furthermore, the fact that Josephus is writing under imperial patronage tended to give the work a pro-Roman bias. A comparison between *The Jewish War* and the *Life* does not present a consistent portrayal of the Galilean campaign. Laquer, in *Der juedische Historiker Flavius Josephus* suspects Josephus of deliberate misrepresentation of details so that he might find favor with his other patron, King Agrippa II. Thackeray asserts that on the whole *The Jewish War*, produced during the prime of life of Josephus, under favorable circumstances must be considered "a fine book."

II. *Jewish Antiquities*

This book appeared 16 years after the publication of *The Jewish War*. Written about A. D. 94 it is the longest *(magnum opus)* of the works of Josephus.[3] It has 20 volumes and seems designed to impress the educated Gentiles with the great military and cultural achievements of the Jewish people. *The Jewish Antiquities* purports to relate the history of the Jews from their beginnings till the War of A. D. 66. The 20 books fall into five divisions: 1. I−IX, from prehistoric times till the captivity; 2. XI, the age of Cyrus; 3. XII−XIV, the beginnings of the Hellenistic Age, starting with Alexander the Great; 4. XVII—XX, from Herod's death till the War of A. D. 66.

The first 10 books contain a paraphrase of the historical material found in Genesis to Daniel, following mainly the Septuagint but with Agadic editions of Alexandrian and Palestinian provenance. For the Persian period Josephus utilized as his chief source the Biblical books of Ezra, Nehemiah, and Esther. The Letter of Aristeas and 1 Maccabees, in Greek translation, were the sources employed by Josephus for the early Hellenistic period. For the Hasmonean and Herodian periods discussed in books XIV—XX, the prime sources of information Josephus used were the writings of Nicholas of Damascus and the geographer Strabo.

III. *The Treatise Against Apion (Contra Apionem)*

This work is Josephus' most inspiring writing. Before Jerome's day, this book was known as *Concerning the High Antiquity of the Jews.* Thackeray says of the *Contra Apionem* that it "is the most attractive of our author's works; exhibiting a well-designed plan, great literary skill, an intimate acquaintance with Greek philosophy and poetry, together with a more sincere and impassioned zeal for his country's religion than we find elsewhere." [4] It was written in two books as a defense of the Jewish religion against the attacks of heathenism. This work gives interesting insights into anti-Semitism of the 1st century A. D. In this writing the author's character is seen at its best, as he energetically refutes the calumnies of Apion and other anti-Jewish pamphleteers. The positive part of the work is a defense of the Mosaic law, depicted by Josephus as a model of ethical and political thinking. *Contra Apionem* preserves numerous quotations from lost writers; this gives this literary production a special value.

IV. The Life of Josephus

The last work of Josephus is the *Vita* or *Autobiography*, which appeared as an appendix to the second edition of *Jewish Antiquities.* It is an echo of the old days in Galilee and is directed against his detractors, who criticized his conduct in connection with the Galilean campaign. The *Autobiography* was produced by Josephus when he was over 60 years old. It contains a reference to the death of Herod Agrippa II, which is alluded to in another source as occurring in 100 A. D. In defending himself in the *Vita*, Josephus says, addressing himself to Justus, the historian: "Why, did you not publish it (the history) in the lifetime of the Emperors Vespasian and Titus and while King Agrippa and all his family were still among us?" The *Autobiography* was in reality an *apologia pro vita sua*, written to refute the attack by the history of Justus on the conduct of Josephus in Galilee more than 30 years before.

Projected Works

At the end of *The Jewish Antiquities* Josephus states that he has plans for two further literary projects: 1) A summary sketch of the war and the post-history of the Jewish people; 2) "A work in four books concerning God and His Being, and concerning the Laws, why some things are permitted to us by them and others are forbidden." These books were never written. From scattered allusions in *The Jewish Antiquities* it would seem that the second book on "Customs and Causes" had begun to shape in his mind. Thackeray claims it is a matter of regret that this work was not written, for it would have shed light on the relation of Alexandrian and Palestinian exegesis. The ascribing of the so-called Fourth Book of Maccabees to Josephus by Eusebius (H. E. iii, 10) and others is an error.

The Relationship of Josephus to His Contemporaries

Josephus probably came into contact with three classes of people during his sojourn and activities in Palestine and Rome: 1) with his Jewish coreligionists; 2) with the wider Greek-speaking people; 3) with the Romans. In discussing the relationship of Josephus with his contemporaries, Thackeray also evaluates his relationship to Judaism, Hellenism, and Christianity.

Of the Aramaic, in which the first draft of *The Jewish War* was written, Josephus was presumably a master. Although he was a priest and a writer, Thackeray, relying on Ewald and Edersheim, believes Josephus was "weak in Hebrew."[5] Thackeray gives a number of examples from the writings of Josephus to show that he was not proficient in Hebrew philology.[6]

Josephus nevertheless claimed proficiency in Hebrew and more than once claims to have translated directly from the Hebrew. In *The Jewish Antiquities* he writes: "This work will embrace a complete account of our ancient history and constitution, translated from the Hebrew records." In the beginning of the *Contra Apionem* Josephus asserts: "At the outset of my work . . . I remarked that I was merely translating the books of the Hebrews into Greek and promised to repeat the story without any addition or omission on my part."

What kind of a Biblical text did Josephus use? Thackeray who has made a special study of this subject states that from Samuel on, Josephus uses the Septuagint. "The Octateuch stands apart from the rest" of the Old Testament. According to Thackeray the type of Septuagint text employed by the Jewish historian is consistent throughout, including also such apocryphal books as 1 Esdras and 1 Maccabees. The text used by Josephus comes closer to the LXX produced by Lucian of Antioch, which appeared about 200 years after Josephus' death. "It is known to have preserved much ancient material" and rests upon a text that critics call "proto-Lucianic." In the Pentateuch much less was made of the LXX. In Joshua, Judges, and Ruth, Thackeray asserts that he cannot find any use of the LXX; it is possible that here Josephus used some form of Aramaic Targum.

Relationship to Hellenism

Josephus' works, as already stated, were primarily intended for educated Greek readers, and therefore he scrupulously wrote his books in good literary style. During the Hellenistic age there was a tendency for Greek writers to despise the Koine Greek and return to the Attic of the age of Pericles. Josephus shared in this Atticistic revival and tried to stem the development of Greek as was evident in the Koine or common Greek of his age. He made sure that there were no Aramaisms in his writings, abjured all vulgarisms, and was fastidious in replacing certain words of the LXX translation with more literary ones.

In order to acquire a polished style he obtained help from individuals reputedly well versed in Greek style and language. In the *Contra Apionem* (II:50) he acknowledges that in composing the Greek edition of the *The Jewish War* 25 years before, he had employed collaborators for the sake of the Greek style. *The Jewish War* is written in classical Greek — in a style uniformly excellent. In *The Jewish Antiquities* the style is much more uneven. Thackeray detects two large portions, including nearly five books, which he believes are not the product of Josephus. These portions are books XV — XVI (called assistant a) and XVII, XVIII, and XIX, 1-275 (called assistant b). In his study on "Josephus" in *Beginnings of Christianity* and in his article for Hasting's *Bible Dictionary* and in *Josephus, The Man and Historian*, Thackeray has shown what the characteristics of both assistants were.

In his writings Josephus shows considerable acquaintance with Greek literature. He must have used a great number of pagan writers in order to improve his style. Josephus imitated Thucydides to a considerable extent; this is apparent especially in *The Jewish Antiquities*, XVII — XIX, and in other parts of the same work. Other historians before Josephus had also leaned heavily on Thucydides. Besides the latter, Josephus used Herodotus, Xenophon, Polybius, and Dionysius of Halicarnassus.

The Greek poets are liberally quoted in the writings of Josephus. He showed familiarity with Homer, the Tragedians, Sophocles, Euripides, and other poets. The mind of the Jewish historian was filled with Greek phraseology and modes of thought. He compares the three sects of the Jews: the Pharisees, Sadducees, and Essenes with the Greek schools of the Stoics, Epicureans, and Pythagoreans.

Josephus' Relationship to Christianity

Josephus had the opportunity of acquainting himself with the life of Christ and with Christian teaching either in Palestine or in Rome. Twice during Josephus' lifetime fierce persecutions broke out against the Christians. When Josephus was composing his various writings, Christianity did not exercise the same influence it had in the beginning of the 2nd century A. D., nevertheless it is highly improbable that he was ignorant of the claims of Christianity.

In *The Jewish Antiquities* there are two references to John the Baptist and James, "the Lord's brother." There is no doubt about the authenticity of the two passages referring to these individuals, who had contact with

Jesus Christ. In *The Jewish Antiquities* XVIII, 116 — 119, Josephus has described the imprisonment and murder of John the Baptist by John the Tetrarch. While the account is different from that of the Gospels, it does not necessarily contradict it but rather supplements the information of the evangelists.

In the other passage, *The Jewish Antiquities* XX.200 — 203, Ananus, the newly appointed high priest, is portrayed as bringing James, the brother of Jesus who is called Christ, before the Sanhedrin, accusing James of transgressing the Law and having him stoned to death. This action of Ananus aroused the indignation of many prominent Jewish citizens, who sent a secret message to King Agrippa, petitioning the latter to restrain the high priest from similar action in the future. Some also complained to the new procurator, Albinus, while he was on his way to Judea from Alexandria. The outcome was that Ananus was reprimanded by Albinus and deposed from office by King Agrippa.

In the XVIII book of *The Jewish Antiquities* there is a passage that refers to Christ, about which there has been much discussion. Many have rejected it as a Christian interpolation, others however, have defended its genuineness. It reads as follows:

> Now about this time lived Jesus, a wise man, if indeed he should be called a man. For he was a doer of marvelous acts, a teacher of such men as received the truth with pleasure; and he won over to himself many Jews and many also of the Greek nation. He was the Christ. And when, on the indictment of the principal men among us, Pilate had sentenced him to the cross, yet did not those who had loved him at first cease (to do so); for he appeared to them alive again on the third day; as divine prophets had declared—these and ten thousand other wonderful things—concerning him. And even now the race (or "tribe") of Christians, so named from him, is not extinct. (*Antiq.* xviii. 63f.)

Burkitt of England and Harnack of Germany have defended its authenticity. Opposed to its genuineness are Schürer, Niese, and Norden, who are convinced that Josephus' writings have come to modern times through the efforts of Christians.[7]

Notes

CHAPTER II

1. Robert & Tricot, eds. *Guide to the Bible* (Paris: Desclee & Co., 1955), II, 229–230.
2. E. J. Bickerman, "The Historical Foundations of Postbiblical Judaism," Louis Finkelstein, *The Jews. Their History, Culture, and Religion* (New York: Harper & Bros., 1949), p. 70.

CHAPTER III

1. E. R. Bury, "Alexander the Great," *Encyclopedia Britannica*, I, 571a.
2. Harold Lamb, "Alexander the Great," *The Encyclopedia Americana*, I, 370b.
3. As quoted by Dorothy Ruth Miller, *A Handbook of Ancient History in Bible Light* (New York: Fleming H. Revell Company, 1937), p. 197.
4. Lamb, pp. 370-371.

CHAPTER IV

1. Ralph Marcus, *Josephus, Jewish Antiquities, Books XII–XIV* (Cambridge: Harvard University Press, Reprinted 1957), Book xii (1.1), pp. 8–9.
2. Moses Hadas, *Aristeas to Philocrates* (New York: Harper & Brothers, 1951), pp. 98–101.
3. Dorothy Ruth Miller, *A Handbook of Ancient History in Bible Light* (New York: Fleming H. Revell Co., 1937), p. 212.

CHAPTER V

1. Conservative students hold chapter 11 of Daniel to be a prophecy, while critical scholars claim a 2nd-century Jewish author is recording historical happenings of his day.
2. Bo Reicke, *The New Testament Era. The World of the Bible from 500 B.C. to A.D. 100*. Trans. David E. Green (Philadelphia: Fortress Press, 1968), p. 51.

CHAPTER VII

1. N. Turner, "Hasmoneans." *The Interpreter's Dictionary of the Bible*. E-J, p. 530–531.
2. Ibid.

CHAPTER VIII

1. H. E. Dana, *The New Testament World*, 3d ed., rev. (Nashville: Broadmann Press, 1937), pp. 89–106.
2. "Herod," in *Dictionary of the Bible*, ed. James Hastings, rev. ed. by Frederick C. Grant and H. H. Rowley (New York: Charles Scribner's Sons, 1963), p. 379.
3. Harold H. Rowdon, "The Historical and Political Background and Chronology of the New Testament," in G. C. D. Howley, general editor. *A New Testament Commentary* (Grand Rapids: Zondervan Publishing House, 1969), pp. 57–66.

CHAPTER IX

1. Norman H. Snaith, *The Jews from Cyrus to Herod* (Nashville: Abingdon Press, 1957), p. 195.
2. A. Robert and A. Tricot, *Guide to the Bible* (Paris: Society of St. John the Evangelist, 1955), II, 288.
3. Elmer W. K. Mould, *Essentials of Bible History* (New York: The Ronald Press, 1951), p. 475.

NOTES

4. Henry Snyder Gehman, *The New Westminster Dictionary of the Bible* (Philadelphia: The Westminster Press, 1970), p. 742.
5. Ibid. p. 817.
6. As cited by Snaith, p. 197.
7. W. E. Oesterley, *The Jews and Judaism During the Greek Period* (London: S.P.C.K., 1941), pp. 240 ff.
8. Charles T. Fritsch, *The Qumran Community* (New York: The Macmillan Co., 1956), pp. 90–103.
9. Frank Moore Cross, *The Ancient Library of Qumran* (Garden City, N.Y.: Doubleday & Co., 1961), pp. 100–103.
10. H. St. J. Thackeray, *Josephus. The Jewish War*. Bks. I–III (New York: G. P. Putnam's Sons, 1927), II, 11, 381–382.
11. Merrill C. Tenney, *The New Testament. An Historical and Analytical Survey* (Grand Rapids: Wm. B. Eerdmans Pub. Co., 1953), p. 140.
12. F. F. Bruce, *Second Thoughts on the Dead Sea Scrolls* (Grand Rapids: Wm. B. Eerdmans Pub. Co., 1956).
13. Robert F. Pfeiffer, *History of New Testament Times* (New York: Harper & Bros., 1949), p. 36.

CHAPTER X

1. W. O. E. Oesterley, "Angelology and Demonology in Early Judaism," T. W. Manson, *A Companion to the Bible* (Edinburgh: T. & T. Clark, 1947), p. 340.
2. G. R. Beasley-Murray, "The Apocryphal and Apocalytic Literature," R. Davidson. (ed.) *The New Bible Commentary* (Grand Rapids: Wm. B. Eerdmans Pub. Co., 1953), p. 54.
3. Robert C. Dentan, *The Apocrypha, Bridge of the Testaments* (Greenwich: The Seabury Press, 1954), p. 107.
4. Ibid., p. 109.
5. Ibid., p. 111.
6. A. Robert and A. Tricot, *Guide to the Bible*, II, 268.
7. Beasley-Murray, pp. 55–56.
8. Ibid., p. 56.
9. As cited by W. O. E. Oesterley, *The Jews and Judaism During the Greek Period* (London: S.P.C.K., 1941), p. 131.

CHAPTER XI

1. Moses Hadas, *Aristeas to Philocrates (Letter of Aristeas)* (New York: Harper & Bros., 1951), pp. 92–227; H. St. J. Thackeray, *The Letter of Aristeas* (London: S.P.C.K., 1917), pp. 21–87. Frederick W. Danker, *Multipurpose Tools for Bible Study* (St. Louis: Concordia Publishing House, 1960), pp. 63–67.
2. W. F. Howard, "The Greek Bible," in H. Wheeler Robinson, *The Bible in Its Ancient and English Versions* (Oxford: Clarendon Press, 1940), p. 44.
3. F. F. Bruce, *The Books and the Parchments* (London: Pickering & Inglis, Ltd., 1950), pp. 146–147.
4. Robert H. Pfeiffer, *Introduction to the Old Testament* (New York: Harper & Bros., 1948), p. 114.
5. Ibid., p. 107.
6. Bleddyn J. Roberts, *The Old Testament Text and Versions* (Cardiff: University of Wales Press, 1951), p. 103.
7. John L. McKenzie, *Dictionary of the Bible* (Milwaukee: Bruce Publishing Co., 1965), p. 787.
8. Ibid., p. 787.
9. B. Wevers, "The Septuagint," *The Interpreter's Dictionary of the Bible, R–Z*, p. 276.

NOTES

10. Sidney Jellicoe, *The Septuagint and Modern Study* (Oxford: Clarendon Press, 1968), pp. 314–329; Wevers, p. 277.
11. McKenzie, p. 787.
12. Henry Snyder Gehman, *The New Westminster Dictionary of the Bible.* (Philadelphia: The Westminster Press, 1970), p. 972.
13. Menahem Mansoor, *The Dead Sea Scrolls* (Grand Rapids: Wm. B. Eerdmans, 1966), pp. 84–85; F. M. Cross, *The Ancient Library of Qumran* (Garden City, N. Y.: Doubleday & Co., 1961), pp. 163–194.
14. J. de Fraine, "Septuagint." Louis F. Hartman, *Encyclopedic Dictionary of the Bible* (New York: McGraw-Hill Book Co., 1963), p. 2169.
15. Sir Frederick Kenyon, *The Text of the Greek Bible* (London: Duckworth. 1949), pp. 29–30.
16. Harry M. Orlinsky, "Current Progress and Problems in Septuagint Research," Harold R. Willoughby (ed.), *The Study of the Bible Today and Tomorrow* (Chicago: The University of Chicago Press, 1947), p. 152.
17. Roberts, at the request of Paul Kahle, made this appraisal, cf. Paul Kahle, "Der gegenwärtige Stand der Erforschung der in Palästina Neugefundenen Handschriften." *Theologische Literaturzeitung*, 79, cols. 81–94, 1954.
18. D. Barthelmy, "redecouverte d'un Chainon Manquant de L'Histoire Septant," *Revue Biblique*, 60:18–29, 1953.
19. Wevers, p. 277.

CHAPTER XII

1. Robert G. Boling, "Twenty Years of Discovery," in *New Directions in Biblical Archaeology*, ed. David Noel Freedman and Jonas C. Greenfield (Garden City, Y. Y.: Doubleday & Co., Inc., 1969), pp. 81–88.
2. Frank M. Cross, "Dead Sea Scrolls," *Encyclopedia Britannica*, (1971 ed.) VII, 117–120.
3. Frank Moore Cross, "Papyri of the Fourth Century B. C. from Daliyeh," in *New Directions in Biblical Archaeology*, pp. 45–69.
4. ——, "The Oldest Manuscripts from Qumran," *Jour. of Biblical Literature*, 74:164, September 1955.
5. J. A. Fitzmeyer, "Dead Sea Scrolls," *The New Catholic Encyclopedia*, IV, 678, 680.
6. Cf. the discussion in Menahem Mansoor, *The Dead Sea Scrolls* (Grand Rapids: Wm. B. Eerdmans Pub. Co., 1966), pp. 137–142.
7. Merrill Unger, "Manuscripts, Dead Sea," *Unger's Bible Dictionary* (Chicago: Moody Press, 1958), p. 693.
8. John Marco Allegro, *The Dead Sea Scrolls* (Baltimore: Penguin Books, 1956), p. 102.
9. Ibid., p. 105.
10. Ibid., p. 106.
11. J. T. Milik, *Ten Years of Discovery in the Wilderness of Judea* (Naperville, Ill.: Alec R. Allenson, Inc., 1959), p. 38.
12. W. H. Brownlee, "A Comparison of the Covenanters' Dead Sea Scrolls with Pre-Christian Jewish Sects," *Biblical Archaeologist*, (1950). XIII, 50–52.
13. Milik, p. 38.
14. Edward Blair, "The Dead Sea Scrolls," *The Interpreter's One Volume Commentary on the Bible*, ed. Charles M. Laymon (Nashville and New York: Abingdon Press, 1971), pp. 1066–1067.
15. Milik, p. 39.
16. Menahem Mansoor, *The Thanksgiving Hymns* (Grand Rapids: Wm. B. Eerdmans, 1961), pp. 99–104.
17. Theodore H. Gaster, *The Dead Sea Scrolls in English Translation* (New York: Garden City: Doubleday & Co., Inc., 1956). p. 111.
18. Ibid., p. 112.

NOTES

19. Cf. Joseph Augustine Fitzmeyer, *The Genesis Apocryphon of Qumran Cave I; A Commentary* (Rome: Pontifical Biblical Institute, 1966).
20. Cf. John Marco Allegro, *The Treasure of the Copper Scroll* (Garden City, New York: Doubleday & Co., Inc., 1960), 191 pp.
21. Frank M. Cross, *The Ancient Library of Qumran and Modern Biblical Studies* (New York: Doubleday Doran, 1961), p. 21.
22. Mansoor, pp. 88–97.
23. Ibid., pp. 88–94.
24. Yigael Yadin, "The Temple Scroll," in *New Directions in Biblical Archaeology*, pp. 139–148.
25. Ibid., p. 143.
26. Cross, "The Dead Sea Scrolls," *The Encyclopedia Britannica* (1971 ed.), VII, 118.
27. Cf. Mansoor, pp. 164–193.

CHAPTER XIII

1. F. W. Filson, *Which Books Belong in the Bible?* (Philadelphia: The Westminster Press, 1957), pp. 73–100.
2. F. F. Bruce, *The Books and the Parchment* (Westwood, New Jersey: Fleming H. Revell and Co., 1955), p. 157.
3. Edgar J. Goodspeed, *The Story of the Apocrypha* (Chicago: The University of Chicago Press, 1939), p. 11.
4. Merrill F. Unger, *Introductory Guide to the Old Testament* (Grand Rapids: Zondervan Pub. House, 1951), p. 96.

CHAPTER XIV

1. A. Robert and A. Tricot, *Guide to the Bible. An Introduction to the Study of Holy Scriptures* (Rome: Society of St. John the Evangelist, 1951), I, 123.
2. W. O. E. Oesterley, "The Apocrypha and Pseudepigrapha," in T. W. Manson, *A Companion to the Bible* (Edinburgh: T. & T. Clark, 1947), p. 81.
3. Robert Dentan, *The Apocrypha, the Bridge of the Testaments* (Greenwich, Conn.: The Seabury Press, 1954), p. 44.
4. Bruce M. Metzger, *An Introduction to the Apocrypha* (New York: Oxford University Press, 1957), pp. 11–12.
5. Meyer Waxman, *A History of Jewish Literature*, (New York: Bloch Publishing Co., 1930), I, 41.
6. Oesterley, *An Introduction to the Books of the Apocrypha*, p. 155–156.
7. Waxman, p. 39.
8. Ibid., p. 41.
9. G. H. Box, "IV Ezra," R. H. Charles, *The Apocrypha and Pseudepigrapha of the Old Testament* (Oxford: At the Clarendon Press, 1913), II, 552.
10. W. O. E. Oesterley, *An Introduction to the Books of the Apocrypha* (London: S.P.C.K., 1953), pp. 179–180.
11. Bruce M. Metzger, *An Introduction to the Apocrypha* (New York: Oxford University Press, 1957), p. 31.
12. W. K. Lowther Clarke, *Concise Bible Commentary* (New York: The Macmillan Co., 1953), p. 640.
13. Meyer Waxman, *A History of Jewish Literature* (New York: Bloch Pub. Co., 1930), I, 13.
14. Clarke, *Concise Bible Dictionary*, p. 645.
15. Goodspeed, *Story of the Apocrypha*, p. 63.
16. Waxman, *History of Jewish Literature*, I, 16.
17. Ibid., p. 17.
18. Otto Eissfeldt, *Einleitung in das Alte Testament unter Einschluss der Apokryphen und Pseudepigraphen* (Tübingen: Verlag J. C. B. Mohr, 1956), p. 739.

19. Meyer Waxman, I, 22.
20. Frederick L. Moriarity, *Foreword to Old Testament Books* (Weston, Mass.: Weston College Press, 1934), p. 103.
21. Edgar J. Goodspeed, *The Story of the Apocrypha* (Chicago: The University of Chicago Press, 1939), p. 101.
22. Bruce M. Metzger, *An Introduction to the Apocrypha*, p. 107.
23. Charles Cutler Torrey, *The Apocryphal Literature* (New Haven: Yale University Press, 1945), p. 56.
24. W. K. Lowther Clarke, *Concise Bible Commentary*, p. 661.
25. Ibid., p. 661.
26. Greek text in Pitca, *Analecta sacra;* quoted in R. H. Charles, *The Apocrypha and Pseudepigrapha of the Old Testament: I Apocrypha* (Oxford: Clarendon Press, 1971), 645.
27. Metzger, *An Introduction to the Apocrypha*, p. 115.
28. Edgar J. Goodspeed, *The Story of the Apocrypha* (Chicago: The University of Chicago Press, 1939), p. 74.
29. W. O. E. Oesterley, *An Introduction to the Books of the Apocrypha* (London: S.P.C.K., 1953), p. 292.
30. Torrey, *The Apocryphal Literature*, p. 69.
31. Metzger, p. 125.
32. W. O. E. Oesterley, *The Books of the Apocrypha* (New York: Fleming H. Revell Company, 1914), p. 412.
33. Waxman, *A History of Jewish Literature*, I, 10.
34. Goodspeed, *The Story of the Apocrypha*, p. 79.
35. Ibid., p. 81.
36. Cf. Clarke, p. 679.
37. Ibid., p. 678.
38. L. H. Brockington, *A Critical Introduction to the Apocrypha* (London: Gerald Duckworth & Co., Ltd. 1961), p. 118.
39. Paul Heinisch, *Theology of the Old Testament*. English ed. by Rev. William Heidt (Collegeville, Minn., 1950), p. 266.

CHAPTER XV

1. H. S. Miller, *General Biblical Introduction* (Houghton, New York: The World-Bearer Press, 1944), p. 120.
2. R. H. Charles, *The Book of Enoch* (London: SPCK, 1952), pp. ix, x.
3. R. H. Charles, *The Apocrypha and Pseudepigrapha of the Old Testament* (Oxford: at the Clarendon Press, 1913), II, v.
4. Torrey, *Apocryphal Literature*, pp. 135 – 145.
5. Waxman, *A History of Jewish Literature*, p. 27.
6. Henry Snyder Gehman, ed., *The New Westminster Dictionary of the Bible* (Philadelphia: The Westminster Press, 1970), p. 776.

CHAPTER XVI

1. Pfeiffer, "The Literature and Religion of the Pseudepigrapha," p. 421.
2. R. H. Charles, *Religious Development between the Old and New Testaments* (London: Oxford University Press, rpt. 1956), p. 228.
3. J. E. H. Thomson, "Apocalyptic Literature," *International Standard Bible Encyclopedia*, I, 176b.
4. R. H. Charles, *Religious Development between the Old and New Testaments* (London: Oxford University Press, 1956), p. 230.
5. E. Littmann, "Das Buch der Jubiläen," *Die Apokryphen und Pseudepigraphen des Alten Testaments* (Tübingen: Verlag von J. C. B. Mohr, 1900), II, 37.
6. J. E. H. Thomson, "Apocalytic Literature," *International Standard Bible*

Encyclopedia (Grand Rapids: Wm. B. Erdmans Pub. Co., 1939), I, 173b.

7. Robert H. Pfeiffer, "The Literature and Religion of the Pseudepigrapha," *The Interpreter's Bible* (Nashville: Abingdon-Cokesbury Press, 1952), I, 422b.

8. Charles Cutler Torrey, *The Apocryphal Literature* (New Haven: Yale University Press, 1944), pp. 127–129.

9. William John Ferrar, *The Uncanonical Jewish Books* (London: SPCK, 1925), p. 66.

10. Pfeiffer, *Interpreter's Bible*, I, 424.

11. Charles, *The Apocrypha and Pseudepigrapha of the Old Testament*, II, 158.

12. Charles C. Torrey, *The Lives of the Prophets* (Journal of Biblical Literature, Monograph Series, Vol. I; (Philadelphia: Society of Biblical Literature and Exegesis, 1946.)

13. ——, *The Apocryphal Literature: A Brief Introduction* (New Haven, Yale Univ. Press, 1945), p. 139.

14. Ibid., p. 139.

15. Thomson, . . . *Bible Encyclopedia*, p. 177b.

16. Torrey, p. 143.

17. Robert H. Pfeiffer, *History of New Testament Times* (New York: Harper & Bros., Publishers, 1949), p. 70.

18. M. R. James, *Apocrypha Anecdota*, 2nd Series (Cambridge: at the University Press, 1897), pp. lxxii–cii. as cited by Torrey, p. 141.

19. Torrey, *The Apocryphal Literature*, p. 131.

20. R. Pfeiffer, *Interpreter's Bible*, p. 426.

21. Torrey, *Apocryphal Literature*, p. 116.

22. R. Pfeiffer, *Interpreter's Bible*, p. 431.

23. Aage Bentzen, *Introduction to the Old Testament* (Copenhagen: G. E. C. Gads Forlag, 1948), II, 248.

24. Thomson, . . . *Bible Encyclopedia*, p. 168a, b.

25. R. H. Charles, *The Book of Enoch* (London: SPCK, 1952), pp. 31, 56, 95, 129. Cf. also pp. xix–xxviii.

26. H. H. Rowley, *The Relevance of Apocalyptic*, p. 54.

27. Torrey, *Apocryphal Literature*, p. 110.

28. Pfeiffer, "The Religion and Literature of the Pseudepigrapha," *Interpreter's Bible*, I, 426.

29. *Psalmoi Solomontos: Psalms of the Pharisees, Commonly Called the Psalms of Solomon* (Cambridge: Cambridge University Press, 1891). (Noted in Pfeiffer, p. 426.)

29a. Pfeiffer, *Interpreter's Bible*, I, 426.

30. Ibid., p. 427.

30a. Ibid., p. 426.

31. Ibid., pp. 433–434.

32. Waxman, Meyer, *A History of Jewish Literature from the Close of the Bible to Our Own Days* (New York: Bloch Pub. Co., 1938), I, 11.

33. Ferrar, p. 20.

34. Moses Hadas, *The Third and Fourth Book of the Maccabees* (New York: Harper & Bros., 1953), p. 3.

35. Torrey, *The Apocryphal Literature*, p. 82.

36. Otto Eissfeldt, *Einleitung in das Alte Testament.* 3., neubearbeitete Auflage (Tübingen: Verlag J. C. B. Mohr, 1964), p. 721.

37. Waxman, p. 25.

38. Ferrar, p. 102.

39. Torrey, p. 104.

40. R. H. Charles, *Religious Development Between the Old and New Testaments*, p. 219.

41. Pfeiffer, *The Interpreter's Bible*, I, 432.

42. Bleddyn J. Roberts, *The Old Testament Text and Versions* (Cardiff: University of Wales Press, 1951), p. 102.
43. H. G. Meecham, *The Oldest Version of the Bible: Aristeas on its Traditional Origin* (London: Holborn Publishing House, 1932.)
44. Moses Hadas, *Aristeas to Philocrates (Letter to Aristeas)* (New York: Harper & Bros., 1951), p. 18.
45. As given by Ferrar, p. 57.
46. R. H. Charles, *Religious Development between the Old and New Testaments* (London: Oxford University Press, 1956), p. 227.
47. Bentzen, p. 237.

CHAPTER XVII

1. R. M. Wenley, "Philo, Judaeus," *The International Standard Bible Encyclopedia*, IV, 2380a.
2. Peter Katz, "Philo of Alexandria," Lefferts A. Loetscher (editor), *Twentieth Century Encyclopedia of Religious Knowledge*, II, 877.
3. George Foot Moore, *Judaism in the First Centuries of the Christian Era, The Age of the Tannaim* (Cambridge: Harvard University Press, 1954; Schocken 1971), I, 211−212.
4. Wenley, p. 2381a.
5. Alfred Edersheim, *The Life and Times of Jesus the Messiah* (Grand Rapids: Wm. B. Eerdmans Pub. Co., 1936), I, 41.
6. Katz, p. 877.
7. Alfred Martin Rehwinkel, *New Testament World* (St. Louis: Concordia Mimeo Company, 3rd revised ed., no date), p. 162.
8. Norman Bentwich, *Philo-Judaeus of Alexandria* (Philadelphia: The Jewish Publication Soc. of America, 1910), pp. 165−166.
9. Wenley, p. 2382.
10. Ch. Guignebert, *The Jewish World in the Time of Jesus* (New York: E. P. Dutton & Co., 1939), p. 226.
11. Ibid., p. 227.
12. Ibid., p. 227.
13. Frank H. Marshall, *The Religious Background of Early Christianity*, (St. Louis: The Bethany Press, 1931), p. 112.
14. Ibid., p. 112.

CHAPTER XVIII

1. Ralph Marcus, "Hellenistic Jewish Literature," *The Jewish People: Past and Present* (New York: Jewish Encyclopedic Handbook, 1952), III, 45.
2. H. St. John Thackeray, "Josephus," in A. Cohen, ed., *Judaism and the Beginnings of Christianity* (New York: Bloch Pub. Co., 1924), p. 178.
3. H. St. John Thackeray, *Josephus, the Man and the Historian* (New York: Jewish Institute of Religion Press, 1929). Cf. chap. 3, pp. 51−74.
4. Thackeray, "Josephus," in *Judaism* etc., pp. 187−188.
5. Ibid., pp. 190−191.
6. Ibid., pp. 191−192.
7. Cf. also Joseph Klausner, *Jesus of Nazareth, His Life, Times, and Teaching*, trans. Herbert Danby (New York: The Macmillan Co., 1929), pp. 55−59.

Selected Bibliography

CHAPTER I

Bickerman, *From Ezra to the Last of the Maccabees*. New York: Schocken Books, 1962.

Bruce, F. F. "Between the Testaments." *The New Bible Commentary: Revised*. Ed. D. Guthrie and J. A. Motyer. Grand Rapids: Wm. B. Eerdmans Pub. Co., 1970. Pp. 59 – 63.

Charles, R. H. *Religious Developments Between the Old and New Testaments*. New York: Oxford University Press, 1919.

Grant, Frederick C. "The World into Which Christianity Came." *The Bible Companion*, ed. William Neil. New York, Toronto, London: McGraw-Hill Book Co., Inc., 1961. Pp. 73 – 94.

Mantey, Julius Robert. "New Testament Backgrounds." *The Biblical Expositor*, ed. Carl F. Henry. Philadelphia: A. J. Holman Company, 1960. III, 3 – 14.

Peters, F. E. *The Harvest of Hellenism*. A History of the Near East from Alexander the Great to the Triumph of Christianity. New York: Simon and Shuster, 1970. 800 pp.

Russell, D. S. *Between the Testaments*. Philadelphia: Fortress Press, 1960.

Schalit, Abraham, ed. *The Hellenistic Age*. New Brunswick: Rutgers University Press, 1972.

Sloan, W. W. *A Survey Between the Testaments*. Paterson, N. J.: Littlefield Adams & Co., 1954.

Wallace, David H. "Between the Testaments." *The Holy Bible. Revised Standard Version*. Verse Reference Edition. Philadelphia: A. J. Holman Company, 1962. Pp. 1207 – 1213.

CHAPTER II

Ackroyd, Peter R. *Israel under Babylon and Persia*. New York: Oxford University Press, 1970. Pp. 162 – 292.

Daniel-Rops, Henry. *Sacred History*. Trans. K. Madge. New York: Longmans, Green and Co., 1949. Pp. 241 – 276.

Driver, G. R. *Aramaic Documents from the Fifth Century*. Oxford: At the Clarendon Press, 1957. 106 pp.

Förster, Werner. *Palestinian Judaism in New Testament Times*. Trans. by Gordon E. Harris. Edinburgh and London: Oliver and Boyd, 1964. Pp. 11 – 21.

Gordon, Cyrus H. *Introduction to the Old Testament*. Ventnor, N. J.: Ventnor Publishers, Inc., 1953. Pp. 257 – 268.

Harrison, R. K. *A History of the Old Testament*. Grand Rapids: Zondervan Pub. House, 1957. Pp. 225 – 235.

Heinisch, Paul. *History of the Old Testament*. Trans. William Heidt. Collegeville, Minn.: St. John's Abbey Press, 1952. Pp. 308 – 353.

Margolis, Max L., and Marx, Alexander. *A History of the Jewish People*. Philadelphia: The Jewish Publication Society of America, 1927. Pp. 119 – 133.

Moore, George Foot. *Judaism*. Cambridge, Mass.: Harvard University Press, 1927. I, 3 – 36.

BIBLIOGRAPHY

Mould, Elmer W. K. *Essentials of Bible History*. Rev. ed. New York: The Ronald Press, 1951. Pp. 345 – 372.

Myers, J. M. *The World of Restoration*. Englewood Cliffs, N. J.: Prentice Hall, 1968. 182 pp.

Noth, Martin. *The History of Israel*. New York: Harper & Bros., 1958. Pp. 299 – 343.

Oesterley, W. O. E. *A History of Israel*. Oxford: At the Clarendon Press, 1932. II, 33 – 172.

Olmstead, A. T. *History of the Persian Empire*. Chicago: The University of Chicago Press, 1948. Pp. 343 – 479.

Price, I. M. and Sellers, O. R., and Carlson, E. L. *The Monuments and the Old Testament*. Philadelphia: The Judson Press, 1958. Pp. 313 – 343.

Robinson, H. Wheeler. *The History of Israel*. London: Duckworth, 1938. Pp. 143 – 165.

Rogers, Robert William. *A History of Persia*. New York: Charles Scribner's Sons, 1929. Pp. 35 – 260.

Snaith, Norman H. *The Jews from Cyrus to Herod*. Nashville: Abingdon Press, (no date). Pp. 7 – 20.

Willett, Herbert L. *The Jews Through the Centuries*. Chicago: Willett, Clark and Co., 1932. Pp. 132 – 165.

CHAPTER III

Albright, William Foxwell. *From the Stone Age to Christianity*. Garden City, New York: Doubleday and Co., 1957. Pp. 334 – 379.

Bevan, Edwyn Robert. "Alexander III Known as the Great," *Encyclopedia Britannica*. Chicago: Encyclopedia Britannica, Inc., 1957. I, 561 – 571.

Bickerman, Elias J. "The Historical Foundations of Postbiblical Judaism." In Finkelstein, Louis, (ed.) *The Jews, Their History, Culture, and Religion*. New York: Harper & Bros. Publishers, 1949. I, 86 – 114.

Botsford, G. W. and Robinson, C. A. *Hellenic History*. New York: The Macmillan Co., 1956. Pp. 287 – 341.

Curtius, Rufus Quintus. *History of Alexander*. Trans. by J. C. Rolfe, Cambridge, Mass.: Harvard University Press, 1946. 2 vols.

Davis, W. Hersey and MaDowell, Edward A. *A Source of Interbiblical History*. Nashville: Broadman Press, 1948. Pp. 3 – 10.

Heinisch, Paul. *History of the Old Testament*. Trans. William Heidt. Collegeville, Minn.: St. John's Abbey, 1952. Pp. 354 – 359.

Laistner, G. A. *History of the Greek World from 479 to 323 B. C.* London: Methuen & Co., 1947. Pp. 291 – 327.

Lamb, Harold. "Alexander the Great." *The Encyclopedia Americana*. New York: Americana Corporation, 1957. I, 367 – 371.

Matthews, Shailer. *New Testament Times in Palestine*. New York: The Macmillan Co., 1933. Pp. 3 – 38.

Miller, Dorothy Ruth. *A Handbook of Ancient History in the Light of the Bible*. New York: Fleming H. Revell Co., 1937. Pp. 186 – 199.

BIBLIOGRAPHY

Oesterley, W. O. E. *The Jews and Judaism During the Greek Period*. London: SPCK, 1941. Pp. 1–11.

———. *A History of Israel*. Oxford: At the Clarendon Press, 1932. II, 175–187.

Olmstead, A. T. *History of the Persian Empire*. Chicago: The University of Chicago Press, 1948. Pp. 486–524.

Pfeiffer, Charles F. *Between the Testaments*. Grand Rapids: Baker Book House, 1959. Pp. 67–70.

Reicke, Bo. *The New Testament Era*. Trans. David E. Green. Philadelphia: Fortress Press, 1968. Pp. 35–41.

Ricciotti, Giuseppe. *The History of Israel*. Trans. C. D. Penta and R. T. H. Murphy. Milwaukee: Bruce Publishing Co., 1958. 2nd ed. II, 206–235.

Robinson, Charles A. *Alexander the Great: the Meeting of East and West in World Government and Brotherhood*. New York: E. P. Dutton and Co. 1953 (?). 252 pp.

Rogers, Robert William. *A History of Persia*. New York: Charles Scribner's Sons, 1929. Pp. 261–376.

Savill, Agnes. *Alexander the Great and His Times*. New York: The Citadel Press, 1955. 300 pp.

Tarn, W. W. "The New Hellenistic Kingdoms." In *The Cambridge Ancient History*. New York: The Macmillan Co., 1928. VII, pp. 75–108.

———. *The Greeks in Bactria and India*. New York: The Macmillan Co., 1938.

Taylor, Lily Ross. *The Divinity of the Roman Emperor*. Middletown, Conn.: American Philosophical Assn., 1931. Pp. 1–35.

Tcherikover, V. "The Hellenistic Environment." In Schalit, Abraham, *The Hellenistic Age*. New Brunswick: Rutgers University Press, 1972. Pp. 5–114.

CHAPTER IV

Bailey, Albert E., and Foster, Charles E. *History of the Hebrew Commonwealth*. New York: Charles Scribner's Sons, 1920.

Bevan, Edwyn. *Jerusalem Under the High-Priests*. London: Edward Arnold, Ltd., 1958 printing. Pp. 21–27; 45–48.

Box, C. H. *Judaism in the Greek Period*. London: Oxford University Press, 1932.

Daniel-Rops. *Sacred History*. Trans. K. Madge. New York: Longmans, Green, and Co., 1949. Pp. 333–343.

Hadas, Moses. *Aristeas to Philocrates*. New York: Harper & Bros., 1951. Pp. 98–101.

Heinisch, Paul. *History of the Old Testament*. Trans. William Heidt. Collegeville, Minn.: St. John's Abbey Press, 1952. Pp. 357–363.

Marcus, Ralph, ed., *Josephus. Jewish Antiquities*, Bk. XII. Cambridge: Harvard U. Press, 1943. rpt. 1957. Pp. 8–9.

Miller, Dorothy Ruth. *A Handbook of Ancient History*. New York: Fleming H. Revell and Co., 1937. Pp. 209–219.

Oesterley, W. O. E. *A History of Israel*. Oxford: At the Clarendon Press, 1951. II, 189–201.

Pfeiffer, Charles F. *Between the Testaments*. Grand Rapids: Baker Book House, 1959. Pp. 71-76.

BIBLIOGRAPHY

Radin, Max, *The Jews among the Greeks and Romans*. Philadelphia: The Jewish Publication Soc. of America, 1915. Pp. 90–117.

Reicke, Bo. *The New Testament Era. The World of the Bible from 500 B. C. to A. D. 100*. Trans. David Green. Philadelphia: Fortress Press, 1968. Pp. 41–48.

Robinson, H. Wheeler. *The History of Israel*. London: Duckworth, 1938. Pp. 166–173.

Rostovzeff, M. "Ptolemaic Egypt." In *Cambridge Ancient History*. New York: The Macmillan Co., 1928. VII, 109–154.

Snaith, Norman H. *The Jews from Cyrus to Herod*. New York: The Abingdon Press, 1956. Pp. 25–30.

Tarn, W. W. "The Hellenistic Kingdoms." *The Cambridge Ancient History*. VII, 75–108.

Thompson, J. A. *Archaeology and the Pre-Christian Centuries*. Grand Rapids: Wm. B. Eerdmans Pub. Co., 1958. Pp. 80–99.

CHAPTER V

Albright, William Foxwell. *From the Stone Age to Christianity*. Baltimore: Johns Hopkins Press, 1940. Pp. 256–275.

Bentwich, Norman. *Hellenism*. Philadelphia: The Jewish Publication Soc. of America, 1919. 386 pp.

Bevan, E. R. *The House of Seleucus*. London: Arnold, 1902. Vol. 1, 300 pp. Vol. II, 332 pp.

Bickermann, Elias. *From Ezra to the Last of the Maccabees*. New York: Schocken Books, 1962. Pp. 93–112.

Förster, Werner. *Palestinian Judaism in New Testament Times*. Trans. George E. Harris. Edinburgh & London: Oliver and Boyd, 1964. Pp. 31–37.

Heinisch, Paul. *History of the Old Testament*. Trans. William Heidt. Collegeville, Minn.: St. John's Abbey, 1950. Pp. 357–362.

Iliffre, J. H. "Seleucidae." *Chamber's Encyclopedia*. XII, 405–406.

Joughet, P. *Macedonian Imperialism and the Hellenization of the East*. New York: Alfred Knopf, 1928.

Margolis, Max L., and Marx, Alexander. *A History of the Jewish People*. Philadelphia: The Jewish Publication Soc. of America, 1927. Pp. 134–141.

Oesterley, O. W. E. *History of Israel*. Oxford: at the Clarendon Press, 1951. II, 202–214.

Peters, F. E. *The Harvest of Hellenism*. New York: Simon and Schuster, 1970. Pp. 220–260.

Pfeiffer, C. H. *Between the Testaments*. Grand Rapids: Baker Book House, 1959. Pp. 77–82.

Reicke, Bo. *The New Testament Era. The World of the Bible from 500 B. C. to A. D. 100*. Trans. David E. Greene. Philadelphia: Fortress Press, 1968. Pp. 49–57.

Ricciotti, Guiseppe. *The History of Israel. From the Exile to A. D. 135*. Trans. Penta, C. D., and Murphy, R. T. A. 2nd ed., Milwaukee: Bruce Pub. House, 1958. II. 37–52.

Schürer, Emil. *A History of the Jewish People in the Time of Jesus Christ*. Edinburgh: T. & T. Clark, 1890. First Division, I. 117–186.

BIBLIOGRAPHY

Snaith, Norman H. *The Jews from Cyrus to Herod.* New York: Abingdon Press, (no date). Pp. 31 – 44.

Tcherikover, Victor. *Hellenistic Civilization and the Jews.* Philadelphia: The Jewish Publication Soc., 1959. 566 pp.

Turner, M. "Seleucus." *The Interpreter's Dictionary of the Bible,* R-Z. Pp. 266 – 267.

——. "Antiochus." *The Interpreter's Dictionary of the Bible,* A-D. Pp. 149 – 152. 152.

CHAPTER VI

Baron. Salo Wittmayer. *A Social and Religious History of the Jews.* 2nd rev. ed. New York: Columbia University Press, 1952. Vol. I., Part 1.

Baron, Salo W. and Blau, Joseph L. *Judaism, Postbiblical and Talmudic.* New York: The Liberal Arts Press, 1954. Pp. 3 – 14.

Bevan, Edwyn. *Jerusalem under the High Priests.* London: Edward Arnold, 1958 printing. Pp. 69 – 99.

Bickerman, Elias. *From Ezra to the Last of the Maccabees.* New York: Shocken Books, 1962. Pp. 112 – 135.

Davis, W. Hersey and McDowell, Edward A. *A Source Book for Interbiblical History.* Nashville: The Broadman Press, 1948. Pp. 43 – 216.

Harrison, R. K. *A History of Old Testament Times.* Grand Rapids: Zondervan Pub. House, 1957. Pp. 237 – 251.

——. *Old Testament Times.* Grand Rapids: Wm. B. Eerdmans Pub. Co., 1970. Pp. 309 – 333.

Heinisch, Paul. *History of the Old Testament.* Trans. William Heidt. Collegeville. Minn.: St. John's Abbey, 1952. Pp. 363 – 369.

Hutchison, J. "Maccabaeus, Maccabees." In *The International Standard Bible Encyclopedia.* Grand Rapids: Wm. B. Eerdmans Pub. Co., 1939. III, 1946a – 1947b.

Margolis, M. L. and Marx, Alexander. *A History of the Jewish People.* Philadelphia: The Jewish Publication Soc. of America, 1927. Pp. 142 – 149.

Orlinsky, H. M. "Maccabees, Maccabean Revolt." *The Interpreter's Dictionary of the Bible,* K-Q. Pp. 197 – 201.

Pfeiffer, Charles F. *Between the Testaments.* Grand Rapids: Baker Book House, 1959. Pp. 91 – 95.

Radin, Max. *The Jews among the Romans.* Philadelphia: The Jewish Publication Soc. of America, 1915. Pp. 118 – 190.

Reicke, Bo. *The New Testament Era. The World of the Bible from 500 B. C. to A. D. 100.* Trans. David E. Green. Philadelphia: Fortress Press, 1968. Pp. 63 – 76.

Ricciotti, Giuseppe. *The History of Israel.* Trans. by Penta, C. D., and Murphy, R.T.A. 2nd ed. Milwaukee: Bruce Pub. House, 1958. II, 236 – 279.

Riggs, James Stevenson. "The Maccabees." In *Funk and Wagnall's New "Standard" Bible Dictionary.* New York: Funk and Wagnalls Co., 1936. Pp. 531 – 532.

Schürer, Emil. *A History of the Jewish People in the Time of Jesus Christ.* Edinburgh: T. & T. Clark, 1890. First Division. I, 219 – 272.

BIBLIOGRAPHY

Snaith, Norman. *The Jews from Cyrus to Herod.* New York and Nashville: Abingdon Press, no date. Pp. 31–44.

CHAPTER VII

Baron, Salo, W. *A Social and Religious History of the Jews.* New York: Columbia University Press, 1952. I, 212–233.

Bevan, Edwyn. *Jerusalem Under the High Priests.* London: Edward Arnold, 1958 Printing. Pp. 100–131.

Cornfeld, Galyahu, et al. *Pictorial Biblical Encyclopedia.* New York: The Macmillan Co., 1964. Pp. 370–377.

Dosker, Henry E. "Asmoneans." In *The International Standard Bible Encyclopedia.* I, 283a–286b.

Farmer, W. R. *Maccabees: Zealots and Josephus.* New York: Columbia University Press, 1956. 239 pp.

Förster, Werner. *Palestinian Judaism in New Testament Times.* Trans. Gordon E. Harris. Edinburgh and London: Oliver and Boyd, 1964. Pp. 68–81.

Goldin, Judah. "The Period of the Talmud." In Finkelstein, Louis, ed. *The Jews, Their History, Culture, and Religion.* New York: Harper & Bros., 1949. I, 119–127.

Heinisch, Paul. *History of the Old Testament.* Trans. William Heidt. Collegeville, Minn.: St. John's Abbey. 1952. Pp. 369–374.

Margolis, M. L. and Marx, Alexander. *A History of the Jewish People.* Philadelphia: The Jewish Publication Soc. of America, 1927. Pp. 150–168.

Oesterley, W. O. E. *A History of Israel.* Oxford: At the Clarendon Press, 1932. II, 273–303.

——. *The Jews and Judaism During the Greek Period.* London: S.P.C.K., 1941. Pp. 26–36.

Pfeiffer, Charles F. *Between the Testaments.* Grand Rapids: Baker Book House, Grand Rapids: Baker Book House, 1959. Pp. 97–102.

Reicke, Bo. *The New Testament Era. The World of the Bible from 500 B. C. to A. D. 100.* Trans. David E. Green. Philadelphia: Fortress Press, 1968. Pp. 67–73.

Ricciotti, Giuseppe. *The History of Israel.* Trans. Penta, C. D., and Murphy, R. T. A. 2nd ed. Milwaukee: Bruce Pub. House, 1958. II, 280–303.

Schürer, Emil. *A History of the Jewish People in the Times of Jesus Christ.* Edinburgh: T. & T. Clark, 1890. I, 212–399.

Turner, N. "Hasmoneans." *The Interpreter's Dictionary of the Bible.* E-J. Pp. 529–535.

CHAPTER VIII

Balsdon, J.P.V.D. "The Roman Empire in the First Century." *Peak's Commentary of the Bible.* Pp. 699–704.

Baron, Salo W. *A Social and Religious History of the Jewish People.* New York: Columbia University Press, 1952. I, 238–285.

Corbishley, T. "The History of Israel (130 B. C.–A. D. 70)." *A Catholic Commentary on Holy Scriptures.* Thomas Nelson & Sons, 1953. Pp. 96–102.

Davis. W. Hersey and McDowell, Edward A. *A Source Book for Interbiblical History.* Nashville: The Broadman Press, 1948. Pp. 217–612.

BIBLIOGRAPHY

Förster, Werner. *Palestinian Judaism in New Testament Times.* Trans. Gordon E. Harris. Edinburgh and London: Oliver and Boyd, 1964. Pp. 92 – 105.

Grant, Michael. *The Jews in the Roman World.* New York: Charles Scribner's Sons, 1973. Pp. 1 – 260.

Hadas, Moses. *Hellenism.* New York: Columbia University Press, 1959.

Heinisch, Paul. *History of the Old Testament.* Trans. William Heidt. Collegeville, Minn.: St. John's Abbey, 1952. Pp. 375 – 383.

Hoehner, Harold. *Herod Antipas.* Cambridge: At the University Press, 1972. 437 pp.

Jones, A. H. M. *The Herods of Judea.* Oxford: At the Clarendon Press, 1938. 271 pp.

Oesterley, W. O. E. *A History of Israel.* Oxford: At the Clarendon Press, 1932. II, 400 – 407.

Perowne, Stewart *The Life and Times of Herod the Great.* London: Hodder and Stoughton, 1957. 186 pp.

——. *The Later Herods.* Nashville: Abingdon Press, 1959. 232 pp.

Pfeiffer, Charles F. *Between the Testaments.* Grand Rapids: Baker Book House, 1959. Pp. 103 – 110.

Radin, Max. *The Jews Among the Greeks and Romans.* Philadelphia: The Jewish Publication Soc. of America, 1915. Pp. 210 – 327.

Reicke, Bo. *The New Testament Era. The World of the Bible from 500 B. C. to A. D. 100.* Translated by David E. Green. Philadelphia: Fortress Press, 1968. Pp. 77 – 107.

Ricciotti, Giuseppe. *The History of Israel.* Trans. Penta, C.D. and Murphy, R. T. A. 2nd ed. Milwaukee: Bruce Pub. House, 1958. II, 304 – 320; 366 – 401.

Sandmel, Samuel. *The First Christian Century in Judaism and Christianity. Certainties and Uncertainties.* New York: Oxford University Press, 1969.

Schürer, Emil. *A History of the Jewish People in the Times of Jesus Christ.* Edinburgh: T. & T. Clark, 1890. Vol. II, Division I, 1 – 248.

Thompson, J. A. *Archaeology and the Pre-Christian Centuries.* Grand Rapids: Wm. B. Eerdmans Pub. Co., 1958. Pp. 95 – 133.

CHAPTER IX

Baron, Salo. W. and Blau, Joseph L. *Judaism Postbiblical and Talmudic Period.* New York: Liberal Arts Press, 1954. Pp. 72 – 100.

Black, M. "The Development of Judaism in the Greek and Roman Periods." *Peake's Commentary on the Bible.* Pp. 693 – 698. Rev. by Matthew Black and H. H. Rowley, New York, Edinburgh, London: Thomas Nelson and Sons, Ltd., 1962.

Cross, Frank Moore. *The Ancient Library of Qumran.* Garden City, New York: Doubleday & Co., Inc., 1961.

Guignebert, C. *The Jewish World in the Time of Jesus.* Trans. S. H. Hooke. London: Routledge & Kegan Paul, Ltd., 1935. Pp. 161 – 210.

Herford, R. Travers. "The Significance of Pharisaism." In *Judaism and the Beginnings of Christianity.* New York: Block Publishing Co., 1924. Pp. 125 – 166.

——. *Pirke Aboth.* New York: Block Publishing Company, 1930. 176 pp.

——. *The Pharisees.* New York: The Macmillan Co., 1924. 248 pp.

BIBLIOGRAPHY

Johnson, Sherman E. *Jesus in His Homeland*. New York: Charles Scribner's Sons, 1957. Pp. 10 – 67.

Kohler, Kaufmann. *The Origins of the Synagogue and the Church*. New York: The Macmillan Company, 1929. Pp. 29 – 52; 108 – 150.

LaSor, William. *Amazing Dead Sea Scrolls*. Chicago: Moody Press, 1956. Pp. 177 – 203.

Leaney, A. R. C., ed. Hanson, R. P. C., and Posen, J., *A Guide to the Scrolls*. Naperville, Ill.: SCM Book Club, 1958. Pp. 54 – 78.

Levison, N. *The Jewish Backgrounds for Christianity*. Edinburgh: T. & T. Clark, 1932. Pp. 143 – 185.

Moore, George Foot. *Judaism*. Cambridge: Harvard University Press, 1954. I, 37 – 47; 56 – 71.

Odeberg, Hugo. *Pharisaism and Christianity*. Trans. J. M. Moe. St. Louis: Concordia Publishing House, 1964. 112 pp.

Pfeiffer, Charles. *Between the Testaments*. Grand Rapids: Baker Book House, 1959. Pp. 111 – 120.

Riddle, Donald. *Jesus and the Pharisees*. Chicago: The University of Chicago Press, 1928. 193 pp.

Russell, D. S. *Between the Testaments*. Philadelphia: Muhlenberg Press, 1960. Pp. 48 – 57.

Schürer, Emil. *A History of the Jewish People in the Time of Jesus Christ*. Edinburgh: T. & T. Clark, 1890. Volume II, Part II, 4 – 43; 188 – 218.

Schubert, Kurt. *Die Religion des nachbiblischen Judentums*. Freiburg: Verlag Herder Wien, 1955. Pp. 69 – 79.

Tenney, Merril C. *The New Testament. A Historical and Analytical Survey*. Grand Rapids: Wm. B. Eerdmans Pub. Co., 1953. Pp. 137 – 143.

Tricot, A. "The Jewish World at the Time of Our Lord." In Robert, A., and Tricot, A., *Guide to the Bible*. Paris: Desclee & Co., 1955. II, 287 – 296.

Vermes, Geza, *Discovery in the Judean Desert*. Paris: Desclee Company, 1956. Pp. 64 – 75.

CHAPTER X

Beasley-Murray, G. R. "The Apocryphal and Apocalyptic Literature." In Davidson, F. ed. *The New Bible Commentary*. Grand Rapids: Wm. B. Eerdmans Co., 1953. Pp. 53 – 57.

Bonsirven, J. *Le Judaisme Palestinien au Temps de Jésus-Christ*. Paris: Beauchesne, 1950. 250 pp.

——. "Judaism in the Christian Era." In Robert, A., and Tricott, A., *Guide to the Bible*. Paris: Desclee & Co., 1955. II, 468 – 484.

Bruce, F. F. *Second Thoughts on the Dead Sea Scrolls*. Grand Rapids: Wm. B. Eerdmans Pub. Co., 1956. Pp. 70 – 84.

Charles, R. H. *Religious Development Between the Old and New Testaments*. London: Oxford University Press, 1914. Pp. 12 – 183.

Clarke, W. K. Lowther. *Concise Bible Commentary*. New York: The Macmillan Co., 1953. Pp. 99 – 117.

BIBLIOGRAPHY

Dana, H. E. *The New Testament World*. Fort Worth, Tex.: Pioneer Pub. Co., 1928. Pp. 125–139.

Davies, W. D. *Torah in the Messianic Age and/or Age to Come*. Philadelphia: Soc. of Biblical Literature, 1952. 99 pp.

"Development of Jewish Religion in the Period Between the Old and New Testaments." Dummelow, J. R. *A Commentary on the Holy Bible*. New York: The Macmillan Co., 1946. Pp. lxvi–lxxiii.

Edersheim, Alfred. *The Life and Times of Jesus the Messiah*. New York: Longmans, Green and Co., 1899. I, 1–92.

Fairweather, F. W. "Development of Doctrine in the Apocryphal Period." *Hasting's Dictionary of the Bible*. V, 272–309.

Fuller, Leslie E. "The Religious Development of the Intertestamental Period." Eiselen, F. L., Lewis, Edwin, and Downey, David G. *The Abingdon Commentary*. Nashville: Abingdon-Cokesbury Press, 1929. Pp. 200–213.

Hawley, Charles Arthur. *The Teachings of the Apocrypha and Apocalypse*. New York: Association Press, 1925. 165 pp.

Heinisch, Paul. *History of the Old Testament*. Trans. William Heidt. Collegeville, Minn.: St. John's Abbey, 1952. Pp. 410–422.

Johnson, Norman B. *Prayer in the Apocrypha and Pseudepigrapha. A Study in the Jewish Concept of God*. Philadelphia: Soc. of Biblical Literature, 1948.

Marcus, Ralph. *Law in the Apocrypha*. New York: Columbia University Press, 1927. 116 pp.

McKenzie, J. L. "The Jewish World in New Testament Times." *A Catholic Commentary on Holy Scriptures*. New York: Thomas Nelson & Sons, 1953. Pp. 736–741.

Oesterley, W. O. E. *An Introduction to the Books of the Apocrypha*. London: SPCK, 1955. Pp. 74–110.

Pfeiffer, Robert H. *History of New Testament Times*. New York: Harper & Bros., Publishers, 1949. Pp. 46–59.

Russell, D. S. *Between the Testaments*. Philadelphia: Fortress Press, 1960. Pp. 119–162.

Rylaarsdam, J. Coert. *Revelation in Jewish Wisdom Literature*. Chicago: The University of Chicago Press, 1946. 128 pp.

Snaith, Norman H. *The Jews from Cyrus to Herod*. New York: Abingdon-Cokesbury Press, no date. Pp. 195–203.

Wicks, Henry J. *The Doctrine of God in Jewish Apocryphal Literature*. London: Hunter & Longhurst, 1915. 371 pp.

CHAPTER XI

Bentzen, Aage. *Introduction to the Old Testament*. 2nd ed., Copenhagen: G. E. C. Gads Vorlag, 1952. I, 75–92.

Bruce, F. F. *The Book and the Parchments*. Westwood, New Jersey: Fleming H. Revell Co., 1953. Rev. ed. Pp. 141–155.

Conybeare, F. C., and Stock, George. *Selections from the Septuagint*. Chicago: Ginn & Co., 1905. Pp. 1–98.

BIBLIOGRAPHY

Danker, Frederick W. *Multipurpose Tools for Bible Study.* St. Louis: Concordia Pub. House, 1960. Pp. 63 – 95.

Deismann, C. Adolf. *Bible Studies.* Edinburgh: T. & T. Clark, 1901. 384 pp.

Dodd, C. H. *The Bible and the Greeks.* London: Hodder and Stoughton, 1935. 264 pp.

Eissfeldt, Otto. *Einleitung in das Alte Testament.* Tübingen: Verlag J. C. B. Mohr (Paul Siebeck), 1956. Pp. 855 – 869.

Filson, Floyd V. "The Septuagint and the New Testament." *The Biblical Archaeologist,* 9:34 – 42, (May 1946).

Gautier, Lucien. *Introduction a L' Ancien Testament.* Lausanne: Libraire Payot & Cie, 1939. II, 467 – 476.

Harrison, Everett F. "The Importance of the Septuagint for Biblical Studies." *Bibliotheca Sacra,* 112:344 – 355, October 1955; 113:37 – 45, January 1956.

Howard, F. W. "The Greek Bible." In *The Bible in Its Ancient and Modern Versions,* Robinson, H. Wheeler, ed. Oxford: at the Clarendon Press, 1940. Pp. 39 – 82.

Jellicoe, Sidney. *The Septuagint and Modern Study.* Oxford: at the Clarendon Press, 1968. 423 pp.

Kahle, P. E. *The Cairo Geniza.* London: Oxford University Press, 1947. Pp. 189 – 264.

———. *Die Massoreten des Westens.* Stuttgart: Verlag von W. Kohlhammer, 1927, I, 89 pp.; (1930), II, 68 pp.

Kenyon, F. *Our Bible and the Ancient Manuscripts.* New York: Harper & Bros., Publishers, 1941. Pp. 91 – 134.

———. *The Text of the Greek Bible.* London: Duckworth, 1949. Pp. 24 – 65.

Klein, Ralph. *Textual Criticism of the Old Testament. From the Septuagint to Qumran.* Philadelphia: Fortress Press, 1974. Pp. 11 – 50.

Meecham, H. G. *The Oldest Version of the Bible.* London: Oxford University Press, 1932.

Metzger, E. E. "The Septuagint." In Flack, E. E. *The Text, Canon and Versions of the Bible.* Grand Rapids: Baker Book House, 1956. Pp. 50 – 53.

Muser, C. A. *The Septuagint Bible. The Oldest Version of the Old Testament.* Indian Hills, Colorado: The Falcon's Wing Press, 1954. 1426 pp.

Nestle, Ed. "Septuagint." *A Dictionary of the Bible.* Hastings, James, ed. New York: Charles Scribner's Sons, 1911. IV, 437b – 454a.

Orlinsky, Harry M. "Current Progress and Problems in Septuagint Research." In Willoughby, Harold R. ed. *The Study of the Bible Today and Tomorrow.* Chicago: The University of Chicago Press, 1947. Pp. 144 – 161.

———. "The Septuagint and the New Testament." *Biblical Archaeologist,* 9:21 – 34, May 1946.

———. *On the Present State of Proto-Septuagint Studies,* New Haven: American Oriental Soc. Offprint Series, No. 13. Pp. 81 – 91.

Ottley, Richard C. *A Handbook of the Septuagint.* New York: E. P. Dutton & Co., 1919. 296 pp.

———. "Septuagint." *Encyclopedia Britannica,* 1957. XX, 335 – 337.

BIBLIOGRAPHY

Paret, Oscar. *Die Bibel, Ihre Überlieferung in Druck und Schrift.* 2te Durchgesehene Auflage. Stuttgart: Privileg. Württ. Bibelanstalt, 1950. Pp. 59 – 59; 65 – 75.

Pfeiffer, Robert H. *Introduction to the Old Testament.* New York: Harper & Bros., Publishers, 1948. Pp. 114 – 119.

Price, Ira Maurice. *The Ancestry of the English Bible.* 3rd revised ed. by William A. Irwin and Allen P. Wikgren. New York: Harper & Bros., Publishers, 1956. Pp. 50 – 82.

Ralfs, A. *Septuaginta.* Würtemberg: Würtembergische Bibelgesellschaft, 1935. 2 vols.

Roberts, Bleddyn J. *The Old Testament Text and Versions.* Cardiff: University of Wales Press, 1950. Pp. 101 – 187.

Swete, Henry Barclay. *An Introduction to the Old Testament in Greek,* Cambridge: at the University Press, 1914. 626 pp.

The Septuagint Version of the Old Testament with an English Translation. London: Samuel Bagster and Sons Ltd., no date. 1132 pp.

Unger, Merrill F. *Introductory Guide to the Old Testament.* Grand Rapids: Zondervan Pub. House, 1950. Pp. 148 – 164.

Wevers, J. W. "Septuagint." *The Interpreter's Dictionary of the Bible.* R – Z, pp. 273 – 278.

Würthheim, Ernst. *The Text of the Old Testament.* Trans. Peter R. Ackroyd. Oxford: Basil Blackwell, 1957. Pp. 34 – 55.

CHAPTER XII

Allegro, John M. *The Dead Sea Scrolls.* Baltimore: Penguin Books, 1956. Pp. 83 – 93.

Bruce, B. B. *Second Thoughts on the Dead Sea Scrolls.* Grand Rapids: Wm. B. Eerdmans Pub. Co., 1956. Pp. 70 – 84.

——. *Biblical Exegesis in the Qumran Texts.* Grand Rapids: Wm. B. Eerdmans Pub. Co., 1959. Pp. 7 – 36.

Burrows, Millar. *The Dead Sea Scrolls.* New York: The Viking Press, 1956. Pp. 371 – 415.

——. *More Light on the Dead Sea Scrolls.* New York: The Viking Press, 1958. Pp. 177 – 187; 387 – 404.

Cross, Frank Moore. *The Ancient Library of Qumran and Modern Biblical Studies.* New York: Doubleday & Co., 1961. Pp. 1 – 37.

——. "The Dead Sea Scrolls," *The Interpreter's Bible.* Buttrick, George Arthur, general ed. New York: Abingdon Press, 1957. XII, 650 – 667.

Danielou, Jean. *The Dead Sea Scrolls and Primitive Christianity.* New York: New American Library, 1962. 128 Pp.

De Waard, J. *A Comparative Study of the Old Testament Text in the Dead Sea Scrolls and in the New Testament.* Leiden: E. J. Brill, 1965. 101 pp.

Dupont-Sommer, A. *The Dead Sea Scrolls.* New York: The Macmillan Co., 1952. Pp. 25 – 96.

——. *The Essene Writings from Qumran.* Trans. G. Vermes. Cleveland and Chicago: Meridian Books, 1961.

187

BIBLIOGRAPHY

——. *The Jewish Sect of Qumran and the Essenes*. Trans. R. D. Barnett. London: Valentine, Mitchell & Co., Ltd., 1954. Pp. 38 – 76.

Eissfeldt, Otto. *Einleitung in das Alte Testament*. 2te Aulage. Tübingen: Verlag J. C. B. Mohr (Paul Siebeck), 1956. Pp. 788 – 822.

Fitzmeyer, J. A. "Dead Sea Scrolls." *The New Catholic Encyclopedia*. IV, 676 – 681.

——. "Qumran Community." *The New Catholic Encyclopedia*. XII, 33 – 35.

Freedman, David Noel, and Greenfield, Jonas, C. *New Directions in Biblical Archaeology*. Garden City, New York: Doubleday & Co., 1969, Pp. 63 – 148; 167 – 170.

Fritsch, Charles T. *The Qumran Community*. New York: The Macmillan Co., New York: 1956, Pp. 16 – 76.

Gaster, Theodore H. *The Dead Sea Scriptures in English Translation*. New York: Garden City: Doubleday Co., 1956. Pp. 1 – 327.

Graystone, Geoffrey. *The Dead Sea Scrolls and the Originality of Christ*. New York: Sheed E. Ward, 1956. 117 pp.

Howie, Carl G. *The Dead Sea Scrolls and the Living Church*. Richmond, Va.: John Knox Press, 1958. Pp. 15 – 44.

La Sor, William Sanford. *Amazing Dead Sea Scrolls*. Chicago: Moody Press. 1956. Pp. 1 – 86.

Leaney, A. R. C. *The Rule of Qumran and Its Meaning*. London: SCM Press, 1966. 310 pp.

Mansoor, Menahem. *The Dead Sea Scrolls*. Grand Rapids: Wm. B. Eerdmans, 1964. 210 pp.

Murphy, Roland E. *The Dead Sea Scrolls and the Bible*. Westminster, Md.: The Newman Press, 1957.

Rabin, Chaim. *Qumran Studies*. London: Oxford University Press, 1957. Pp. 1 – 135.

——. *The Zadokite Documents*. Oxford: at the Clarendon Press, 1954. 95 pp.

Ringgren, Helmer. *The Faith of Qumran*. Trans. Emilie T. Sander. Philadelphia: Fortress Press, 1963. 310 pp.

Rowley, H. H. *The Zadokite Fragments and the Dead Sea Scrolls*. Oxford: Basil Blackwell, 1952. Pp. 1 – 30.

Thompson, J. A. *Archaeology and the Pre-Christian Centuries*. Grand Rapids: Wm. B. Eerdmans Pub. Co., 1958. Pp. 100 – 120.

Unger, Merrill F. *The Dead Sea Scrolls and Other Amazing Archaeological Discoveries*. Grand Rapids: Zondervan Pub. House, 1957. Pp. 5 – 15.

Van der Ploeg, J. *The Excavations at Qumran*. Trans. Kevin Smith. New York: Longmans, Green & Co., 1958. Pp. 1 – 29; 150 – 188.

——. *Le Rouleau de la Guerre*. Translation, Connotation, and Introduction in French. Leiden: E. J. Brill, 1959. 198 pp.

Vermes, Geza. *Discovery in the Judean Desert*. New York: Desclee Co., 1956. Pp. 157 – 204.

Wernberg-Moeller, P. *The Manual of Discipline*. Grand Rapids: Wm. B. Eerdmans Pub. Co., 1957. 180 pp.

BIBLIOGRAPHY

Yadin, Yigael. *The Message of the Scrolls.* New York: Simon and Schuster, 1957. 192 pp.

CHAPTER XIII

Bentzen, Aage. *Introduction to the Old Testament.* Copenhagen: G. E. C. Gads Forlag, 1952. II, Pp. 218–236.

Bonsirven, Joseph. *La Bible Apocryphe en Marge de L'Ancien Testament.* Paris: Libraire Artheme Fayard, 1953. 335 pp.

Brockington, Leonard Herbert. *A Critical Introduction to the Apocrypha.* London: Duckworth, 1961. 170 pp.

Bruce, F. F. *The Books and the Parchments.* Westwood, New Jersey: Fleming H. Revell Co., 1955. Pp. 156–167.

Charles, R. H., ed., *The Apocrypha and Pseudepigrapha of the Old Testament.* New York: Oxford University Press, 1913. I, 684 pp.

——. *Religious Development Between the Old and New Testaments.* London: Oxford University Press, 1914. Pp. 184–219.

Clarke, W. K. Lowther. *Concise Bible Commentary.* New York: The Macmillan Co., 1953. Pp. 629–684.

Conway, Joan. *Who's Who in the Old Testament Together with Apocrypha.* New York, Chicago, San Francisco: Holt, Reinhart & Winston, 1971.

Davies, Thomas Witton. "The Apocrypha." *The International Standard Bible Encyclopedia.* I, 179–183.

Dentan, Robert D. *The Apocrypha-Bridge of the Testaments.* Greenwich, Conn.: The Seabury Press, 1954. 122 pp.

——. "Apocrypha, Old Testament." *Encyclopedia Britannica,* 1971, II, 117–119.

Dimmer, Catherine. *The Old Testament Apocrypha.* New York: Hawthorne Books, Publishers, 1964. 154 pp.

Dosker, Harry E. "Between the Testaments." *The International Standard Bible Encyclopedia* I, 455a–458b.

Eissfeldt, Otto. *Einleitung in das Alte Testament unter Einschluss der Apokryphen, Pseudepigraphen sowie der apokryphischen and pseudepigraphischen Qumran-Schriften.* 2te Auflage. Tübingen: J. C. B. Mohr (Paul Siebeck), 1956. Pp. 707–745.

Ferrar, William John. *The Uncanonical Jewish Books.* London: S.P.C.K., 1918. Pp. 11–48.

Frey, J. B., F. Vigheuk. ed. "Apocryphes de L'Ancien Testament." in L. Pirot's *Supplement au Dictionnaire de la Bible.* I, cols. 354–459.

Fritzsche, Otto Fridolin, und Willibald Grimm. *Kurzgefasstes Exegetisches Handbuch zu den Apokryphen des Alten Testaments.* Weidmannsche Buchhandlung, 1851-60. 6 volumes.

Goodspeed, Edgar J. *The Story of the Apocrypha.* Chicago: The University of Chicago Press, 1939. 150 pp.

Harrison, R. K. *Introduction to the Old Testament.* Grand Rapids: Wm. B. Eerdman's Pub. Co., 1969. Pp. 1173–1276.

BIBLIOGRAPHY

Kautzsch, Emil. *Die Apokryphen und Pseudepigraphen des Alten Testaments.* Tübingen: Verlag von J. C. B. Mohr (Paul Siebeck), 1900. Band I, 506 pp.

Malden, R. H. "The Books of the Apocrypha, Introduction." *The Story of the Bible: Told by Living Writers of Authority.* New York: Wiseman & Co., 1948. III, 845–891.

Manz, K. G. "The Opinions of Modern Scholars on the Origin of the Various Apocryphal Books." *Concordia Theological Monthly,* 12:658–686, September 1941; 12:744–768, October 1941.

Marcus, Ralph. "The Future of Intertestamental Studies." In *The Study of the Bible.* Willoughby, Harold, ed. Chicago: The University of Chicago Press, 1947. Pp. 190–208.

McCown, C. C. "Apocrypha." *The Universal Jewish Encyclopedia.* I, 422–424.

Marcus, Ralph. "Hellenistic Jewish Literature." in *The Jewish People, Past and Present.* New York: Jewish Encyclopedia Handbooks, Inc., 1952. III, 40–53.

Oesterley, W. O. E. *An Introduction to the Books of the Apocrypha.* London: SPCK, 1953. Pp. 133–327.

——. "The Influence of the Apocrypha on New Testament Thought." *The Story of the Bible.* New York: Wiseman & Co., 1948. III, 934–942.

——. *The Books of the Apocrypha. Their Origin, Teaching and Contents.* New York: Fleming H. Revell Co., 1914. 553 pp.

——. "The Apocrypha and Pseudepigrapha." in *A Companion of the Bible.* Manson, T. W., ed. Edinburgh: T. & T. Clark, 1947. Pp. 78–97.

——. "The Witness of the Apocrypha to Religious, Eternal Verities." *The Story of the Bible.* New York: Wiseman & Co., 1948. III, 892–910.

Pfeiffer, R. H. "Apocrypha." *The Twentieth Century Encyclopedia of Religious Knowledge.* I, 50b–52a.

——. *History of New Testament Times, with An Introduction to the Apocrypha.* New York, Harper & Bros., Publishers, 1949. Pp. 233–524.

——. "The Literature and Religion of the Apocrypha." Buttrick, George, ed. *The Interpreter's Bible.* Nashville: Abingdon Press, 1952. I, 391–419.

Rylaarsdam, J. Coert. "Intertestamental Studies Since Charles' Apocrypha and Pseudepigrapha." In Willoughby, Harold R. ed. *The Study of the Bible Today and Tomorrow.* Chicago: The University of Chicago Press, 1947. Pp. 32–51.

Ryle, H. E. "Introductions to the Books Called Apocrypha." in Barnes, W. Emery, ed. *A Companion to Biblical Studies.* Cambridge: at the University Press, 1916. Pp. 154–162.

Steinmueller, John E. *A Companion to Scripture Studies.* New York: Joseph F. Wagner, Inc., 1941. II, 103–155.

Torrey, Charles Cutler. *The Apocryphal Literature.* New Haven: Yale University Press, 1945. Pp. 1–103.

Tricot, A. "The Apocrypha of the Old and New Testaments." In Robert, A., and Tricot, A., *Guide to the Bible.* Paris: Desclee & Co., 1951. I, 61–66.

Unger, Merrill. *Introductory Guide to the Old Testament.* Grand Rapids: Zondervan Pub. House, 1951. Pp. 81–114.

Young, C. Douglas. "The Apocrypha." in Henry, Carl F. H. ed., *Revelation and the Bible.* Grand Rapids: Baker Book House, 1959. Pp. 169–185.

BIBLIOGRAPHY

Walker, Thomas. "The Historical Background of the Books of the Apocrypha." *The Story of the Bible.* New York: Wiseman & Co., 1948. III, 911–933.

CHAPTER XIV

The Complete Apocrypha Available in English Versions

The Apocrypha According to the Authorized Version. London: Oxford University Press, no date. 292 pp.

The Apocrypha, King James Version, with an introduction by Robert H. Pfeiffer. New York: Harper & Bros., no date. 295 pp.

The Apocrypha, The Revised Standard Version. Oxford University Press, 1885.

The New English Bible with the Apocrypha. Oxford and Cambridge: at the University Press, 1970. Pp. 1–275 (Apocrypha Section).

Goodspeed, E. J., *The Apocrypha. An American Translation.* Chicago: The University of Chicago Press, 1938. 493 pp.

The Apocrypha, Revised Standard Version. New York: Thomas Nelson & Sons, 1957. 250 pp.

Monsignor Knox. *The Holy Bible. A Translation from the Latin Vulgate in the Light of Hebrew and Greek Originals.* New York: Sheed and Ward, 1956. Pp. 419–452; 574–629; 737–743; 805–809; 858–908.

Commentaries on the Apocrypha

Bissel, Edwin Cone. *The Apocrypha of the Old Testament, with Historical Introductions, a Revised Translation, and Notes Critical and Explanatory* (being J. P. Lange's Commentary on Holy Scriptures, Vol. XV). New York: Charles Scribner's Sons, 1886.

Brown, Raymond E., Fitzmyer, Joseph A., Murphy, eds. *The Jerome Biblical Commentary.* Englewood Cliffs, New Jersey, 1968. Cf. pp. 461–486, 541–555, 556–568, 614–619, 620–632.

Gore, Charles, Goudge, H. L., and Gillaume. Alfred. *A Commentary on Holy Scripture Including the Apocrypha.* New York: The Macmillan Co. 1928. Part II, pp. 1–158.

Lamparter, Helmut. *Die Apokryphen I. Das Buch Jesus Sirach.* Stuttgart: Calwer Verlag, 1972. 210 pp.

——. *Die Apokryphen, II. Weisheit Salomos, Tobias, Judith, Baruch,* Stuttgart: Calwer Verlag, 1972. 228 pp.

Laymon, Charles M. *The Interpreter's One-Volume Commentary on the Bible.* Nashville and New York, 1971. Pp. 519–606. A commentary on 15 apocryphal books by six different scholars.

Orchard, Bernard, Sutcliffe, Edmund F., Fuller, Reginald C., and Russel, Raith, eds. *A Catholic Commentary on Holy Scripture.* New York: Thomas Nelson and Sons, 1957. This commentary does not include I Esdras, II Esdras, or The Prayer of Manesseh.

Reider, Joseph, *The Book of Wisdom.* Jewish Apocryphal Literature Series. New York: published for Dropsie College for Hebrew and Cognate Learning by Harper & Bros., 1957. 233 pp.

Tedesche, Sidney, and Zeitlin, Solomon. *The First Book of Maccabees.* Jewish

BIBLIOGRAPHY

Apocryphal Literature Series. New York: published for Dropsie College by Harper & Bros., 1950. 291 pp.

——. *The Second Book of the Maccabees.* Jewish Apocryphal Literature Series. New York: published for Dropsie College by Harper & Bros., 1954. 271 pp.

Wace, Henry, ed. *Apocrypha* (The Speaker's Commentary). London: John Murray, 1888. 2 vols.

Zimmermann, Frank. *The Book of Tobit.* Jewish Apocryphal Literature Series. New York: published for Dropsie College by Harper & Bros., 1958. 190 pp.

CHAPTER XV

Andrews, H. T. "Apocalyptic Literature." *Peake's Commentary of the Bible.* 1920. Pp. 431–435.

Berry, G. R. "The Apocalyptic Literature of the Old Testament." *Journ. of Biblical Literature.* lxii: 9–16, 1943.

Black, M. "The Inter-Testamental Literature." In T. W. Manson–H. H. Rowley, *A Companion to the Bible.* 2nd ed. Edinburgh: T & T Clark, 1963. Pp. 81–89.

Charles, R. H. "Apocalyptic Literature." In *Cheyne and Black's Encyclopedia Biblica.* London: Adam and Charles Black, 1891. I. cols. 213–250.

Charles, R. H. "Eschatology of the Apocryphal and Apocalyptic Literature." *Hasting's Dictionary of the Bible.* I, pp. 741–749.

——. *The Religious Development between the Old and New Testaments.* London: Oxford University Press, 1914. Pp. 220–252.

Eissfeldt, Otto. *Einleitung in das Alte Testament unter Einschluss der Apokryphen und Pseudepigraphen sowie der apokryphischen und pseudepigraphenartigen Qumran-Schriften.* 2.te Auflage. Tübingen: J. C. B. Mohr (Paul Siebeck). 1956. Pp. 745–787.

Ferrar, William John. *The Uncanonical Jewish Books.* London: SPCK, 1918. Pp. 49–109.

Fox, G. George. "Pseudepigrapha." *The Universal Jewish Encyclopedia.* 9:20 a.b.

Frey, J. B. "Apocalyptic." In *Pirot's Supplement au Dictionnaire de la Bible.* I, 326–354.

Frost, Stanley Brice. *Old Testament Apocalyptic: Its Origin and Growth.* London: The Epworth Press, 1952. Pp. 210–230.

Gautier, Lucien. *Introduction a L' Ancien Testament.* Lausanne: Libraire Payot et Cie, 1939. II, pp. 382–389.

Gehman, Henry Snyder. "The Pseudepigrapha." *The New Westminster Dictionary of the Bible.* Philadelphia: The Westminster Press, 1970. Pp. 775–776.

James, Montague, Rhodes. *The Lost Apocrypha of the Old Testament.* London: SPCK, 1920. 111 pp.

Kaufmann, J. "Apokalyptik." In *Encyclopedia Judaica.* ii, cols. 1142-54.

Kohler, K. "Eschatology." In *Jewish Encyclopedia* (1903). V, pp. 209–218.

MacCulloch, J. A. "Eschatology." In *Hasting's Encyclopedia of Religion and Ethics.* V, 373–391.

McGown, C. C. "Apocalyptic Literature." *The Universal Jewish Encyclopedia.* I, 418–422.

BIBLIOGRAPHY

Mangenot, E. "Apocalypses apocryphes." In *Dictionnaire de Theologie Catholique.* I. cols. 1479 – 98.

Miller, H. S. *General Biblical Introduction.* Houghton, N.Y.: The World-Bearer Press. 1944. Pp. 120 – 121.

Oesterley, W. O. E. "The Apocrypha and Pseudepigrapha." In T. W. Manson ed. *A Companion to the Bible.* Edinburgh: T. & T. Clarke, 1947. Pp. 89 – 96.

Pfeiffer, Charles F. *Between the Testaments.* Grand Rapids: Baker Book House. 1959. Pp. 121 – 124.

Pfeiffer, Robert H. "The Literature and Religion of the Pseudepigrapha." *The Interpreter's Bible.* I. 421 – 436.

——. "The Pseudepigrapha." Loetscher, Lefferts A. *The Twentieth Century Encyclopedia of Religious Knowledge.* Baker Book House. 1955. II. 924 – 926.

Rost, Leonhard. *Einleitung in die alttestamentlichen Apokryphen und Pseud-Epigraphen, Einschliesslich der grossen Qumran Handschriften.* Halle: Quelle & Meyer. 1970.

Russel, D. S. *The Method and Message of Jewish Apocalyptic.* Philadelphia: The Westminster Press. 1964. 464 pp.

Thomson, J. E. H. "Apocalyptic Literature." *The International Standard Bible Encyclopedia.* I. 161 – 178.

Torrey, C. C. "Apocalypse." In *Jewish Encyclopedia* (1901). I. 669 – 674.

——. *The Apocryphal Literature.* New Haven: Yale University Press. 1945. Pp. 103 – 145.

Waxman, Meyer. *A History of Jewish Literature.* New York: Block Publishing Co., 1930. I. 26 – 44.

Wilder, A. N. "The Nature of Jewish Eschatology." *Jour. of Biblical Literature.* 1931, 50:201 – 206.

CHAPTER XVI

The Testaments of the Twelve Patriarchs

Charles, R. H. *The Testaments of the Twelve Patriarchs.* Translation of Early Documents. First Series. London: Soc. for the Promotion of Christian Knowledge. 1917. 108 pp.

——. "The Testaments of the Twelve Patriarchs." In Charles, R. F. *The Apocrypha and Pseudepigrapha of the Old Testament.* Oxford: at the Clarendon Press. 1913. II. 282 – 285.

Schnapps, F. and Kautzsch, E. *Die Apokryphen und Pseudepigraphen des Alten Testaments.* Tübingen: Verlag von J. C. B. Mohr. 1900. II. 458 – 506.

The Book of Jubilees

Charles, R. H. *The Ethiopic Version of the Hebrew Book of Jubilees.* London: Oxford University Press. 1895.

——. "The Book of Jubilees." Charles, R. H. *The Apocrypha and Pseudepigrapha.* II. 1 – 82.

Littmann, E. "Das Buch der Jubiläen." Kautzsch, E. *Die Apokryphen und Pseudepigraphen.* II. 31 – 119.

BIBLIOGRAPHY

The Ascension of Isaiah

Beer, G. "Das Martyrium Jesajas." Kautzsch, E. *Die Apokryphen und Pseudepigraphen.* II, 119–126.

Box, G. H. *The Apocalypse of Abraham,* and R. H. Charles, *The Ascension of Isaiah.* London: The Soc. for the Promotion of Christian Knowledge, 1918. 99 pp. and 62 pp.

Charles, R. H. "The Ascension of Isaiah." Charles, R. H. *The Apocrypha and Pseudepigrapha.* II, 155–162.

The Paralipomena of Jeremiah

Harris, James, Rendel. *The Rest of the Words of Baruch: A Christian Apocalypse of the Year 136 A.D.* London: C. J. Clay & Sons, 1899.

The Lives of the Prophets

Torrey, C. C. *The Lives of the Prophets.* Jour. of Biblical Literature, Monograph Series, Vol. I; Philadelphia: Soc. of Biblical Literature and Exegesis, 1946. 53 pp.

The Testament of Job

Mai, Cardinal. *Scriptorum Nova Collectio.* Vol. VII. Rome, 1833.

James, M. R., *Apocrypha Anecdota.* 2nd series. Cambridge: at the University Press, 1897.

The Assumption of Moses

Clemen, C. "Die Himmelsfahrt Moses." Kautzsch, E. *Die Apokryphen und Die Pseudepigraphen.* II, 311–331.

Ferrar, William, John. *The Assumption of Moses.* Translations of Early Documents, Series I. London: Soc. for the Promotion of Christian Knowledge, 1917. 42 pp.

The Apocalypse of Baruch

Charles, R. H. *The Apocalypse of Baruch.* London: Soc. for the Promotion of Christian Knowledge, 1917. 96 pp.

———. "2 Baruch I. the Syriac Apocalypse of Baruch." Charles, R. H. *Apocrypha and Pseudepigrapha.* II, 470–532.

Kautzsch, E. "Die syrische Baruchsapokalypse." Kautzsch, E. *Die Apokryphen und die Pseudepigraphen.* II, 404–446.

The Psalms of Solomon

Harris, Rendel J. *Psalmoi Solomontos: Psalms of the Pharisees, Commonly Called the Psalms of Solomon.* Cambridge: at the University Press, 1891.

The Sibylline Oracles

Blau, F. "Die Sibyllinen." Kautzsch, E. *Die Apokryphen und Pseudepigraphen.* II, 177–217.

Lanchester, H. C. O. "Sibylline Oracles." Charles, R. H. *Apocrypha and Pseudepigrapha.* II, 368–406.

Rowley, R. R. "The Interpretation and Date of the Sibylline Oracles." *Zeitschrift fuer alttestamentliche Wissenschaft.* 1926. 44:324–327.

3 Maccabees and 4 Maccabees

Emmet, C. W. *The Third Book of the Maccabees.* London: SPCK, 1918. 75 pp.

BIBLIOGRAPHY

Hadas, Moses. *The Third and Fourth Book of the Maccabees.* Jewish Apocryphal Literature. Published for Dropsie College of Hebrew and Cognate Learning by Harper & Bros., 1953. 248 pp.

The Letter of Aristeas

Hadas, Moses. *Aristeas to Philocrates* (Letter of Aristeas). Jewish Apocalyptical Literature. Published for Dropsie College by Harper & Bros., 1951. 233 pp.

Thackeray, H. St. J., *The Letter of Aristeas.* London: Society for the Promotion of Christian Knowledge. 1917. 117 pp.

Wendland, P., in Kautzsch, *Die Apokryphen und Pseudepigraphen,* II, 1–31. (Der Aristeasbrief)

CHAPTER XVII

Philo and His Writings

Arnaldez, R. "Philo Judaeus." *New Catholic Encyclopedia.* New York, St. Louis, etc.: McGraw-Hill Book Co., 1966.

Baron, Salo W. and Blau, Joseph. *Judaism. Postbiblical and Talmudic Period.* New York: The Liberal Arts Press, 1954. Pp. 31–53.

Barrett, C. K. *The New Testament Background: Selected Documents.* London: S.P.C.K., 1957. Pp. 173–189.

"Philo." *The Encyclopedia Americana.* New York, Chicago, Washington, D. C.: Americana Corporation, 1959. XXI:766–767.

Belkin, S. *Philo and the Oral Law.* Cambridge: Harvard University Press, 1940.

Bentwich, Norman. *Philo-Judaeus of Alexandria.* Philadelphia: The Jewish Publication Soc. of America, 1910. 273 pp.

Daneliou, Jean. *Philon d-Alexandrie.* Paris: Libraire Artheme Fayard, 1958. 220 pp.

Drummond, James. "Philo." *A Dictionary of the Bible.* New York: Charles Scribner's Sons, 1909. V, (Extra vol.), pp. 197–208.

Gilbert, George Holley. *Interpretation of the Bible.* A Short History. New York: The Macmillan Company, 1908. Pp. 35–57.

Goodenough, E. R. *Introduction to Philo Judaeus.* New York: Oxford University Press, 1940.

——. *Light by Light.* New Haven: Yale University Press, 1935.

Goodhart, H. L. and Goodenough, E. R. *The Politics of Philo Judaeus with a General Bibliography.* New Haven: Yale University Press, 1938.

Goodhart, H. L. and Goodenough, E. R. *An Introduction to Philo Judaeus.* New Haven: Yale University Press, 1935.

Husik, Isaac. "Philosophy, Alexandrian." *The Universal Jewish Encyclopedia.* New York: Universal Jewish Encyclopedia Co., Inc., 1942. VIII: 499–500.

Heinemann, Isaac. "Philo." *The Universal Jewish Encyclopedia.* VIII, 495–496.

Heinemann, F. H. H. "Philo Judaeus." *Chamber's Encyclopedia.* London: George Newnes Limited, 1959. X, 661–662.

Katz, Peter. "Philo of Alexandria." *Twentieth Century Encyclopedia of Religious Knowledge.* Loetscher, Lefferts A. ed. Grand Rapids: Baker Book House, 1955. II, 876–877.

BIBLIOGRAPHY

Marshall, F. H. *The Religious Backgrounds of Early Christianity*. St. Louis: Bethany Press, 1931. Pp. 101 – 112.

Pfeiffer, Robert H. *History of New Testament Times*. New York: Harper & Bros., 1949. Pp. 173 – 177; 197 – 209; 212 – 215.

Schürer, Emil. *A History of the Jewish People in the Time of Jesus Christ*. Edinburgh: T. & T. Clark, 1890. III, 321 – 381.

Schürer E., Biggs, Charles, and Altmann, Alexander. "Philo." *Encyclopedia Britannica*. 1971 ed. XVII, 860 – 862.

Wenley, R. M. "Philo, Judaeus." *The International Standard Bible Encyclopedia*. Grand Rapids: Wm. B. Eerdmans Pub. Co., 1939. IV, 2380a – 2383a.

Williamson, Ronald. *Philo and the Epistle to the Hebrews*. Leiden: E. J. Brill, 1970. 602 pp.

Wolfson, A. "Philo Judaeus." *Dictionary of Philosophy*. New York: The Macmillan Co. & The Free Press, 1967. VI, 151 – 155.

Wolfson, Harry Austryn. "Philo." *Foundations of Religious Philosophy in Judaism, Christianity, and Islam*. Cambridge: Harvard University Press, 1947. 2 vols.

Zöckler, O. "Philo of Alexandria." *The New Schaff-Herzog Encyclopedia of Religious Knowledge*. Grand Rapids: Baker Book House, 1953. IX, 38 – 41.

Text of Philo

Colson, F. H. and Whitaker, G. H. *Philo*. In the Loeb Classical Library. London: William Heinemann, 1929 – 1956. 10 vols.

Marcus, Ralph. *Philo*. Supplementary volumes in the Loeb Classical Library. London: William Heinemann, 1958. 2 vols.

CHAPTER XVIII

Baron, Salo W., and Blau, Joseph L. *Judaism, Postbiblical and Talmudic*. New York: The Liberal Arts Press, 1954. Pp. 54 – 63.

Barrett, C. K. *The New Testament Background: Selected Documents*. London: S.P.C.K., 1957. Pp. 127 – 132; 190 – 207.

Bentwich, Norman. *Hellenism*. Philadelphia: The Jewish Publication Society of America, 1919. Pp. 24 – 34; 101 – 107; 241 – 245; 361 – 370.

Chadwick, Owen. "Josephus." *Encyclopedia Britannica*. 1971 ed. XIII, 89 – 90.

Farmer, Wm. R. *Maccabees, Zealots, and Josephus*. New York: Columbia University Press, 1956. 235 Pp.

Feldman, Louis H. *Josephus with an English Translation*. London: William M. Heinemann, 1965. Vol. IX.

Foakes-Jackson, Frederick John. *Josephus and the Jews*. London: Society for the Promotion of Christian Knowledge, 1930.

Hölscher, G. "Josephus." in Pauly-Wissowa, *Realenzyklopedie der klassischen Altertumswissenschaft*. Stuttgart: Alfred Druckenmüzzer Verlag, 1916. XVIII, 1934 – 2000.

Klausler, Joseph. *Jesus of Nazareth, His Life, Times and Teaching*. Trans. from the Hebrew by Herbert Danby. New York: The Macmillan Co., 1925. Pp. 55 – 59.

BIBLIOGRAPHY

Marcus, Ralph. "Bibliography on Josephus." *Proceedings of the American Academy for Jewish Research.* (1947), 16, 178 – 181.

――. "Josephus, Flavius." *Twentieth Century Encyclopedia of Religious Knowledge.* Grand Rapids: Baker Book House, 1955. I, 614.

――. *Josephus, with an English Translation.* London: William Heinemann, 1937 – 63. Vols. VI – VIII.

Montefiore, Hugh. *Josephus and the New Testament.* London: A. R. Mowbray, 1962.

Niese, Benedictus. "Josephus." *The Encyclopedia of Religion and Ethics.* New York: Charles Scribner's Sons, 1915. VII, 569 – 579.

Pfeiffer, Robert H. *History of New Testament Times.* New York: Harper & Bros., 1949. Pp. 207 – 210.

Reznikoff, Charles. "Josephus." *The Universal Jewish Encyclopedia.* New York: The Universal Jewish Encyclopedia, Inc., 1939. VI, 197 – 202.

Roth, Cecil. "Josephus Flavius." *Chamber's Encyclopedia.* London: George Newnes Limited, 1959. VIII, 138.

Schürer, Emil. "Josephus." *The New Schaff-Herzog Encyclopedia of Religious Knowledge.* Grand Rapids: Baker Book House, 1950 rpt. VI, 234 – 236.

Shutt, Rowland, J. H. *Studies in Josephus.* London: SPCK 1961. 132 pp.

Strugnell, S. "Josephus Flavius." *New Catholic Encyclopedia.* New York, St. Louis, etc.: McGraw-Hill Book Co., 1967. VII, 1120 – 1123.

Thackeray, H. St. John. *Josephus, The Man and the Historian.* New York: Jewish Institute of Religion Press, 1929. 151 pp.

――. "Josephus." in *Judaism and the Beginnings of Christianity.* New York: Block Publishing Co., 1924. Pp. 167 – 231.

――. "Josephus." *A Dictionary of the Bible.* New York: Charles Scribner's Sons, 1909. V, 461 – 473.

――. *Josephus, with English Translation.* London: William Heinemann, 1926 – 29. vols. I – V.

Wenley, R. M. "Josephus, Flavius." *The International Standard Bible Encyclopedia.* Grand Rapids: Wm. B. Eerdmans Pub. Co., 1939. III, 1742.

Williamson, Geoffrey Arthur. *The World of Josephus.* London: Secker & Warburg, 1964.

Whiston, William. *The Works of Flavius Josephus.* London: Ward, Lock and Co., no date, 858 pages.